Idiot

Idit

Beating "The Curse" and
Enjoying the Game of Life

JOHNNY DAMON

with Peter Golenbock

Three Rivers Press / New York

All rights reserved.
Published in the United States by Three Rivers Press, an imprint
of the Crown Publishing Group, a division of Random House, Inc., New York.
www.crownpublishing.com

Three Rivers Press and the Tugboat design are registered trademarks
of Random House, Inc.

Originally published in slightly different form in hardcover in
the United States by Crown Publishers, New York, in 2005.

Library of Congress Cataloging-in-Publication Data is available upon request

ISBN 0-307-23773-7

Printed in the United States of America

Design by Leonard W. Henderson

10 9 8 7 6 5 4 3 2 1

First Paperback Edition

ACKNOWLEDGMENTS

I want to thank my mom and dad for letting me experience life; my brother, James, for being there at all times; Michelle for showing me what life is and how much fun it can be; my kids for allowing me to live through their eyes once again; Angie for being a good mother; my friend Roger Hernandez for taking care of everything for me, especially when I'm gone; Lisa for helping make my hair look great; Arden and Puma for making me realize it's okay to be cool playing this game; David Powers for being a loyal friend, even though you're a Cubs fan (one day you'll get to feel what we experienced); Ian Kleinert and Peter Caparis for arranging to do this book; Jason Giambi for showing me what it's like to be a big leaguer; and finally, the Boston fans for letting me be me.

Johnny Damon
Orlando, Florida

I want to thank my sister Wendy, her mate Cheryl, and their son Max for showing us the true face of courage; my cousin Douglas, who finally found the joy he was seeking when he became a Red Sox fan back when Pumpsie Green was playing; Ray Foster, who has Red Sox tattoos; Bobby Duffey, Ray Arsenault, and Rich Hershenson, who prayed for this day since we were roommates at Dartmouth; Jeffrey Lyons and Chris Zucker, who wears Red Sox underwear as he makes his rounds; and Josh Pierce's girlfriend's mother, whose life has become enriched by Johnny and his Beantown buddies; Herb Snitzer and Shaun Kelley, educators with Red Sox blood in their veins for taking the time to read the manuscript and make suggestions; Neil and Dawn Reshen and their staff, for everything they do; Frank

Weimann and Ian Kleinert, for bringing me this wonderful project; Rick Horgan, who signed the project and did an absolutely magnificent job line editing the manuscript; Genoveva Llosa, who helped expedite the project; Amelia Zalcman, Random House's Red Sox maven and in-home attorney, who couldn't believe Johnny's dad let him do some of the things he did; Mark Davis and Dick Whitcomb, the heart and soul of my dear, dear alma mater, St. Luke's School of New Canaan, Connecticut; Rhonda and Charlie, the two great loves of my life, and our canine companions Doris and Fred the Gekko Hunter, bassets both, and mastiff Mandy; and finally to Johnny Damon, whose indomitable spirit, zeal to write a great book, and good heart shines through every page. My heart goes out to you all.

Peter Golenbock
St. Petersburg, Florida

CONTENTS

Contents

Idiot

Chapter 1

So Close, but So Far

OCTOBER 2003

I was standing out in center field under the bright lights in Oakland. The Red Sox were playing the A's, my old team, in the first round of the playoffs in the fall of 2003. Jermaine Dye, probably my best friend in baseball, hit a lazy fly ball my way. I remember thinking it was going to be an easy catch. I ran over to get it. Then I blacked out. Damian Jackson, our second baseman, had run out for the ball, and just as it came down, we both went for it and collided. His hard-ass head struck me in the temple, knocking me out cold for a few minutes. If you look at the replay, I fly into the air, and my whole body goes numb. One of my arms starts shaking. It was the hardest whack I ever got. When I was playing football in high school, Warren Sapp hit me pretty good but Damian Jackson's head-on-head collision was definitely harder.

While I was on a stretcher being put into an ambulance, I gave a thumbs-up. When they carted me off the field, everyone thought I was okay, but I wasn't. I'd suffered a bad concussion. My mind was scrambled. I actually thought I was wearing an Oakland uniform and that I was walking off the field waving to the Oakland fans, saying, "Thank you for supporting us this year."

After the medics loaded me into the ambulance, they put some fluids in me and hooked me up to an IV. But as they were sticking it into my left arm—people think everyone's right-handed—the ambulance hit a speed bump on the way out of the coliseum and the IV rammed into my veins. I ended up with a bruise from my wrist to my bicep that pained me for weeks.

When I arrived at the hospital, I asked one of the staff to turn on the TV, but I hardly remember anything about the game. Richard Halpern, a friend of mine from L.A., came to see me. He was wearing a shirt that said "Boston Red Sox vs. Oakland A's, 2003 ALCS." I kept looking at it thinking, "2003? When did Boston and Oakland play?" And I continued to think I was part of the Oakland A's, who I'd been with in 2001. I remember thinking, *What just happened to those two years?* I had no clue.

My girlfriend Michelle, whom I'd later marry, was in the room, and I kept asking her, "Did we win? Did we win?"

"We won," she kept assuring. "The team is going to New York." But then a few minutes later I'd ask her, "Did we win? Did we win?"

I kept asking the same question over and over, 10 times, driving Michelle crazy. She told the doctor, "Every question he's asking me, I'm answering the same way, but he's not taking it in."

That's because my brain was scrambled. I knew what I was asking, but the answers I was receiving didn't register. They say that when you suffer a serious concussion, you get thrown into a loop of questions. No matter how much your questions get answered, you don't comprehend. That's exactly what was happening here.

The doctors sent Michelle back to our hotel so she could take a nap. After she left, I kept asking for her. "Where is she? Tell her to get back up here." When she returned, I figured she'd been away 10 minutes. But she'd taken a 2-hour nap before coming back.

When I was released from the hospital and returned to my

hotel room, I kept asking, "What kind of game did I have? Was I doing good?" I really had no idea what had occurred that night. I didn't know if I'd struck out four times or hit two home runs.

"You had a good game," Michelle assured.

About five months later I got to watch a replay of the game. That was the game in which Derek Lowe finished off the A's in the ninth by striking out the last two batters looking on two of the most hellacious pitches he's ever thrown. It was a satisfying first-round win that had my teammates celebrating while I was lying in a hospital bed.

Hours after defeating Oakland, the Sox left for New York without me. Our head trainer, Jim Rowe, an incredible guy, made it his job to stay with me. He didn't get to celebrate our advancing on to the next round of the playoffs, but he never complained.

The next morning one of our owners—I'm not exactly sure which owner—sent his private jet over to fly us into New York.

Before the series with the Yankees, the team doctors were debating whether to even put me on the roster because they knew how messed up I was. I went to Grady Little, our manager, and I said, "I can pinch hit if you need me."

"You don't look like you're all there, son," he said in that southern drawl.

"I'm ready to pinch run for you. I'll be ready to play whenever you need me."

"You don't even sound right, boy."

Grady may have had that slow drawl, but he was a very smart man. What a great guy to play for. He knew he couldn't keep me off the roster, nor did he want to, even though I sat and watched those first two Yankee games from the bench.

I don't remember those two games at all. I know we won the first one with Tim Wakefield on the mound. In Game 2 Andy Pettitte beat us, but I had no clue. Every time I'd stand up and grab a bat or do something to get loose, Grady would look at me and say, "Sit down, boy."

When we got back to Boston, I went to the team doctor, and he said everything was checking out fine, that I was regaining some of my faculties. But the truth was I wasn't close to normal—it took me four or five months before I had a clear, vivid picture of what was going on. When it rained the day we were supposed to play our first game in Boston, I got in one more day of recuperation. I don't get much time off, even in the off season, and in all I ended up resting five days, which was huge. Everything started to feel fine. I felt like I was pretty strong.

Only a couple of people knew how beat up I really was when I started against the Yankees in Game 3. Not only was I not playing with a full deck upstairs, but my left arm was still bruised from the IV and was absolutely killing me. I was playing with one arm. I couldn't move it.

I have an unorthodox swing where I release the bat just after contact. The pain didn't allow me to do that. People said, "Your swing really changed for the Yankee series." It wasn't because I was scared in the box. It was because I had no motion owing to what had happened in the ambulance.

Before the game I didn't even take batting practice. I just stepped out on the field and tried giving it what I could. Thinking about it now, I was in no condition to play. I'd start the games, and every game by the third or fourth inning I'd experience a painful migraine brought on by the concussion. I'd always been able to relax before a game, but not now. As soon as I started feeling stress or exerting energy, I'd get a migraine. Every day before the game was half over I'd just be wiped out. I would be standing out in center field, and my head would be throbbing. But being the kind of person I am, I still thought we were a better team with me out there. I just wish I'd been a little bit healthier for that Yankee series.

My memory of Game 3 is spotty. Roger Clemens started for the Yankees, not a very fun situation. When I came into the league in 1995, Roger was having a couple of down years. I'd say to myself, *Hey, I see the ball pretty decent off him.* Then when he got to Toronto he started throwing his split-finger pitch, and I thought, *My gosh, this is one of the greatest pitchers ever. This is what they've been talking about!*

Roger has been a workhorse. Against him that day the score-card says I got three hits, but they were all softly hit to the left of the third baseman and to the right of short. I beat out a couple of tough hops on slow rollers which were credited for hits. I wasn't going to complain, but I very easily could have been 0–3.

So even though I was in such bad shape to play, I went 3 for 3 against Clemens right out of the chute. I didn't even consider myself a player in those games. Normally I'm filled with adrenaline. I hustle. Normally, I can do some special things on the baseball field. Against the Yankees, nothing was there, though the last thing I wanted to do was tell Grady, "I'm not really the guy you want to play."

You just can't ask out of big games, even if you have nothing going for you and your head is throbbing. That's not how I was brought up as a ballplayer. You go out there because you think you're the best option for the team.

Though I don't remember a lot of that game, one incident does stand out: after Pedro Martinez hit Karim Garcia, tempers got hot and both benches cleared. I came running in from center field, thinking, *No way in heck can I get in the middle of this thing. I have absolutely no strength, and I'll get beat down something awful.*

I ran toward the home plate area to find my best friend on the field, Jason Giambi, who was playing first base for the Yankees. When Jason and I were teammates in Oakland in 2001, we were very close.

"Hey, protect me if you can," I said to Jason, "because I've got no clue where I am right now."

Jason, being the great player he is, had to clear some guys off, but he kept coming back to me, making sure I was all right. While Jason and I were dancing, I could see a big commotion going on to the left of me. I turned to see Don Zimmer sprawled on the ground.

Pedro was looking at Zim laying there on the ground, but he wasn't concerned about it. Pedro is a warrior. He's one of the greatest competitors there ever was. He wasn't quite the pitcher he'd been back in the late '90s, early 2000s, but he went out there with his heart. You knew when he had it. He got that serious look in his eyes that said, *Hey, I've got my stuff today.* If you scored him a couple of runs, he was going to be fine.

As a person, Pedro was generous and giving. He was one of those guys who'd always pick up the check when the team went out to dinner. He has three kids, and he made sure they were taken care of. He didn't go around with a big entourage. He was very smart. When he got to talking about baseball, he wouldn't shut up. He knew how good he was. He wanted to win, and he did what he needed to do to win.

I wasn't really sure what had happened until after the game. As much respect as Don Zimmer got from the Yankees, he used to be the Red Sox manager, so he got a lot of respect from our players as well. We liked that guy. He's tough not to like. After the game Zim said all the right things, that he was wrong to go out there, that he was out of place. It had been building for years between Pedro and the Yankees, and Zim decided it was time to act. And so he went after Pedro, who defended himself and pushed Zim down on the ground before Zim could take a swing at him.

When you're part of a rivalry, the best of friends can become upset with each other. We play each other 19 times a year, and we expected to play each other 7 times in the playoffs, so unfortunately you can see your friends too much. We got sick of each other. By the time September rolled around, they knew all of our weaknesses, a lot of our strengths, and it made it harder to get hits. We had to go into Yankee Stadium, the most intimidating ballpark there is, and a lot of players can't take it. We could. The 2003 Red Sox weren't afraid to walk into any ballpark. We knew what we had to do to win.

The fans and the press see these rivalries in terms of Hatfields and McCoys or good against evil, but for most of us it isn't like that. It may be that way for the guys who came up in an organization and played 10 years—guys like Derek Jeter, Bernie Williams, Jorge Posada, and for us Nomar Garciaparra and Jason Varitek. But these days most players jump teams a lot, rarely staying long enough to develop strong feelings. Sometimes, though, the passion of the fans can get a player caught up in the craziness.

That happened in the ninth inning when Paul Williams, one of the Fenway Park groundskeepers, one of the nicest, most respected guys, was in the Yankee bullpen waving a towel and rooting us on. That's all he was doing. But because he was in the Yankee bullpen, the Yankee pitchers took offense at the show of support. Jeff Nelson of the Yankees and Karim Garcia, who ran over from right field, got in some pretty good shots, and Paul ended up in the hospital. The way we saw it, it was so uncalled for, way out of line. To avoid a trial, Nelson and Garcia each accepted 50 hours of community service. The important thing is, Paul seems to be doing great.

We ended up losing that game, but in the next Tim Wakefield threw a beauty, and Scott Williamson struck out David Dellucci and Alfonso Soriano to end it. Wake, who has the longest tenure on the Sox, was a guy who started every spring as the odd-man-out in the rotation, or was relegated to a role as fifth starter. It was probably because he's too darn nice. He'd say, "Whatever you need from me to make the team better." If they wanted him to be the fifth starter, he was happy to accommodate. Then management would realize it was a good idea to stick him between two hard throwers, and by the time the season was halfway done, he'd end up the third guy.

When we were going good in 2003, we knew we were better when Tim was in the bullpen. It's really hard to find a good long man. He could also close. When they moved him into the rotation, our starting pitching got better but our bullpen went straight to hell. He made that big a difference. The guy did everything we asked of him. His heart is all Red Sox. And if the Sox needed to rebuild one year, guess what? Wake would go through the rebuilding process and help out the kids, until the Red Sox became winners again.

I looked forward to facing David Wells in Game 5. I'd had decent at-bats against Wells. I was one of those guys who got him tired because I fouled off a lot of pitches.

Wells was like Clemens. He knew how to pitch the big games. Wells was one of the smartest pitchers I'd ever seen. You thought you had him, and then you didn't. He *never* gave in. He was not going to give you that cookie shot, the home run pitch. He was never going to walk you intentionally. He was going to stay on the outer edges of the plate, go up and down, mix in a slow curve ball, then a sharp curve ball, and just pitch. That was true of all those Yankee pitchers: they may not have had the best stuff in the world, but they knew how to pitch.

Wells beat us that day. He allowed one run. We had two chances to score, and Nomar ended both rallies. He got up with runners on second and third and struck out, and he grounded out with runners on first and second and two outs. It was sickening the way the Sox fans booed him.

Whenever Nomar stepped into his uniform, all of Red Sox Nation's hopes rested upon his shoulders. Ted Williams once said that Nomar was the best athlete the Red Sox had ever had. If the Red Sox were ever going to win a World Series, it was thought, it was going to be because of him.

It wasn't easy for Nomar to play in Boston. Nomar was very sensitive, but he was also a guy who read every paper and listened to every talk show to a fault. The result was that whenever a reporter tried to be friendly, Nomar would say, "Excuse me, didn't you just rip me?" He was someone who cared too much about his talent to take any bull crap from anybody.

Nomar was isolated in Boston, because he was so popular that everybody wanted a piece of him. The attention was suffocating, and he couldn't enjoy being himself anymore.

Nomar had a lot of friends on the team. We always wanted Nomar to come out with us, grab dinner, but he couldn't. We wondered, *How come he doesn't want to hang out with us?* But as we became more of a team, we started understanding each other more. I don't think anyone really knew what Nomar was going through.

We felt Nomar's slump in September and through the playoffs, because it was a pretty steady drop. The guy was hitting .330 going into September, and he ended up hitting .301. We could tell he was upset. Nomar was one of those guys who thought he could get a hit at every bat. When he didn't, you were surprised.

Like everyone else, I wondered what caused Nomar's slump. I always look at the game of baseball as a very humbling game. I never questioned when a player got in a slump. And I certainly wasn't going to question a six-time All Star, one of the greatest shortstops ever, one of the greatest Red Sox ever. I didn't see anything physically wrong with his swing. He was just going through a bad time.

To me, Nomar was like Joe DiMaggio. He always had that great class. He knew he had to keep his cool. He knew he had to be a teammate. We knew that any time he swung the bat he could cause damage. We never got down on him. No one ever said, "Let's bench him. Let's play someone else." Nomar is a superstar, and superstars find a way to get the job done.

We were down three games to two, with John Burkett going against Andy Pettitte in Game 6. This was another one of those smart guys. He threw a pitch that ran in on the hands of a left-handed batter. He had a cutter he threw to right-handers, and he started throwing it to lefties as well. To this day I don't know whether he throws a change up or a splitter. It was never fun facing that guy.

John Burkett, whose nickname is "Sheets," started for us. John is one of the game's amazing characters. Some pitchers want to be left alone before they start a game. Not John. As soon as the pro football season began, he'd come into the clubhouse with his football pool. Each player got a sheet of paper listing point spreads for fifteen games, and you had to pick which teams you thought were going to cover. Some guys played two or more sheets. John would pass them out as a way to get the team together. The stakes were small. We'd put in twenty bucks a sheet, and whoever picked the most games correctly had a nice little payday.

There aren't a lot of activities you can do in the clubhouse that involve the whole team. As much as we'd like to go out to dinner together, there are other factors like family members who need you, or guys having other things to do, so you can't always get everyone together. Arguing over the Vikings or the Packers really brings the team together.

So Sheets was in charge of the football pool—we *never* bet on baseball—and on the Saturdays he pitched, he'd be in the clubhouse fifteen minutes before the game, making sure the bets were in. He'd run out five minutes before the game, throw his bullpen, and then be ready to go.

Jose Contreras, pitching in relief, struck out the side in the sixth. When we batted in the seventh, we were losing by two runs. Nomar, who broke out of his slump, tripled, one of his four hits. He scored on Matsui's wild throw. Manny doubled, and Ortiz singled him home to tie the game.

We loaded the bases, and the Yankees brought in Felix Heredia, a lefty, to pitch to me. Heredia was another pitcher who gave me trouble. Every time I faced him, he threw me that fastball up and on my hands.

The score was tied when I came up to bat. I stood on top of the plate to make him think—if he threw the ball in, he might hit me. I wasn't in any mood to swing. Like I said, my swing was way off. My strength was way down. I stood on the plate, making him throw perfect pitches. I took four straight balls, driving in the winning run. I did my job, and I was very happy about that. We won the game 9 to 6.

After Game 6, naturally we were very happy celebrating in the clubhouse. As we sat there, we all knew we'd gotten to the point where we had the better team. There was nothing stopping us, and we had Pedro going in Game 7.

Why shouldn't we win it? The guys had started to hit, though I hadn't hit too well the first couple of games. We were ready to attack Game 7. We could not wait for it to come. Roger Clemens was pitching against us, and we'd done some real damage against him during the course of the season. We knew how good Roger was, but we also knew Trot Nixon and David Ortiz had had some success against him. We just felt we were going to have Roger's number.

Being Roger, he had a way to dampen your spirits right away, and he did that, but by the fourth inning Nixon and Kevin Millar homered, and we'd scored four runs against him; after Roger left, we scored one more. It should have been enough, but unfortunately, it wasn't.

Pedro had given up only two solo home runs to Jason Giambi

over the wall in center field, and we took a 5–2 lead going into the eighth inning. If I'd had more strength, I feel pretty certain I could have robbed one of those homers. Normally, I could sky, but when I went after his ball, I was only able to jump three or four inches. That's all the strength I had.

When Pedro went out to pitch the eighth, I felt very comfortable with him out there. Pedro was the best pitcher in the game, and Pedro wanted the ball.

We were five outs away from winning the pennant, with a three-run lead. Pedro was looking good. He still had his velocity. And for five straight hitters, Pedro got strike two. He just wasn't able to finish them off.

Derek Jeter hit a ball over the head of Trot Nixon, who could have been playing deeper. What do you do? Pedro was throwing hard that inning. He had good stuff that inning. When Bernie Williams got up, I thought about cheating up on him a little more. I thought, *If it's over my head, he deserves to get this hit.* But as much as I wanted to move in 15, 20 feet, I didn't, because I couldn't take the chance he would actually hit it over my head. And then Williams hit the ball exactly where I thought he was going to hit it. It dropped about 15 feet in front of me for a single.

Hideki Matsui was next. His hit might have been the biggest. He doubled down the right field line. Jorge Posada then had a two-run single, a broken bat bloop in front of me to tie the score. This was just a case of Yankee magic. It was just going to happen. The Yankee magic was working, and when it's working and when it's late in the ball game, you know what they're going to do next—bring in Mariano Rivera. When he's on, if you have a runner on third, he can get six outs before that runner will score. That's how dominant Rivera is, and he dominated in this game for three straight innings. As beat up as our team was, we couldn't get anything going. That night he had an extra yard on his fastball. He was that awesome.

The sad part about it was that the Yankees were the home team and hit last. Tim Wakefield was pitching for us, and sometimes knuckleballs can go a long way, which we experienced when Aaron

Boone hit Wake's first pitch in the bottom of the eleventh into the left field stands.

People say Boone's hitting that home run was like Bucky Dent's hitting his home run to beat the Sox in 1978, but it wasn't like that at all. I know Bucky Dent, and back in those days it was pretty unusual for a nine hitter or a shortstop to hit a home run. When you consider that Kevin Elster hit 24 home runs in 1996 and drove in 99 runs from the 9 hole for Texas, you know times have changed.

Boone is six foot three, 215 pounds, a pretty solid guy. So his homer wasn't nearly the shock as the home run hit by Bucky Dent.

As I stood out there in center field and watched Boone's ball go into the stands, my first thought was, *What a great series!*

I always try to look at things from the fans' perspective, because, of course, I want the game to thrive. I didn't think the better team won. I wish I would have been healthier. If I'd been healthier, I know things would have been a lot different.

I know I would have hit better. One run in a playoff game is pretty huge. We lost in an extra-inning game. If we could just have pushed across another run. . . .

Back in the fifth inning, Mike Mussina came in with the bases loaded. Jason Varitek struck out, and I hit into a double play. I hit a hot shot right at Jeter. These are the at-bats that get you thinking afterward. *Had I been healthier* . . . In the end I was happy for Aaron Boone, who became part of baseball history. I just wasn't happy his golden moment came at our expense.

I was upset, but I really didn't know what to do. Should I cry? Throwing something wasn't going to do any good. There was no one to blame but our whole team. That night was kind of a blur. We had to get on a plane. I remember as the team bus left Yankee Stadium, Tim Wakefield sat in his seat, and he was crying.

He just felt so bad. He wasn't crying for himself. He just felt so bad because beating the Yankees and going to the World Series was a dream for all of us. He felt bad for the fans, and he felt bad for his teammates. He felt like it was all him.

I made sure I told him how important he was to our team.

"You know what," I told him, "we would have gone home a couple days earlier if it hadn't been for you." We'd used Wake a lot, and he just ended up on the wrong side of history. "By no means did you lose that game for us," I said. "You win as a team, and you lose as a team."

As I rode the bus to the airport, it didn't occur to me that Grady Little had done anything wrong. I didn't even think it was an issue. Grady wasn't swinging the bats for us. And Pedro wanted to get the job done, and he looked like he was going strong. But because he didn't, all eyes turned on Grady. That's why being a manager has to be one of the toughest jobs. Any time a team loses, it's not the players' fault, it's the guy running them. That's why managers know the day they get hired, one day they're going to be fired.

I remember the day they fired Grady. We talked on the phone. He said he'd had a great time being a part of our team, and he wished we could have done more. He just said that the owners didn't see things the way he saw them. He wished us luck. He said he'd see us around.

You have to understand Grady. When the Sox introduced him as our manager, the guys on our team who knew him applauded him. Everybody was happy. We all thought he was the perfect manager for the Red Sox. Then, because of what happened in that eighth inning, Grady went from being the perfect manager to being the biggest scapegoat in the history of the game.

We were still in a state of shock from losing that seventh game. Every time I saw one of my friends, he'd say, "I still can't believe you guys lost."

"No shit," I'd say. "I was there, and I can't believe it, either."

The day after we lost, I was in Boston packing before driving home to Florida when the phone rang. It was my business agent Peter Caparis with some sad news. During the year I had been the spokesperson for a program that brought gravely ill children to Fenway Park to meet the players. During my year working with HP Hood in this program, I got to meet a lot of very brave kids. They never said, "Why me?" They always moved forward.

Eddie Urbanowski, one of the boys I'd met, was on his deathbed, and Peter said his last wish was to speak with me for a final time, that it would give him some happiness. I felt honored.

I began driving south from Boston down Route 95 to my home in Orlando when I called him. He was 12. I could hear how much worse he'd gotten. He hurt every time he spoke, so I did most of the talking.

The first thing I told him was I was sorry we couldn't beat the Yankees, but then I said, "Guess what? We will. It's just a matter of time. Our day will come." And then I told him how happy I was to have met him, and I said I wanted him to stay strong, stay positive.

"You just have to hope for a miracle," I said. Unfortunately, it didn't happen, and Eddie passed away a couple days later.

When you see kids dying young, it makes the game of baseball seem a lot less important. I don't ever look at this game as life and death. After my concussion, I could have been done playing baseball for good. You never know when your time is up.

On that ride home I made a vow to myself that when the 2004 season rolled around, I'd go out there and enjoy myself. You find it's the not caring so much about winning that makes winning possible.

Chapter 2

Childhood

NOVEMBER 1973

I was born on an army base in Fort Riley, Kansas, in 1973. We only spent about a month there, so I don't remember anything about the place. I remember driving by it once when I was playing for the Kansas City Royals. It only took two minutes to drive past.

My dad was in the army for 20 years and 20 days. When he left, he held the rank of staff sergeant. He said he could have moved up higher in rank, but that would have meant moving us even more as kids, and he didn't want to do that.

My dad and mom met during the Vietnam War. My mom, who was born in Thailand, was working as a nurse helping the army troops. My mom says the reason she married my dad was that she felt sorry for him. I'm serious. At least that's what she said when I asked her about it. My mom said she felt the guy needed to be loved by someone. My dad had actually been married twice before, once when he was real young, and a second time early in his army career.

He was divorced when he and my mom met. It was my mom's first marriage, and they wed in Thailand while he was serving in the army.

My dad doesn't like to talk about what he did during the war. Not many soldiers do. He spent most of the war in Thailand. He said he made a couple of trips to Vietnam. He told me that one of his duties was to stand watch on the outskirts of the jungle and watch for the enemy. He said a couple times he called in for permission to fire, but never got it. I do know he never got shot at, and I'm glad about that.

My mom lost her first child, a daughter, in childbirth, and a year later my brother, James, was born in Thailand. After that, my dad was transferred to Fort Riley, so that was why I was born there.

From Fort Riley, we moved to Germany for a month or two, and then we went to Okinawa, Japan, and spent a couple years there. A couple of times I went with my mom to Thailand when she visited her parents.

Okinawa was a very cool place. I remember going to the beach with my mom. There were rocks that led out into the ocean, and she'd walk out onto the rocks, reach down, and catch lobster. By the time the day was over, we'd have a bathtub full of lobsters. I remember a couple times getting bitten by one of those creatures. Even then, I was fearless and curious, a bad combination. I'd go up to the lobsters and play with them, trying to see how tough they were. My mom definitely had to keep a close eye on me.

One time my brother and I got in a little trouble in Okinawa. We were six and four, and we decided to walk over to a local hotel and cause a little havoc. We were playing around, making noise, acting like kids. Nobody would claim us. Okinawa was a small town, and our mischief even made the news on the radio. It wasn't until I was fifteen years old that my parents realized it was James and I who'd terrorized the hotel guests that day.

Even though my brother was older, I was the guy who always stuck up for him. If I ever saw anyone picking on him, I'd attack the bully, biting him if I had to.

My dad was very nonchalant about being a dad. He is a tough guy who wanted me to experience life. He wanted me to try things. If I climbed up on the roof of the house and fell down, he wasn't going to be the parent standing there ready to catch me, which is what a lot of parents do today. The new generation of parents is scared their kids will get hurt, and they wrap them in a cocoon, never giving them the chance to experience life. If my dad saw me on the roof, his attitude was, *If he falls, he won't do it again.* It's where I get my toughness. You try to instill that in your kids, and hope they survive their childhoods to become tough adults.

I was four when we left Okinawa and moved to Fort Campbell, Kentucky, where my dad was stationed. We lived in the town of Clarksville. That's where I learned the joy of running. My brother would head off to school, and I'd be home all day with my mom. When I got bored, my mom would tell me to run around the outside of the house. It got so I could run around the house 300 times. I would run from my house to the bus stop where the bus would let off my brother. We had a family friend who had a son, and he and I would run five miles, keeping up a fast pace. I guess my athleticism began back then. I always was active.

Before we left Clarksville, my mother spent her hard-earned money signing my brother and me up for baseball. I was going to play T-ball, and James was signed up for the real thing. But right before the season was scheduled to start, we moved again.

My mom, coming from Thailand and not knowing much about the States, told my dad she wanted to go someplace magical. She was mesmerized by the Disney mystique, so she wanted to go either to Disneyland in Anaheim, California, or Disney World in Orlando, Florida. It turned out she had some friends from back home in Thailand who lived in Orlando, so that made the decision easier. My father wanted out of the army, so when we moved to Orlando, he left the service. It was time for them to start a new life.

When we first arrived in Florida, for a couple weeks we lived in Panama City with friends of my mom's. We were at the beach all the time. The weather was nice and warm. Then we headed for

Orlando, and again we lived with friends at first. There was, and is, a strong Thai presence in Orlando. My mom goes to the temple quite a bit and helps out. It makes her happy to use some of the money I've made to help them build a nicer facility.

I thought the world of Orlando right away. There were lakes close by, and I made friends with a bunch of young kids, who remain friends of mine to this day. You meet a lot of people, but you can count your friends on two hands, and most are from my childhood. Even when we were poor, these guys always had my back. We'd stay out all day and night, playing games, playing baseball. Our moms would always have to come looking for us.

My dad became a security guard. He worked at Howard Johnson, and he also worked at the Florida Mall when it was being built. My mom worked for the Moran Printing Company binding books, and she was also a housekeeper at Howard Johnson cleaning rooms.

I hadn't played sports before coming to Orlando. I just ran, which was a big help to me when I began playing soccer. To this day I'm a very good soccer player. I can run at top speed all game long, and I have a strong leg.

I first became aware that I had baseball talent when I began playing T-ball. In T-ball, they put the ball on a stick and you get up and hit it. Pretty much every time I got up, I hit a home run. In my son's league, they have changed the rules so the batters can only take one base at a time, but when I was playing, you could keep running.

I was born left-handed, but when I first started playing, I played righty, because we couldn't afford a glove, and the one somebody gave me was a righty glove. I was 8 when I started playing Little League, and I'd wear the glove on my left hand. If I only had to make a short throw, I'd throw righty, but if the ball was hit far and I had to field it, I would catch the ball, take the glove off, and throw it in with my left hand. I sensed back then I had unusual talent, because even though I was only 8, I was the second player selected in the Little League draft. The first player picked was aged 12.

I played first base that first season and hit above .300. I played great defense, and what really made me stand out was my pitching ability. I had a tough curve ball that just buckled hitters.

We didn't have anyone to teach us. We experimented, tried out things until they worked, and living in Florida we could play from sun up to sun down all year round.

During the summer all we did was play baseball. I remember when one friend, Shawn Roth, got a three-wheel ATV. We took it everywhere. We lived near Lake Buena Vista, and back then there were empty fields near the Disney properties where we could go and play. Or we'd find construction sites with big holes and big piles of dirt, and we'd play there. I remember as a kid not having to shower for a month because we were outside all the time playing, and we would just find one of those pools and jump in to cool off.

In the woods we played the game Army for hours. We'd pretend we were marines. If a car was parked on the street, we'd run up the back, over the roof, down the hood, and keep on going.

My brother, who was two years older, would come home from school and pick a fight with me.

"Did you steal my sandwich?"

"I didn't steal it. You took a bite and left it there."

"You got three seconds to run," he'd say.

He'd grab the BB gun and get ready to fire it at me. We grew up rough and tumble. And to think how nice I am to him now! But it was instrumental to my childhood to be able to play ball with him and his friends. That's where the baseball player in me really came out, because it was an opportunity to play with older kids, and I had to play better and harder to keep up.

We'd play home run derby, and it seemed like every swing I took resulted in a home run. I was always shocked when I swung and didn't hit it. That's how talented I was when I was 12 and 13. I don't say this to brag. I just don't know any other way to describe it.

Because my parents each worked two jobs, and sometimes three, I didn't have any supervision. One of the advantages of their being so busy was that they never pushed me into doing anything. In fact, my dad never even watched me play. Until I was a senior in high school and the college scouts began to call, he had no idea how good I was. My dad hated talking on the phone, and he'd tell whoever called, "Son of a bitch, stop calling my house."

Around this time my dad went to Orlando College on the GI bill and got his degree. My dad was why I ended up being so easy-going, so nonchalant about things. All he said was, "Just don't get D's and F's, and you'll be fine." He never got on me about being a better student. And I ended up being an A student. Similarly, he never pushed me to play baseball. He just said, "You do whatever you want." He actually let me start driving his car when I was 12. He'd be tired from working all night, and so I would drive him. Orlando was a very unbusy place, and my mom didn't mind.

When I was 14, I was helping my mom clean rooms at the Howard Johnson's so I could help make some extra money during Christmas break. I was driving fast to get back to work on time, and I was pulled over by a cop.

"I'm going to need your license, registration, and insurance."

Though I was 14, I looked 18. I told him I'd left my license at home, and I gave him my brother James's name. My brother was cool about it. That was one time I really got lucky. If I'd have gotten busted right there, who knows what would have happened to me?

That same year my mom bought me a motor scooter. The first day I had it, I drove it 500 miles. I'd arrange parties for all the kids in the neighborhood, and I would shuttle them all to where we were having the party. I never threw parties at my house, but we had so many cool areas nearby for having a good time.

We'd build forts back in the woods. Once we tried digging holes to China. And I continued playing baseball.

When I was 13, I actually thought I was good enough to play right then in the big leagues. Physically, I was a man. I was six foot one, 185 pounds, and I had a rifle arm. I played in the South Orange Little League, and in the playoffs we played against the best team in the Dr. Phillips Little League, which was the best in the state. The fastest player on their team was a guy by the name of Will Brand. I'd pitched the game before, and under the rules you couldn't pitch two games in a row, so I was in center field when we played them. I caught a ball in deep center, near the outfield wall, and Brand went to tag from third, and I threw the ball in with such force that he had no chance to score. I threw out a couple runners in that game, and I hit great. Those Dr. Phillips guys felt sorry for me because no one else on the South Orange team was gifted with much talent. What I didn't know then was that I'd end up going to Dr. Phillips High School in Orlando and playing on the same team as those Dr. Phillips Little League players.

For years everyone was in awe of how I hit and threw. Then one day, while playing in a sandlot football game, I landed on my shoulder and heard a pop that scared me. After that I had to change my throwing motion.

My seventh-grade year I played at Walker Junior High School in Orlando. The school board had voted to drop baseball at the end of the year. The coach said to me, "No seventh grader has ever started here, but since this is the last year of baseball, if you can win a starting position, you'll start." I wanted to play center field, but the coach started me out in right field and then moved me over. I ended up being second on the team in hitting and—this will sound like bragging again—just electrified the team. It's pretty cool to be young and athletically gifted.

When I was 13, I was playing in the senior division with kids 13 to 15, but a bunch of my brothers' friends, my friends too, were in the 16 to 18 division. They were scheduled to play a game in Deland and they only had eight players, and they went around the neighborhood looking for a couple more guys to play. I told them I'd play, even if I wasn't old enough.

"Just tell them you're James." My brother was playing baseball in high school at the time. These guys either lacked the skills or the grades to make the high school team.

We rolled into Deland, a hotbed for the Ku Klux Klan, from what I've heard. The first time I came to bat, I ripped a double. Then a single. And I was hitting against a kid who ended up getting drafted in the pros in the fourth round.

I was on base, and I started talking to the Deland first baseman.

"Man, you've got a great swing," he said. "Are you going to be drafted this year, or are you going to college?"

"Oh, I'm not sure," I said. "I'm just playing. We'll see what happens." I was 13.

I went 3 for 3, and then the game was cut short by a big brawl. We were winning, they were getting mad, and one of their players slid hard into my friend Chuck Shea, the second baseman, and Chuck just cold-cocked the guy, and here we go. Somehow we got in the car and drove back to Orlando without anyone getting arrested.

Soon something happened to me that happens to a lot of kids that age: I began viewing baseball as not that important. Much more interesting was causing trouble with my friends and going out with girls. I first started chasing girls when I was 12, though I discovered that catching them wasn't easy at that age. I ended up kissing a lot of girls, but I didn't get really involved with them until I was a little older. It was healthy fun—the good old days of adolescence. I'd take my scooter and try to pick up girls.

In my eighth-grade year the middle school I was attending dropped baseball, so I didn't play very much. My brother's insistence was one of the biggest reasons I kept playing at all. I wanted to go out and smoke weed and run with the kids in the neighborhood and just get into any kind of trouble I could find, staying out all night, but he wouldn't let me quit. He pushed me to keep playing.

"You have a gift," he'd say.

My brother knew how much pot I was doing and about the wine I'd steal from my mom's stash, and one day he sat me aside and kind of kicked me into high gear.

"You have no idea how good you are," he said. "You make guys like me sick. You play better than me. You play better than anyone who's here. Your talent is amazing. You're fast. You're strong." He told me if I kept at it, I was sure to get a scholarship to college.

At the time I was resentful that he was trying to tell me what to do with my life, but his talk made an impression, and because of him I never did stop playing.

I needed to make some money to go to the movies and buy stuff, and fortunately for me, I had a friend whose dad needed kids to help him out. His father sold sunglasses at Sea World, and he'd take me with him, and two or three times a week I would clean the racks of sunglasses for $7 an hour. As a result, I never had to ask my parents for money, and I was never a kid who sold drugs or robbed people, like some of the kids I grew up with who are no longer friends.

My mom and dad kept me from going in that direction. My dad smoked two packs of cigarettes a day. When it came to drugs, my dad would say, "I can't watch you all the time. I used to smoke pot myself, so who am I to tell you what to do? You're old enough to know what's right and wrong. You can try it out, because that's the only way you'll learn, but I'd strongly advise you not to do drugs. And if you get in trouble, call me, and I'll do what I can."

When I was 14 I entered the ninth grade at Dr. Phillips High School, where I played JV football and went up to varsity at the end of the year. I was a running back and scored some touchdowns, but I was also a free safety. My sophomore year I was on varsity but they only played me at free safety. I liked football, but I didn't love it. I wanted to be a receiver, and they wanted me at safety. I wanted stardom. I wanted to go out and catch passes. And they wouldn't let me, so I stopped playing football. Another reason I quit was that I was playing baseball all year round.

As a freshman I started on the varsity baseball team. My brother James was playing left field. I struggled my freshman year and didn't do much. I put a lot of pressure on myself. I was pressing so hard, I stopped having fun, and they ended up sending me down to JV. I was also running track, so at the end of the year I told them not to bother bringing me back up, because the baseball team wasn't fighting for anything, and the track team was winning a lot. I could fly. In the 100 meters I finished second behind Horace Copeland, who could run the 100 in 10.2 seconds. I was a freshman and he was a senior, and I got a bad start, which cost me the race. I ran the 100, the 200, and the

400. In four years of high school I never lost a 400-meter race. Everyone thought I was a machine, the way I ran. I never won the state championship in the 400, because you can only run in two events, and I ran the 100 and the 200. My senior year I finished fifth in the state of Florida in the 100 meter, behind a skinny kid named Tony Gaiter.

My freshman year in high school I met the girl I'd later marry. Her name was Angie Vannice, and she wowed me. She was in the tenth grade, and when I first saw her at school, I told myself, *I need to meet her.* A couple of friends of mine were in her class, and they told her, "I know someone who likes you."

I was different from a lot of the high school guys. As much a hoodlum as I was, I was also mature, friendly, and very courteous. I went up to her and asked her for her telephone number. She wrote out her locker combination. Her locker was only a few lockers away.

"What am I going to do with that?" I wanted to know.

She eventually gave me her phone number, and we started dating. We hung out and did a lot of things together. That's all we wanted to do. Angie was in the dance corps at Dr. Phillips, performing at football games and rallies. Eventually she danced at UCF and was a dancer at Disney. Her dad owned a construction company, and during the summer he hired me. I worked there as a surveyor even after I became a pro ballplayer.

My sophomore year I had a pretty good season, and our baseball team ended up 22–8, but we didn't get very far in the state championships. We had good players, but guys who were still a year away. The coaches didn't want me pitching. They wanted me in center field.

By my junior year I was playing on the Central Florida All Stars. Malcolm Cepeda, Orlando's son, was on the team along with Mark Bellhorn, even though he came from Seminole County.

That year I played baseball and ran track. The deal was that if there was a conflict, and the baseball team was facing a tough opponent, then baseball won out over track. Early in the season we had a track meet and a game, and I wanted to play baseball, and the track coach gave me a hard time.

"I thought we had an agreement that baseball comes first," I said. But he really wanted me to run.

"These guys are depending on you," he said.

"I can't."

"Then you're off the team."

"I want to be off the team." So it was mutual. Besides, the year before, I'd won the 100- and 200-meter races in our conference, had been the most important runner on the team, and the coach gave the MVP trophy to this other guy, a good jumper who was always hurt.

You've got to be kidding me, I thought. Not to take anything away from the jumper, but I thought I had shown a lot of heart. It really hurt my feelings. I figured if this coach wasn't going to be loyal to me, I had no obligation to return any loyalty to him. Both of us were stubborn. I didn't run for the rest of the season. I concentrated on baseball.

Brian Barber, who would get drafted in the first round by the St. Louis Cardinals, was our team's top starting pitcher. David Moore, our third baseman, was drafted by the White Sox. Brian Costello, our left fielder, signed a scholarship to go to the University of Florida but ended up signing with the Philadelphia Phillies. Kevin Chabot went to Auburn, where he was on a pace to break all of Frank Thomas's records. But being the crazy man he is, Kevin hurt himself in an arm-wrestling competition. He swung the bat well and was signed by the St. Louis Cardinals, but he wasn't high enough on the totem pole to warrant their keeping him, so he never made it to the major leagues. He was probably our best hitter. Bob Hanousek, our catcher, went to Valencia Community College. Bryan Bruce, our second baseman, went on to play at the University of Central Florida. I was the center fielder. Our team was stacked.

My high school coach Danny Allie was the most influential person in my entire baseball career. He was the one who instilled in me the importance of hard work and hustle. He's the reason I run in and out of the dugout to go to the outfield and why I hustle down to first base. After our practices and workouts were over, he used to time us running on and off the field. He wanted to make sure we hustled. He really knew how to push our buttons. Coach Allie was also the guy who got on the phone and said to the college and pro teams, "I've got a player by the name of Brian Barber. I have another player named Johnny Damon. They're going to be special." He's the one who induced colleges to give scholarships to a lot of players who might not otherwise have been able to go. He pretty much dedicated his life to getting us into college, to putting us on the right track.

He was a life-management skills teacher. Because I was a good student, I'd hang out in his classroom and talk about my future, about what was next for me.

He's not at Dr. Phillips anymore. Somebody must have had it in for him, a disgruntled parent probably, because he was in charge of selling tickets to the games, and one day there was a head count of spectators, and the money drawer came up $20 short. At times he'd let parents who couldn't afford the $5 go in for free, and when they accused him of letting people skate without paying, instead of fighting it, he quit. He wasn't going to spend $20 thousand in legal fees fighting over $20. His daughter was going through chemotherapy at the time, and he just packed his things. John Hart, then the general manager of the Cleveland Indians, was a good friend of his and got him a job running a baseball clinic in the Cleveland area.

The most important thing is that his daughter fully recovered from cancer. Coach Allie's got four great kids, and he's happy. The kids who came along later at Dr. Phillips High School were the big losers.

My junior year our Dr. Phillips High School team was rated number one in the country. We got as far as the semifinal game in the state tournament. We had a 28–4 record, we were leading 5–2 in the fourth inning, and Brian Barber was kicked out of the game for wearing a necklace.

He had a turtleneck on because it was cool at the start of the game, and after it warmed up, he took it off, and you could see his necklace. Wearing a necklace has never won anyone a ball game, but apparently it's a high school rule that if you're caught wearing one, the umpire has to throw you out of the game. Because that's what happened. We were playing Jacksonville Terry Parker, and the coach came out and told the umpires, "I am taking my team off the field unless you throw this guy out of the game for wearing jewelry." I hope that coach is leading a happy life. I also hope he chokes on his trophy.

After Brian came out, we lost the game, and there went our dreams for the state and national championships. It was a dream season anyway, but after the game we all knew we'd lost something that would have stayed with us forever. It wouldn't be the last championship snatched away from me but I can feel the disappointment to this day.

Chapter 3

Up the Ladder

JUNE 1990

During the summer after my junior year in high school, a coach from New York, Steve Bort, recruited me to play on an All Star team that included Alex Rodriguez, Todd Helton, and Danny Kanell. It was the first time I'd ever been away from home. Alex, our number nine hitter, was the only sophomore on the team. You could see his talent. When we played basketball, he could jump up and dunk the ball. Of all the players on the team Todd Helton had the best swing. Danny Kanell, who was also pretty awesome, would talk about his plans to become an NFL quarterback. He ended up starting at quarterback for Florida State and going on to the New York Giants.

We played 10 games, and I scored 19 runs and drove in 19 runs, all against good pitching from all over the country. We lost the championship to a team from California.

When I returned to Dr. Phillips High for my senior year, the track coach and I reached a new understanding. He just said, "Show up and run whenever you can." He knew how many points I could earn in a meet. If he had me for just part of the season, he knew we could compete for the state title.

The reality is that the track season really starts in the districts, and from there the team can advance to the states. Our team finished seventh in the state of Florida. I finished fifth in the 100 meters, second in the 200 meters, and sixth in the triple jump, not because I was good, but because not a whole lot of people were competing in that event. The winner, James Beckford, was a high school freshman who was on the Jamaican national team.

Our baseball season my senior year started off badly. We faced Doug Million from Sarasota. This kid was something else. He tore us apart. Doug signed with the Colorado Rockies, but died a couple years later from asthma.

I remember that as I was walking up for my first at-bat, the PA announcer said, "Now batting, the number one player in the country, Johnny Damon." Talk about pressure. That was pretty rough. Also my health was not as good as it should have been. The track team had gone to the Florida Relays in Gainesville, and I'd eaten a bad taco, got sick from food poisoning, and lost 10 pounds.

It was one of those no-luck years. I hit .305 my senior year when I should have hit .500. Everything I hit seemed to go right at a fielder somewhere. Opposing outfielders were catching the balls I hit against the wall, diving and making catches. One time I hit a hot shot off the second baseman's chest, and I beat out the throw, and then he had to go to the hospital. The official scorer called it an error. It was just one freak play after another. I went from being rated the best player, a sure-shot number one draft choice, to falling all the way to being chosen the thirty-fifth player in the pro draft.

I did have other options. Stanford University asked me to fly out to California and meet with their coaches, but that would have been too far for my folks. Angie and I were still dating, and she was going to the University of Central Florida, and UCF wanted me to go there. The University of Miami offered me a full ride back when they never offered anyone full rides. Florida State University didn't say

I'd get a scholarship. All I was told was, "You'll be taken care of." I didn't know what that meant, whether it was academics or athletics. Georgia Tech, a school I was really leaning toward, called me a couple days before I was supposed to visit and said, "We can't afford to bring you here, because there's a good chance you're going to turn pro." So I didn't go.

The Florida Gators offered me a full ride, and their school was the one I picked.

Joe Arnold was the Gators' head coach, and he really impressed me as being down to earth, as were all the coaches there. Arnold told me if I went to Florida, I'd start as a freshman in center field. Florida had a family atmosphere. Everything was perfect there.

Arnold told me, "We'd love for you to come to Florida."

As it turned out, the Gators would offer scholarships to Dr. Phillips players three years in a row, and three years in a row those players would end up signing pro contracts. First came Brian Barber, the next year me, and then Brian Costello.

Before draft day I'd gotten some calls from teams expressing interest in signing me. The Milwaukee Brewers had called. The Houston Astros called and said they definitely would be interested, but that they weren't sure whether they'd use a number one pick to get me. I'd known John Hart, the general manager of the Cleveland Indians and later the Texas Rangers, because during Christmas vacation he ran a camp for top high-school prospects in Kissimmee, Florida, near where I lived. I'd attended the camp, so he knew what I could do, and I was thinking I was going to go to Cleveland. At the time, I was being compared to Barry Bonds and Ken Griffey Jr., but others thought I was more like Willie Wilson, the Kansas City speedster. I bought into the hype, except that I saw myself as more like fleet-footed slugger Kirk Gibson.

I remember the day I was drafted. I was playing golf just to get my mind off it. I didn't have a cell phone. I'm not sure anyone even had cell phones then. My brother was home on the phone keeping track of what was going on. When I got home from golf, they'd gone through the entire first round, and no one had taken me.

"Hey," I said to my brother, "maybe I should just go to college."

I knew I needed to go pro, because my parents really didn't have much money, and even if I got a college scholarship, going to college was going to cost them money. My dream was to go to college and be a college baseball and even football star, but I was also a realist. I knew Mom and Dad couldn't afford it. They'd supported me all those years, and I needed to start helping them out.

The next hour I became a sandwich pick awarded the Kansas City Royals after their shortstop Kurt Stillwell left as a free agent. I was happy to go to Kansas City. It had been a team I'd rooted for as a boy—Kansas was where I was born. And the Royals trained in the spring a half hour west down Interstate 4 in Haines City, which back then was known as Baseball City. All I had to do was drive up the street thirty minutes. It worked out perfectly.

When I was drafted by Kansas City, the local writers started saying I was the "new George Brett," the guy who was going to put the Royals back on the map.

James, with assistance from superagent Scott Boras, negotiated my first contract. It took about three weeks. I'd met Scott when I was a junior in high school.

"You're an incredible player," he'd said to me in passing. "Hopefully we can work together in the future."

After I was drafted, James called Scott, who was happy to give his advice.

You really don't have very much leverage when you're a second-round pick. The leverage I had was that if I didn't like the Royals' offer, I could enroll at the University of Florida.

What I was also up against was the fact that the Royals, a small-market team in a good old-fashioned midwestern town, had chosen 5 players among the first 42 picks. For me, it was never about the money. I wanted to get what was fair, but I never wanted to push the boundaries or make anyone mad or cause the Royals to have second thoughts about my signing if I struggled. What I eventually signed for—a $250,000 bonus and $800 a month—was very fair to me, my family, and the Royals. For an 18-year-old, it was all the money in the world. I bought my first vehicle, a '92 Ford Bronco. I helped Angie buy a new car.

I went to rookie ball in Baseball City, living in a little dorm room thirty minutes away, so I got to go home quite a bit and I still got to see Angie. For the first time, my folks came and watched me play. My dad had been shocked that someone would actually give me money to play baseball.

When I reported in the spring for A ball at Rockford, what I noticed most was that the players who had to return held a grudge against the new players coming in. They felt the new guys were out to take their jobs, and they had a chip on their shoulders. Even though we all had a common goal, to do well and get to the next level, the newbies weren't greeted with open arms.

More than anything our manager, Mike Jirschele, taught me how to be a man.

At Rockford, we had a good team but lost out for the championship, and when Jirschele managed me again at Wilmington in the high A league, we won the Carolina League championship. Mike was a second baseman who never made it to the big leagues. He told me that one time in the minors the manager even sent a pitcher up to hit for him.

One of the biggest problems I had as a leadoff hitter was knowing what advice to take and what to ignore. I was often told, "Take the first pitch." But very often the first pitch was the best pitch I was going to see. It's a problem I'm still wrestling with today.

That first year I learned that in baseball things are constantly changing. Pitching reports change, and you have to be able to adjust and go with the flow.

I took pitches in high school. It can help your teammates quite a bit, which I've always been happy about, because being patient at the plate will result in the opposing pitcher throwing a lot more pitches, and eventually tiring. But taking pitches is not something you want to do if you're worried about your batting average and your stats. Guys who hack away at the first best pitch do the best on that score.

I was always able to foul pitches off that were strikes but that I didn't want to hit. I was always able to put the ball in play. So there always were things I could do in high school, and in the minors I worked even more diligently to perfect these skills.

During my rookie ball half season Angie and I got engaged. Her argument was that when I left the next year to go to a different city, it wouldn't be right if she went with me and we started living together unmarried.

I was oblivious. My reaction was, "Oh, okay." It didn't occur to me what I'd be giving up. The movie *Bull Durham* is real in a lot of its aspects. It shows women throwing themselves at ballplayers, something I never dreamed of. I knew I loved women. I just didn't know the temptations that were out there.

After my half year in rookie ball in the summer, Angie and I got married. We were 19. She had no idea what she was getting into when she became a ballplayer's wife. Though I didn't want to hear about it, she definitely had her opinions about certain guys. For me, I respected them, no matter what they wanted to do. She was always judging my teammates, and me as well. Not only judging, but accusing. That's just not fun. The jealousy had started when she was 16. I'd go off to baseball tournaments, and she would always be accusing me of doing things with other girls behind her back. For years, I listened to her suspicions, and for years that's all they were, empty suspicions. If she hadn't been so jealous when I was out of her sight, we might still be together.

I played a full year at Rockford and then a full year at Wilmington, Delaware. The thing about playing in the minors is that you're always playing against local legends. One of them was Trot Nixon, who was playing for the Red Sox minor league team in Lynchburg, Virginia. Nixon had turned down a football scholarship to play quarterback at North Carolina State University. We knew he was big stuff when we played him. When you go up against a guy like that, you try even harder. We read in *Baseball America* that Trot had even earned comparisons to Mickey Mantle back in high school. The experts talked about his grit and his hard-nosed attitude. He was someone we looked forward to playing.

Another guy who impressed me was Billy Mueller of Shreveport. This guy was the same guy he is now—the perfect baseball player. You couldn't defense him. He didn't hit home runs; he hit line drives and just went about his business. When we played against each other, I admired him so much I was hoping one day we'd play on the same team. He turned out to be everything I expected.

One pitcher who impressed me was Jesus Martinez, Pedro's younger brother. He was pitching for the San Antonio Dodgers, and he had really good stuff. When you faced him, you heard the Martinez name, and you tried to get it out of your head. This guy had a running fastball and a great curve. He was mature beyond his years, and yet he never made it, and I don't know why.

There were a bunch of us who started out together, and the year we moved up to Wilmington, our team came together. Among my teammates were Chris Sheehan, Mike Bovee, and Brian Bevil, pretty good players, but they didn't make it. They were good but didn't get the breaks, and they gave up.

That's the thing about baseball. It's never about your talent. Everybody in the minor leagues has talent. If you're planning on building a career in baseball through just your talent alone, you've got *no chance*. Most important, you need *will*. You've got to work harder than the next guy, and you have to want it more than the next guy. Guys who make it do so with their heart and mind.

And a lot of luck. If you signed with the New York Yankees, they had the luxury of leaving you in the minors for a while. If you signed as a shortstop and were playing behind Derek Jeter, your stay in the minors might be for a *long* while. The Kansas City Royals—luckily— didn't have that luxury.

I began my third year in the minor leagues at Double A Wichita, Kansas, where we were the only team in the league to fly everywhere we played. It was a fun year, and I was putting up some monster numbers. I made the All Star team, and I remember meeting the legendary Todd Walker, who would be a Red Sox teammate in 2003. He was sitting down surrounded by three or four of the most gorgeous girls I ever saw. I was so jealous, until I found out at least two of them were his sisters, and the others were his sisters' friends.

In August 1995, after only half a season in Double A ball, I was called up to the majors. The Royals needed an outfielder, and I was the best thing in the minors they had.

I remember very vividly the day I was called up. Ron Johnson, who'd coached in the Royals organization for years, was my manager at Wichita. He was fiery, and he was always talking.

The day before I got the call, Ron rested me. He knew I was a little beat up and that we'd be traveling the next day. When I went to the ballpark that day, and I looked at the lineup card, and my name wasn't on it, I was pissed.

"Ron," I said, "how come I'm not playing? Did I do something wrong? Is there something I don't know about? Did I miss a sign? What's going on?"

He grabbed the scorecard with the lineup on it and in mock anger, ripped it up.

"This is so unbelievable," Ron said. "This guy here is complaining about playing time. He plays *every day*. Why do I have to play you? Are you saying you're better than everyone else?"

I couldn't tell whether he was serious or saying these things jokingly, and then he said, "The reason I'm not playing you is that you need to get on a plane and head to Kansas City."

At first I didn't understand what he was telling me. I always figured my career's natural progression would be from Double A to Triple A and then to Kansas City. Earlier in the season I'd been upset that the Royals hadn't promoted me to Triple A, where I'd be one step away from the big leagues. Darren Burton was playing center field in Triple A at Omaha, and I always figured I'd be following behind him going up. Darren had one of the best arms I had ever seen and had good talent. His only weakness was his hitting. He didn't hit for average.

I was hitting .350, and Darren was hitting .230, and when I bypassed Triple A, I also bypassed Darren. His progression had stopped. I skipped over him and went to Kansas City.

When I got the word I was going to the big leagues, Angie was with me in Midland, Texas. I was living a dream, but when we called our relatives, we couldn't get anyone on the phone. We tried calling everyone. Her parents were out of town. My parents wouldn't answer the telephone. My brother didn't answer his phone. It was very strange.

There'd been a huge shakeup on the Royals with 11 players switching around, 6 leaving, and 5 new ones coming. Guys like Vince Coleman and Craig James were in the clubhouse getting ready to leave, bitter at being cut. The Royals were in the wild-card hunt, and all of a sudden, players were being let go and a group of young players were coming in. Coming along with me were Brent Cookson, Michael Tucker, Joe Randa, and Joe Vitiello.

From Midland, I flew straight to Kansas City. Angie flew to Wichita to pack our things. I got to the ballpark in KC knowing the Royals were supposed to play the Seattle Mariners and wondering if we were going to face Seattle's star pitcher Randy Johnson that night.

Before the game Bob Boone, the Royals manager, called me into his office. He said, "You're going to be batting lead off. Just relax. Go out and keep doing what you've been doing, and hopefully it'll be the right thing."

I remember being nervous the first game. Tim Belcher, not Randy Johnson, was pitching for Seattle. I didn't want to swing at the first pitch because I didn't want to pop it up. The first two times I batted he got me to pop out lazily anyway. My third time up I hit a roller down the first base line, but Tino Martinez, the first baseman, was playing wide of the bag because of my late swing, and the ball rolled all the way to the wall, as I raced into third with a triple. The crowd went crazy. I ended up getting two more hits that night to go 3 for 5 in my first game.

"Keep bringing up those young guys," the newspaper said the next morning. It meant a lot to me to do well in my first game. We'd collected a win, and Kansas City was looking for good things.

In the first week I was up, we actually went from $2\frac{1}{2}$ games back to a $2\frac{1}{2}$ game lead for the wild card. We went out and played well. That first month in the majors I hit clutch home runs and played the good D.

I was sparking the team. We couldn't catch Cleveland, though, who were led by Jim Thome. The Indians were an awesome ballclub that won the division with 100 wins and finished 30 games ahead of us.

The veterans on the Royals had missed spring training because of the long baseball strike, but because I was in the minors, I'd gone to the instructional league and then played a full slate of spring training games, in addition to all the games I played for Wichita. By the end of the year I had about 900 at-bats. Before the season was over I wore out, and we just missed making the wild card.

In 1996 and 1997, the Royals ended up at the bottom of the division. There was no money, and no veterans to help us greenhorns understand what we were going through. We were just a bunch of kids who'd had success in the minor leagues, and it became a tinkering, learning process.

On opening day of 1997 Bob Boone pinch hit for the number three, four, and five guys back to back to back. I was hitting three, Joe Vitiello was four, and Bob Hamelin was five. We were there because we were among the better hitters on the team, but we never got really comfortable. We weren't happy. We knew it was a long learning process and we weren't going to win no matter what we did.

Our team just wasn't good. Our payroll was about $18 million, with $3 million of that locked into Jeff Montgomery, our closer who was at the tail end of his career. Pitcher Kevin Appier was making maybe $7 million, so we had $8 million spread around the other

20 players. We were young, and that might have been one of the worst offensive teams ever put together.

When we started the 1997 season our outfield was Tom Goodwin in center, Bip Roberts in left, and Jermaine Dye. I was odd-man out.

"You're going to play if Jermaine gets a hit," is what Bob Boone kept telling me. He wanted Jermaine to start hitting before letting me play. So there I was, sitting on the bench, and Dye didn't get a hit in his first five games. Even though he didn't hit the first month, I still played sparingly. That first month Dye, Goodwin, and Roberts didn't have a single RBI. As sparingly as I played, I had seven RBIs.

I knew they were thinking about sending me down, so I went to see Herk Robinson, the general manager.

"I'm just as good as those guys if not better," I told him. "I'm not the reason we're losing. Why should I be sent down to Omaha? I'm ready to play. The swing feels good. I'm ready."

Around this time Dye got hurt, so I went in and started playing in center field. I wasn't that great, only hit about .275, but I scored 70 runs and was more team oriented than some of the other outfielders. I started maybe 120 games and either pinch run or went in defensively in the rest of them. It was not the way I wanted my career to be going. I wanted to be able to go to the ballpark, find my name on that lineup card, and be comfortable. Boone kept moving me around in the lineup. I batted from one to nine and everywhere in between.

With the team not winning, Bob Boone wasn't going to get much more time to make those decisions. The team brass thought he'd be the perfect manager for that ballclub, someone who could develop players, but we really weren't learning how to rebound, weren't learning much, except how to fail.

We improved in 1998, finishing third in the division behind Cleveland and Chicago, who didn't slip. That year our pitching was the problem. We blew a lot of games at the end. We couldn't save games.

Ewing Kauffman, the former owner, died and left money to run the team, and the deal was, if it wasn't spent, it would go to Kansas City charities. I'm all for charities, but obviously, not much money was spent on the team, which was a shame, because all we needed was a couple of bullpen pitchers.

Offensively we'd become a very scary team, and in '99 we became even scarier. We were third in the league in runs scored. We had a pretty potent lineup. I led off, Ray Sanchez was second, then you add Jermaine Dye, Carlos Beltran, Mike Sweeney, and Joe Randa. But in '99 we won exactly 64 games, which is not easy to do with a lineup like that. It was the first time in history that a team blew the majority of its save opportunities. If I remember correctly, we blew 30 games and only saved 28.

In 2000 I had my breakout year. We improved, winning 77 games, and finally I was healthy and very confident in what I was doing. Tony Muser took over as manager for Bob Boone. Boone had always pinch hit for me late in the game, so I was always looking over my shoulder to see if someone was going to hit for me.

On Muser's first day as manager, he came up to me and said, "Hey, Johnny, do you think you can play center field for the Kansas City Royals?"

"Yeah," I said.

"You don't sound too confident about it," he tested.

"I've been thinking I was good enough to play center field for a long time," I said. "I never knew when I was playing. I still don't know to this day if I'm playing. I have to go look at the lineup card every day."

Tony told me I wouldn't have to look anymore.

"Be prepared to play every day," he said. "I am going to play you every single day."

That was a great feeling. He put that confidence in me. He knew he could count on me through thick and thin, through pain and injuries, no matter what.

That year I played in 161 games to lead the league. As the Royals' leadoff hitter I hit .327 and drove in 88 runs—unusual for a guy at the top of the order. I also led the league in stolen bases with 46 and in runs scored with 136.

A lot of players didn't like Tony Muser because of his drill sergeant–like attitude. I didn't mind it. A good kick in the butt is what we needed. I remember one game that was rained out in Kansas City even though the skies were showing signs of clearing.

"All these fans are staying here expecting to see a game," he said, "and we can't do it. We're going out there, and we're going to run to show them that our team is dedicated, that we didn't want this game to be rained out."

So we went out on the field as a team and ran. The fans went nuts. They were feeling good about Tony Muser. *We have somebody who's going to make sure these guys work,* the Royals fans saw, *and even if we didn't win, at least they knew we were working hard.*

Chapter 4

Leading off for the A's

By the year 2000 Angie and I didn't have the happiest of relationships. As I've said, she repeatedly questioned my faithfulness. I'd always hear, "Why are you out having a beer? Why are you out with those guys? Why are you doing this, or that?" She always had the feeling I was cheating on her, but you know what? I wasn't.

Her accusations, however, were beginning to grate on me. Our relationship was okay—there wasn't as much yelling as would come later—but there was a lot of unhappiness.

In 1999 my twins were born. I wanted to name my son Jaxson, because I grew up in Generation X, but Angie preferred "Jackson" so we spelled it the traditional way. His middle name is Scott, named after Scott Muhlhan, a good friend of mine. He played on my high school baseball team and died of melanoma.

I was playing in Puerto Rico in the winter league because Tony Muser had said, "You've got to go and work hard during the off-season to show everyone what you're made of." And while I was there, Scott called me up to say he was dying and had only a few more days to live.

"I just wanted to say good-bye and that I love you," he said.

"What can I do?" I asked. "Can I come see you?"

"No," he said, "don't worry about me. I'll be with you in spirit. You get your baseball career on track and make me proud of you. I'll be watching."

A couple days later I was sitting on my couch watching Terrell Owens of San Francisco catch a ball up the middle against the Green Bay Packers for a last-second touchdown. His dad later told me that was the game Scott was watching when he died.

My daughter's name is Madelyn. She wasn't named after anyone in particular. It was just a name we liked. But by the time she was two, my daughter saw how her mother treated me, and she began scolding me as well.

Angie felt things could be talked about and worked out, but a barrier had gone up between us, and once that barrier went up, I couldn't look at her anymore, couldn't talk to her in a civil voice. It was never about us enjoying ourselves. It was just about quarreling.

The off-seasons were the worst. I'd bust my butt playing baseball, so what I wanted to do in the off-season was go surfing, fishing, boating. I wanted to *live*, have fun, not pick out furniture. I suppose I could have worked harder to see it from her perspective, but at the time I felt she could have done that by herself.

I'm not a very good explainer. I just let things build up. I let them build and build and build. Then I just can't take it anymore. I was completely through with our marriage, but I couldn't figure out how to end it. I felt protective of my two young kids. I knew I was very unhappy at home. Angie was unhappy. We didn't know *where* we were. We'd tell each other we hated each other, and there'd be lots of tears.

I also wanted out because her relationship with my family wasn't very good. Because of her I didn't get to see my parents or brother very much. Her family was great to me, but they were the *only* family to her. My family was never part of her life. I wanted to take better care of my parents and brother financially, but she didn't want me to, so I had to hide my money if I wanted to help them. When I started making good money, I had no problem helping them out, but as far as she was concerned, they were taking advantage.

"You're giving them too much," she'd say, and I was caught in the middle, an unhappy husband and an unhappy son, though a very lucky father.

After having a great 2000 season, I was expecting to get traded from Kansas City, though I wasn't sure where I'd be going. I'd heard rumors about going to the Mets, the Yankees, and the Dodgers. I hadn't heard anything about the Oakland A's. I didn't even know Oakland had made the playoffs the year before. They were a team that just quietly became good, without anyone noticing. You didn't hear much about them.

In January of 2001 Angie and I were in Hawaii—no kids, no nothing, just trying to enjoy ourselves. We got back from horseback riding, and I had all these messages waiting for me. I'd been traded to Oakland.

Going to Oakland was fine with me. But she started in.

"Oakland? What's Oakland? Are they a good team?" Blah. Blah. Blah. She wasn't too happy about my going to Oakland.

"Hey, this is part of the game," I said. "I've got no control over it. I'm going to go and do what I can. This is going to be the greatest place in the world for me to play."

We'd just bought a house in Orlando, and she refused to go with me. She wanted to stay back and put it together. She wanted to get the kids into preschool. She came out to Arizona for short periods to be with me during spring training. I was with her knowing she really didn't want to be there.

The first day of spring training Eric Chavez came up to me all excited about my being on the team.

"Do you think you'll be here for a while?" he asked.

"This is going to be my only year because I smell a divorce coming on if it isn't," I said. "I need to be closer to the East Coast."

It was too bad, because I really enjoyed my experience with Oakland that year. The Oakland front office and manager treated you like men. In Kansas City during spring training we ran our asses off all day long. With Oakland, you did your work and you left. Baseball was so much better once I was able to get away from Kansas City.

I spent a lot of time in Phoenix during spring training. There were girls there. I decided there no longer was any reason not to go out and have some fun. I figured Angie no longer wanted to be with me, so why not? Rightly or wrongly, I figured I'll just have me a good time.

Oakland was like a frat house. We had a lot of young guys, and we were incredibly close. Billy Beane was our general manager, and everybody knew he was very smart, a class guy, someone who always pulled off the best trades. When he traded for me, he said I was the missing link as far as their winning the World Series. And he was right. That year we should have won it all. Seattle would win 116 games in 2001, but they didn't want any part of us. They weren't as good a team as we were in Oakland.

When I went to Oakland, I wanted to fit in. Before coming over, I knew the A's subscribed to the Bill James theory of taking pitches. I never read any of James's books, but I understand the theory: you take a lot of pitches, wear down the starting pitcher, and get him out of the game early. It's what I'd been doing instinctively since high school.

I'd lead off, then Frank Menechino, then Jason Giambi, and by the time the first inning was over, that starter had thrown 30 pitches. Many times we would get him out of there by the fifth inning.

That year, unfortunately, I started the season with the worst slump of my career. I just couldn't buy a hit. I was hitting .190 in June and I ended up at .256, the worst batting average of my career, but I still scored 108 runs, the players around me did very well, and we won 102 games. The philosophy worked.

At Oakland I really started to learn what it is to play the game of baseball. I've always been a team player, but I really learned how important it is to give yourself up, take pitches so your teammates can see everything the pitcher might have that day. It's that unselfishness that helped me earn the respect of my teammates.

We got off to a bad start, in part because I wasn't hitting in April and May. After we acquired Jermaine Dye, my best friend from Kansas City, we went 58 and 13 after the All Star break.

Every time we crossed the foul line and stepped onto the field, we knew we were going to beat someone up. We were going to get the starting pitcher out of the game by the second and third inning. We were going to take pitches and just wear those pitchers out. That was the primary reason my batting average dropped so much, but guess what, I still scored my runs. I was hitting .256, but big frigging deal, I was still playing team baseball. I knew that once the postseason came, it was going to be different.

We played hard on the field, harder off it. I was playing on the Oakland A's, and I was like a kid in a candy store. Everyone knew we were going out, partying, drinking, and having a good time, though never *too* crazy. After the games guys would coax you into going out and letting off steam. When I was at home, friends would fly in to keep me company. I enjoyed myself in Oakland.

Seattle won the division, and we earned the wild-card spot. We were matched against the Yankees in the first round of the playoffs. This was a month after the destruction of the World Trade Center, and all of New York City was in turmoil.

I remember the morning of 9/11. Jermaine Dye called me.

"Look at the news," he said. "We're being attacked."

"Being attacked? What are you talking about?"

"Turn on the news."

I turned it on in time to watch the World Trade Center towers fall. You tend to take for granted planes flying in the sky. You never expect one to fly into a building, never mind two.

People's lives were turned upside down. It was one of the worst days for America, possibly the worst.

That day we were supposed to fly to Anaheim and head over to the Playboy mansion, but all flights were canceled, so we didn't get to go. When you think of what the people in New York City and Washington, D.C., suffered on 9/11, complaining about our not getting to go to the Playboy mansion sounds ridiculous, but it's probably good we didn't go, because that A's team was cra-zee. Giambi loved tattoos and hamburgers, owned a Lamborghini, and liked to take a boat out on the water and really open it up. I used to skateboard to the stadium sometimes. Jeremy Giambi one time showed up for a game wearing a full-length mink coat he bought after winning big in Las Vegas. Jermaine Dye was our barber. Barry Zito practiced Zen and called us all "Dude." In Oakland nobody had to watch themselves because nobody was watching.

One day people will look back at that Oakland team and say, "I can't believe all those great players were on that same team." When our careers are done, they will say, "You've got to be kidding me." In addition to Tim Hudson, Zito, and Mark Mulder, we had Jason Giambi, Frank Menechino, Miguel Tejada, Eric Chavez, Jermaine Dye, Ramon Hernandez, Terrence Long, Jason Isringhausen, and myself.

Jason Giambi was the team leader. This guy just ran the best clubhouse. When I went over there, I was in awe. I thought, *This guy has everything. He has confidence. He's a good ballplayer on the field, but off the field, he's a leader. He has this team together.*

Jason always took us to dinner and made sure we were having a good time. He always made sure we had a drink in front of us. He was everything a team could want from a guy. He was a tough guy, but a guy who just loved life. He still drove his old Porsche to the ballpark because it was a good luck charm. He rode his Harley. And what was most appreciated by me, everything about him was positive, because I was living in a world with a lot of negativity.

It was also fun being with his brother Jeremy, another great friend.

Miguel Tejada was our shortstop. He loved to play the game, wanted to be in there every day. Even when it was a blowout, he didn't want to come out. He was one of the guys who possessed a bundle of energy and a bundle of talent. You couldn't pitch to him, because he could hit the fastball up and away out of the park, and if you threw it down and away, he could also hit it out of the park. He was a very important guy in the middle of that lineup. He was an incredible player, and it was too bad the A's couldn't compete in the market to keep him. He was too good for them.

Eric Chavez was Mr. Smooth. I loved the way he wore his pants. He was a California guy who always seemed to be happy.

These Oakland guys are taught how to have confidence and how to look good, I thought when I first arrived. When we were ahead and the situation didn't call for him to hit a home run, Chavez would take a pitch down the middle—no big deal. And then, when the time came for him to hit one out, the pitcher would be lulled into a false sense of security. He'd throw Eric the same pitch, thinking he could throw it by him, and Eric would crush it. He would amaze me. I just hope he can stay healthy. He's had a rash of injuries, but if he can ever stay healthy for 150 games, he will be a force. He has the best pop to the opposite field of any player in the league, even more than Alex Rodriguez.

Our manager was Art Howe, who was a father figure. Ken Macha was his assistant. Art was so casual and perfect for our team. When I began the season going hitless in my first 17 at-bats, Art never flinched. When in mid-June my batting average hovered around .200, he continued to stick with me. Other lesser managers might not have. He had faith that when I got hot, the whole team would come alive, and that's exactly what happened. We ended up winning 102 games in 2001.

From the ownership and the press Art was always hearing, "You need to get control of the team," but his answer was, "Why? If they mess around at night and don't get the job done, I can see where you're coming from, but this team goes out and plays hard and wins. Nothing needs to be said to them."

Art let us go out and play. He had a set lineup, and he didn't use a lot of pinch hitters. His door would be open, and you could go in and talk to him. If you were feeling banged up, he'd let you rest until you felt better. He didn't rush you. You trusted him, so you knew you'd get your job back when you returned.

I get along with most managers, but as managers go, Art was one of the real good ones.

Going into the first round of the 2001 playoffs against New York, we were on a mission. We knew we had a better team than the Yankees, even though they'd won the World Series three years in a row. And those pinstripers knew they were in trouble. Before the first game, Art Howe made the statement, "It's going to take a great series from the Yankees for them to have a shot at beating us."

In the opener in New York, we faced Roger Clemens, who had a 20–3 record in the regular season. I went 3 for 3, and I drew an important walk, stole second, and scored on a hit by Jason Giambi. Clemens walked off the mound limping. Terrence Long hit two home runs, Jason Giambi hit one, and Mark Mulder, who won 21 games for us, only gave up one run in six plus innings. We won the day, 5–3.

The next night Tim Hudson, all 165 pounds of him, threw eight innings of shutout ball and we beat the Yankees 2–0. He had incredible control, and the Yankees had trouble hitting the ball out of the infield.

Andy Pettitte was almost as good. Ron Gant's long home run would have been enough to win, but in the ninth I tripled then I scored when a rocket hit by Tejada went through Scott Brosius's legs at third.

Our closer, Jason, who was outstanding all season, struck out Jorge Posada to end the game.

Now we were feeling good, because we were going back to Oakland, and because we had Barry Zito going for us in Game 3. What I remember most was how quiet the guys were on the plane ride back home. It just seemed that a lot of guys were tired.

Normally, with an off-day coming up, we'd be up, pounding the booze. I looked around at the guys sleeping or lying quietly, and thought, *Is this the team that's about ready to shock the world and beat the*

World Championship Yankees? Talentwise the Yankees knew that they didn't have what we had, but they had a history. They had their 20-odd championships. They had their experience. They'd been there. Even though we were up two games to none and only needed to win one more game, I sensed a momentum shift. I told myself, *Don't let them win, not even once.*

In Game 3 I had great at-bats, which is all you can ask for. I hit a one-hopper hard to the first baseman, a line drive to the third baseman. I couldn't find a hole.

Neither Barry nor Mike Mussina, the Yankee starter, allowed a hit until the fourth inning. The Yankees scored their one run on a home run by Jorge Posada in the sixth.

We should have tied it up in the eighth. With two outs Jeremy Giambi singled. Terrence Long then doubled down the right field line. Jeremy rounded third, and Ron Washington, our third base coach, waved him home.

Shane Spencer, who was playing right, ran to the wall and picked up the ball. He threw it in to Alfonso Soriano, the Yankees' second baseman, but the ball missed him and also missed Tino Martinez, who was the alternate relay man. There is never a provision for a third cut-off man, but Derek Jeter, who had nothing else to do, raced across the infield near the first base line, caught the ball and flipped it backhand to Posada, who tagged Jeremy, who didn't slide because he didn't think there was any way in the world Spencer's throw could possibly get him. It was our only scoring chance all night, and we lost 1–0.

We didn't want to admit it, but Jeter's play was pretty amazing. You watch it, and you say to yourself, *What just happened?* Of course, we all wanted Jeremy to slide, but I'm not sure it would have made any difference.

What was Jeter doing on the first base line intercepting that ball? I don't know. How did he make a backhand flip with enough accuracy to get Jeremy? I don't know. Jeter is one guy who amazes me. He's always in the right place at the right time, and you can't teach that. Ordinarily his running over like that would have been a huge waste of time and energy, but that play was a momentum shifter and a game saver.

I hate to think it, but that play may have unhinged us. We took our suitcases with us before Game 4, figuring if we lost we'd go back to New York, and if we won, I would fly to Oakland and wait to see who won between Seattle and Cleveland.

On paper beforehand the game looked like it would be close, but we really had no chance. We were out of it from the beginning and lost 9–2. Art started Cory Lidle, who got batted around. We couldn't hit Orlando Hernandez, and Bernie Williams drove in five runs. Now we had to do the one thing we had wanted to avoid: go back to New York.

All our momentum was gone. The Yankees started Roger Clemens in Game 5, and we had Mark Mulder going. Clemens, who had a strained hamstring, flew back to New York a day early to rest up. Mulder stayed with us in Oakland just in case we won and celebrated. He should have done what Clemens did. It might have made a difference.

Game 5 was not a happy one. We were playing without Jermaine Dye, who'd freakishly broken his leg the game before. We hung Jermaine's jersey in the dugout to inspire us, and we actually led 2–0, but Mulder didn't have his good control, kept falling behind on hitters. He hit five batters all season long. In the final game he hit two batters, including one that loaded the bases in the second inning, before Alfonso Soriano singled in two runs to tie the score.

The Yankees went ahead after a throwing error by Greg Myers, who was catching because Ramon Hernandez had sprained his wrist on an earlier play, and an error on a slow ground ball fielded by Eric Chavez. They scored another run when Jason Giambi made an error on a throw to second.

We had chances to score, but the Yankees did all the right things. David Justice hit a long home run off Tim Hudson, who pitched in relief. Clemens was throwing okay, nothing great, but we couldn't generate any offense.

When Mariano Rivera came in to close it out in the eighth with the Yankees leading 5–3, the Yankee Stadium crowd was just going crazy. They had so much momentum against us. When he struck out Eric Byrnes to end the game, our magical season was over, and we went home crushed. That's when I first realized that the better team doesn't always win. I didn't think the Yankees were close to us as far as talent level, but they knew how to win.

After the game I went up to Art Howe and said, "Thank you." I shed a tear or two, because I knew we'd had a magical year in Oakland, and now it was time for me to move on.

Chapter 5

Joining the Red Sox

The magic number is six. That is the number of years you have to play before you can become a free agent. So for three years in the minors and three years in the majors, I had no rights. Then you go for arbitration. The way that works is a judge or a panel of judges decides your salary. Your agent goes in and says you're the greatest player who ever played the game, and the general manager of the team or his representative goes in and says you're awful.

I first had to do that when I was with Kansas City. I took Scott Boras, who is still my agent today, with me. Scott had a reputation as a very good negotiator, and he had a long track record of success. What I also liked about him was that he was *just* a baseball agent. Other agents who represent baseball players also represent actors and actresses, and football and basketball players. This guy concentrated on baseball, and I thought that was important.

In the minor leagues I was making about $850 a month. By the time I got called up to the majors in 1995 I didn't have much left. I'd signed as a rookie for $250,000, which became $150,000 after taxes and attorney's fees. My house was in Orlando, so I had to pay the mortgage on that and also pay to rent a place where I was playing. You start eating cheap sandwiches and a lot of McDonald's and Burger King.

When you're in the minors, there isn't much to negotiate. You try to raise your salary from $850 to $950 a month. That extra hundred a month was huge back then. A lot of players remember what it was like with a certain amount of bitterness. I was never that way. Get mad over a hundred bucks? Why bother?

During the off-season in the minors I worked as a construction worker and a surveyor for Angie's father. I helped develop a lot of the Orlando neighborhoods, helped build some of the first developments in Clermont. We walked the land, measured how the plans should be laid out. I'd survey and tell them where the road should be. We had to take a measure of the land to see if it had to be leveled. We'd clear the trees. When the backhoes came in and started clearing, we would go in there and actually mark where the streets were to go. We'd say where the water mains and the pipes should be located. We'd mark where the retention ponds were to be dug. Then we put the lot lines in for the homes.

It was a great job. It helped me get by financially before I got called up to the big leagues, and I did that for a couple years even after going up to Kansas City.

After my third season in Kansas City, I didn't need the job any more. The first year I was with the Royals I was paid $109,000. The second year was $160,000. The following year my salary jumped to $400,000. It was a lot of money, but I still knew I had to live within my means. I remembered how quickly my $250,000 signing bonus went. I also had to help my brother get through college. I was very good with my money. I wasn't enticed to go out and buy a new car. I didn't do that until I was making $4 million a year.

After my third season with Kansas City, we went to arbitration. The Royals wanted to give me $2.1 million. I was asking $3.2 million.

That's a big difference. Under the rules the judges had to choose one of those figures based on what they learned at the hearing.

Scott Boras was great. He made me sound like I was the best player in the world. I felt like Ken Griffey Jr. after he finished talking. Of course, the Royals made me feel like Bob Uecker.

It would have been better if we could have met halfway, but the system doesn't provide for that. As a result, arbitration results in a lot of bitterness. Jay Henrich, the assistant general manager of the Royals, pretty much said I couldn't do anything, that I was responsible for the team's finishing in last place. Right after they get done trashing you, you really don't want to play for a team that has just crushed you like that.

My advice to players is to avoid arbitration if they can. But that's not always possible.

After the hearing, which I lost, Jay came over and said, "We didn't really mean all those things we said. We're on a tight budget. We've got to do what we can."

"I know it's business," I said. "I tried getting what I could." I understood, but it hurt my feelings. When spring training rolled around, though, I went out and played as hard as I could. I worked hard. I still hustled down the base paths. I didn't let it affect the way I played the game.

The next year the Royals and I signed a contract for $4 million for one year. They knew two straight years of arbitration pretty much spells doom for a team's chances of retaining a player, because a player who gets slammed twice in a row doesn't forget. When he becomes a free agent, it's see ya.

Kansas City would have liked to have signed me and their other top players to multiyear deals, but they said they couldn't afford to do that. So one year it was.

At the end of my sixth year, the Royals and I were talking about a long-term contract. I accepted arbitration as an alternative, and then I waited and waited and waited for my contract offer, which came very late. I was happy to hear about it, but I thought, *What took them so long?*

By then I was thinking that I'd experienced six straight losing seasons, and I suspected that life somewhere out of Kansas City would probably result in more victories. When they finally came to me with that five-year contract, I turned it down. Another reason I said no was that I was pretty sure if I signed it, the Royals would trade one of my two buddies on the team, Jermaine Dye or Mike Sweeney. I thought, *If you're not improving the team by signing me, if you're going to trade away a great offensive player, then my signing makes no sense.* I knew we were close. I wanted them to keep everyone, and I wanted them to go out and get some pitchers. The Royals had some great young arms coming up through the farm system. We needed a couple of vets to fill out the staff.

After I rejected their offer, the Royals started trying to move me. They could have shipped me to Montreal, another team with no money to spend. Thankfully they moved me to a winner in Oakland.

When I got to Oakland, I was scheduled to go to arbitration. I was facing a situation where I'd be trashed by a team I hadn't even played for yet. Fortunately, we didn't do that. Scott Boras talked to A's general manager Billy Beane, and I signed a one-year contract for $7.1 million. At this point I was making all the money in the world. But all the money in the world seriously complicates your life.

First of all, almost everybody you've ever known comes to you with an idea for using your money to start a business. Those who don't come to you with a business scheme want to invest your money.

Only one business made any sense to me and that was the cell phone business, and I happily jumped into that. But I had to turn down offers to invest in restaurants, land deals in places I didn't know, deals I couldn't follow, or deals I'd never have time to enjoy. The offers just kept coming, and they haven't stopped.

I especially hate to mix friendships and business. As a way of making money off me, I've had friends try to sell me insurance that's a lot more expensive than what I have now, more expense for less coverage. I found there was only one way to handle these "friends": stop talking to them. My true friends, the ones who've stuck by me since high school, leave me alone. If I need a friend of mine to help me out, I ask him. I have one friend whom I've asked to take care of all my landscaping. My brother takes care of all my fan mail. A brother of another friend does all my home repair.

After the 2001 season, Billy Beane had offered me arbitration, because he knew if another team signed me as a free agent, he'd get a number one draft pick. Billy knows the value of number one picks. He's one general manager who doesn't keep them in the minors too long, and he's such a great judge of talent, they come up and play great for the A's.

After I said good-bye to Oakland, I became a free agent. Being a free agent can be very stressful, especially when you know there are about 10 teams needing a leadoff hitter and a center fielder, and no one comes knocking. Everyone was gung ho to sign Roger Cedeno, who had stolen 55 bases for the Tigers in 2001. He'd stolen 66 bases with the Mets two years earlier. I'd played great defense, but in 2001 I'd had a really slow start, plus I'd always put the team first, moving the runners at the expense of my batting average, and that year I only hit .256. That was the statistic GMs wanted to focus on.

I thought I was going to sign with the New York Mets. I figured the Mets would be interested in me because they had the money and I was just what they needed, a leadoff hitter who could both score and drive in runs. But back then the Mets—who've lately been aggressive spenders—who seemed to be snakebit every move they made, decided to take the cheaper route, and they signed Cedeno for a second stint. They figured he'd get a lot of steals, but found his stealing didn't make up for his fielding.

No one called, not even Oakland, but I understood why. It was going to cost them more money than they wanted to spend, and they knew the A's fans would say, "He hit .256 last year. Why is management even considering re-signing him and giving him three years of guaranteed money and a possible no-trade clause when they couldn't even sign their franchise player, Jason Giambi?"

The days during the off-season kept passing. Texas expressed a slight interest. "I'd love to get you," John Hart told me, "but we have no money right now because of all the money we have to pay Alex Rodriguez. We can offer you a contract that's filled in the back end, but as far as your first couple of years, we probably can only offer you two or three million." Compared to the $7 million I was making, it didn't make a lot of financial sense.

My neighbor at the time was a part-owner of an airline and was involved in the rise of the Back Street Boys. He'd made a movie. He saw me on the other side of the fence, working in the yard, and he asked me what was going on. I told him I wasn't worried. I had a carefree attitude about my future. I knew I was in good hands and that something positive would happen. Heck, even if I never made another nickel, I'd still be set for life.

"Whatever happens, happens," I told him.

I didn't even care where I ended up. I'd have been just as happy to be going back to Oakland.

Unfortunately, my wife and her family were *very* stressed out about where I might be going. My returning to Oakland was the last thing Angie wanted. That season in Oakland had been very tough on her, and the physical distance between us was one of the reasons we grew apart. When I returned home, there wasn't much mutual respect left.

We were still living together, but things weren't the same. I knew she was doing a great job as a mom, but my interest in her and my love for her had faded so much that I stayed with her pretty much just so I could see the kids. I'm a Scorpio by nature. Stuff builds and builds and builds, and then we have stingers that nothing can survive.

I ended up going to Boston. I landed there because GM Dan Duquette had traded away his center fielder, Carl Everett, who was making the front office crazy, keeping them on their tippy toes. They wanted a change and put Everett on the trading block. Texas shifted money around, signed him, and sent pitcher Darren Oliver so Boston could eat his contract. The way Texas saw it, they only had to pay $2 million more for Everett, and they were able to get rid of Darren.

It's astounding how often players have career years, sign gigantic long-term contracts, and then their teams want to dump them a year or two later after they put up their more typical numbers.

I was Dan Duquette's last sign, after Everett left the door open for me. We went and talked to Duquette, and his first offer was four years for $24 million. It wasn't what we wanted, but Scott Boras and I were happy that somebody finally stepped up.

Scott told Dan he'd have to do better.

"You guys have a second baseman, Jose Offerman, whom you don't like and whom you've given four years, twenty-six million," Scott said. "John's a better player. He'll give you great defense. He's a great teammate."

I don't know how Scott did it, but we ended up with four years for $31 million. Maybe there was another team interested. Scott did do some negotiating with Oakland. I really wanted to go back there, though I knew that was impossible with the situation at home.

I wanted to buy a home where I was playing, but not until I got a long-term deal. It didn't make sense to buy a home in Oakland, knowing I was only going to be there one year and knowing Angie would never come out to be with me.

You read in the papers how when a team wants to sign a free agent, players from the team will call him and ask him to come play with the team. Not a single Red Sox player called me. When I arrived in spring training one player—I won't say who it was—came up to me and said, "Why did you sign with Boston? It's miserable here. You should have called me, and I would have told you never to sign here."

"Nice to meet you," I said. "Good to be here, too."

It was the last gasp of the regime run by Red Sox President John Harrington and General Manager Dan Duquette, and the players were miserable. It seemed that everyone was on edge. Harrington was running the team, and to me he was great, very professional. I thought Duquette was a great guy. I never had any bad experiences with him. I wasn't there two weeks when he left.

In 2001, the Red Sox had been 6 games up on the A's for the wild-card spot until August, when they stopped winning. The Sox ended up 17 games out, and the A's just kept winning.

A bunch of people were probably asking what Duquette was thinking when he signed me to that huge contract.

When I arrived, I had no idea the Red Sox were even up for sale. All I knew was that I was going to a town where the fans were passionate about the game. I didn't know the extent of their passion. I just felt, *This is a good place to play.* I also knew about the Red Sox–Yankee rivalry, and I was happy to be a part of that. I didn't know just how big that rivalry was, either. I also never knew how many media personalities could be around the game and how intense everything could become. I had no clue.

A week after I signed, I was surprised when it was announced that the team had been sold. The new owners were John Henry and Tom Werner, and the CEO was Larry Lucchino. If the old ownership was as stodgy as Lawrence Welk, the new guys were cooler than Justin Timberlake.

Henry, a college dropout, started as a soy beans farmer in Arkansas, and made a billion dollars trading commodities. He owns a rotisserie baseball team, and as a kid sang in a rock-and-roll band.

Tom Werner made his money in television. He was involved with *The Cosby Show* and *That '70s Show,* and the fact that he knew every actor and actress in Hollywood was really neat.

Larry Lucchino was the baseball guru, the negotiator, the guy who knows how baseball players think. He was the negotiator who'd try to get the most for the buck for the team.

When I arrived in the spring of 2002 Dan Duquette was still the general manager and Joe Kerrigan was the manager, but I knew that new owners want their own GMs and managers, so it was just a matter of time before they'd be replaced.

The new owners came in and talked to us. Early on, they were quiet, because they wanted to find out exactly what they'd bought before they did anything. They hadn't just bought the Red Sox; they also bought radio stations and NESN, the Red Sox TV network.

They were very personable. You knew good things were going to happen. They were fixed on improving the Red Sox. John Henry had owned the Florida Marlins, and he got out of Florida because he couldn't get a new stadium. I also knew John Henry was close to Bud Selig, and Bud wanted someone who understood the numbers game, someone who wouldn't pay an Alex Rodriquez $254 million for 10 years. He wanted an owner who'd spend $10 million total on 15 players. That way you actually can win.

When Larry Lucchino, who'd run the Orioles and San Diego, came in, the players who knew him didn't have much good to say about him. I didn't pay any attention to the talk. I wasn't going to judge him by what happened in the past. And he's turned out to be a great guy.

The first big move came on March 1, 2002, when Lucchino fired Dan Duquette. Four days later he fired Joe Kerrigan as manager and replaced him with Grady Little. Grady had been bench coach for the Red Sox a couple years earlier, and he'd managed in the minors a long time. When Grady walked in to introduce himself, all the players stood up and gave him a standing ovation. I don't think there was ever another manager who got as rousing a reception. That's how much our players who knew him liked him.

There was a new, lighter atmosphere on the team with the coming of the new owners, and I decided I'd do what I could do to make the Red Sox into more of a team. I wanted us to loosen up a little bit, and I started carrying one of those boom boxes on the team plane. I talked to the media, and when I did that, the other guys would say, "You'll get tired of doing that sooner or later," because it seemed that the Boston press wore everyone out.

At the tail end of spring training, we played a game in Houston. We went to Ruth's Chris Steak House for dinner, and we were on our way back to the hotel to call it a night when we drove by the Hotel Derek. There were tons of people milling around. I was riding with Justin Sherrod, who's in the Red Sox system, and Lou Merloni, and we decided, "It's only eight o'clock. Let's go out for a little bit."

We went inside, and that's when I saw the woman who is now my wife. Michelle Mangan was working for a modeling agency recruiting talent, and she was discussing business with a couple of clients.

Later I learned she'd done some modeling herself. She sold insurance. She used to fix up homes and sell them. She's talented, but she hates being in a rut.

We met that night. Looking back, I have to say it was love at first sight, though it was several months before we saw each other again. We stayed in contact by phone. I'd see her now and then, but we started out as strictly friends. She loved my honesty, because when I saw her, I told her I was legally married, was very unhappy, and wouldn't be married for too much longer. I told her I had two kids. I didn't want her to get into a relationship and have her find out down the road I was lying to her. She was cool with taking it slow. We didn't start dating until seven months later.

We opened our season in Baltimore. No one was having any fun. I was absolutely miserable. When we arrived in Baltimore, we had a whole night before the game. No one wanted to grab dinner. No one wanted to do anything. I couldn't believe it. The guys would go back to their hotel rooms—I figured they were laying there thinking about the great stories they'd tell their grandkids about the big leagues.

In Oakland, sometimes 15 or 20 of us had gone out together. We were a team that went out to have a good time. We weren't trying to hide from anyone.

I know my way around. The next night I talked a couple of guys—Lou Merloni and Shea Hillenbrand—into going out with me. When we arrived at one of the clubs, they were pulling their wallets out of their pockets, getting ready to pay at the door.

"What are you guys doing?" I asked. "You're major league ballplayers. They expect us to show everyone else a good time." I told the doorman who we were, and he said, "We never saw a Boston Red Sox player come in here before." Of course, he let us in gladly. When I was with Oakland, we went to clubs in every American League city. We'd have private rooms where we could go and relax. The Red Sox just never did it. That night, Lou and Shea had the time of their lives.

In Boston, the players tended to hide, to hang out by themselves. I didn't understand why, because I didn't understand how huge the Red Sox were in Boston. I first got a glimpse of it when a group of us, Darren Oliver, Merloni, Hillenbrand, Nomar, and I went out one evening after a game. I didn't realize that it was virtually impossible for Nomar to go out in public. If he went, he needed a private room or he had to be shielded by the other players so the public wouldn't get to him. Nomar had to deal with his superstar status every day. If one fan wanted an autograph, there'd be a hundred behind him. Nomar spent much of his time in his room getting food delivered. It was the only way he could get to eat.

I had an ally in Carlos Baerga, who was able to drag the Latin guys along and loosen them up. Carlos got everyone ready to play. He'd look at you before the game and say, "Do you have the eye? Are you ready?" Also before the game Carlos would lead us in prayer. "Dear God, please help us. We need your help today. Johnny isn't feeling good. . . ." Or he'd say, "Dear God, Manny's swing is horrible. Please help us, God." He had the kind of energy that helped everyone around him feel happy. He was a big reason why things began changing in 2002. He was 36 years old, but he was nonstop energy.

Carlos was a major factor in Manny Ramirez becoming comfortable playing with the Red Sox. Carlos and Manny had played together in Cleveland, and when Manny came to Boston that first year, he felt isolated and alone, and he was upset by the scrutiny of the Boston press. It wasn't until Carlos arrived in Boston that Manny was able to have some fun. The two of them often hung out with Pedro Martinez, and even Jose Offerman, who just couldn't get a break in

Boston. Jose hit .300, but he was in the unenviable position of having to replace Mo Vaughn at first. He didn't field that great, and any time the ball got past him, the fans would boo and the press would join in.

The player everyone—the fans and the press—focused on was Pedro Martinez. In 2001 Pedro had been plagued by a sore arm and only won seven games, but I'm sure at least two of them were against us in Oakland.

Pedro to me was always very intimidating. You think of him as a fastball pitcher, but he was so much more than that. He worked off his fastball, which was clocked at around 95 miles an hour, and he had a great change up. You never saw a change up as great as his.

Pedro and I became friends in no time. I understood him and his personality. People questioned him, why he wasn't always on the bench during games when he didn't pitch. But Pedro didn't become a superstar overnight. He had a routine, and part of that routine was to work out in the clubhouse during games. Whenever he'd sit on the bench, he'd talk nonstop, so we didn't mind his being upstairs, working out, giving us a little peace.

Some pitchers on the day they start get to the park four hours early and get ready. When Pedro pitches, he likes to show up two minutes before he's supposed to warm up, and then he works out. Who cares? Why should anyone criticize him when he's as successful as he's been? The other players on the Red Sox never cared.

"Why is Pedro not on the bench?" we'd get asked over and over.

"Well, he's doing something," we'd say. "Leave him alone."

Why would anyone want to upset Pedro? He always wears a smile on his face.

When John Henry took over the team, he set up a number of events for us. In spring training he held a big family picnic where the kids could come. He hired a magician and a balloon blower, and he ordered lobsters for everyone. He has a 164-foot boat, and he invited the players for a ride. Sometimes I wish I knew about commodities!

On the day of our 2002 home opener, John Henry asked the

players to greet the fans at the gates of Fenway Park, and it was hard to say no.

"This is not a good idea," some of the players like Nomar and Trot Nixon were saying. In one way it wasn't, and in another way it was.

Even though it was a great public relations gimmick, we went out and got absolutely mauled by the fans. I had no idea it was like this in Boston.

We weren't protected in any way, and there wasn't much we could do. Fans were rushing all around. We had security standing with us, but it's tough for one security guard to fend off 10 thousand fans.

We didn't sign autographs, but we did shake hands. I thought to myself, *These people are passionate about us and even a little bit crazy.*

Chapter 6

93 Wins

THE 2002 SEASON

When John Henry and his group took over, a lot of people were convinced that their intention was to level Fenway Park and move to a fancier, newer facility on the water. The truth was that the Henry group was the only competing ownership group that respected the tradition and history of the park enough *not* to want to tear it down. Years from now, we'll all be grateful to him for that.

Henry, Tom Werner, and Larry Lucchino are smart. They know what they're doing. They talk to people. Unlike a lot of owners who are infatuated with power and using that power, John Henry tries to do what his players and his fans want. Red Sox management doesn't decide what's best for them and then overnight start doing it. They plan. It may be unique, but they even talk to the players.

Once a month the owners, coaches, and about seven players get together, and we talk about what we can do to make Fenway better, travel better, the team better. One time the pitchers in the bullpen complained that they couldn't see the game very well, and when we came back from a road trip, there were TVs in both the visitors' and home bullpens.

We told them the TVs in the clubhouse were old and didn't always work, and they installed flat-screen TVs. We didn't have a food room—we ate in the center of our clubhouse—and when we asked for one, they made one for us and now every night we get catered food. The food room has a huge TV and a sound system that beats the sound system in most people's homes.

Management is even putting in a small swimming pool for us, and a better drainage system on the field to protect the outfielders. We couldn't ask for anything better.

They know the needs of today's players, and they're doing the extra things that will keep us happy and wanting to stay in Boston.

And when they consider doing something, they come to us for input. Before John Henry came in, players were wishing they were playing somewhere else. Now you only hear the players say, "I want to be back."

The highlight of spring of 2002 came on April 27 when Derek Lowe pitched a no-hitter against the Devil Rays. I was dinged up, and not playing that day. I was on the bench the first couple of innings, and then I left and went into the trainer's room to get treatment. When it was time for me to leave the trainer's room, Derek still had his no-hitter, so being a little superstitious, I thought, *I'm not going to the dugout. I'm not going to change the mojo.* I remained in the clubhouse and on TV watched our guys make great play after great play. Ricky Henderson ran down some balls in center field that were pretty exciting.

"I've got some really good stuff working," Derek said to me in the clubhouse. "It's going to be tough for them to do anything against me."

He had all that confidence, and when he was on, he was awesome. What was even better was that after he threw his no-hitter he took care of all the players who shared in his day. He bought Jason Varitek, his catcher, a nice Rolex, and he bought all the guys on the team a Tag Heuer watch that was engraved "Thanks for sharing this perfect moment with me."

The Red Sox ownership then made a plaque and gave it to all the players with a ticket stub and a picture of Derek Lowe throwing his no-hitter.

We had a good team, and we were cruising along pretty darn good in April and May. Our record was 40 and 17. We had some talent, and we had depth. Early in the season Ricky Henderson, who was 40 but who still loved to play, provided the spark. Ricky was great. He, Casey Fossum, Lou Merloni, and I would play the card game Pluck every day. Toward the end of the season, Casey leaned over to me and said, "I still don't think Ricky knows my name." Ricky called him K. K for Casey, I guess.

"I don't really think he knows my name either," I told Casey. "He just calls me J." That's the kind of guy Ricky is. The world is his. He's seen so much in this game. He's played against so many great players. I remember when I was a kid, the coolest baseball card was Ricky Henderson's. He's crouched down and just as chiseled as he is today. For years he was the best player in the American League, and if you ask him now, he'll say that he still can be.

Meanwhile, I was having my best spring. Usually I start very slowly, but in 2002 I was leading the league in runs scored with 57, I had 16 stolen bases, and I was getting some buzz for the All Star game. I brought energy to the Red Sox that they hadn't had before. When I came over, only a couple guys appreciated what I could bring to a team, but it wasn't long before more people found out. Our video guy, Billy Broadbent, studied the game films. Part of his job was to ready video of the upcoming team for our pitchers. For years when I came into Boston with Kansas City or Oakland, I'd do well and give Boston heartache. In 2002 every day Billy would say to me, "I've wanted you here for so long. I can't believe we got you. You are the missing link."

Our great start was halted on May 11, when Manny Ramirez broke his finger sliding into a base, and he was out a month. Manny was very important—more important in 2002 than he was later, because in 2002 we didn't have anyone else to supply the power he brought us. As soon as he got hurt, we all got together and said, "Okay, we have to step up as a team. We need the other guys to get the job done." And we were able to do that for a little while, but after losing a player like Manny, you can't go long without experiencing a dropoff.

That year it was very cold in Boston in the spring, the temperatures sometimes dropping into the 40s, so Manny was doing his rehab in Florida. When he came back, he looked good, but I still think that finger bothered him for most of the year.

We were doing just fine until mid-June when we played sub-.500 ball against four National League teams in interleague play. One of the teams, the Arizona Diamondbacks, featured pitcher Curt Schilling, who was almost perfect against us. My only contribution was a walk, the first he'd issued after 130 batters. I should have walked the time before that as well, but I chased a pitch a couple inches off the plate. It's funny that against a guy like Schilling you can take such pride getting a walk!

About three months into the 2002 season, I made up my mind that Angie and I were through. When the season began, we'd picked out a house that we thought would be perfect for the kids, but while we were going through the whole process, my heart just wasn't in it. She was taking charge and picking the furniture and getting the place straightened out, but with the suppressed frustration I was feeling, all she was doing was driving me nuts.

She knew I wanted out, and she was always on me. We were fighting every day.

"I'll always love you as the mother of my kids and as a friend," I kept stressing to her, "but we're enemies. We can't even stand to talk to each other. We can't even stand to see each other."

I couldn't wait to get back out onto the road where it was peaceful.

It was in early June when she asked me—for the millionth time—whether I was cheating on her, and finally I snapped and said yes.

"There's no love with you," I told her. "There's nothing."

She went home for about a week and came back.

"There is no reason for you to be here," I said. Just to push her buttons, I added, "I was with three more girls while you were gone." When you're feeling these raw emotions, you say things you wish you could take back.

We decided to get a divorce. It took a while to agree to the numbers, and when all was said and done, she ended up with three times more than I did, but I was happy with it. I just wanted out.

If you're good looking and a ballplayer, girls want a piece of you. For the rest of the season, I met some women, some good, some bad. I had some one-nighters that I had never gotten to experience before. It was fun. I ended up having to carry around a separate cell phone for the women to call me. I didn't want them to have my main number, because my phone would have been ringing off the hook, and it just got tiring. Being single turned out to be as tiring as being in a bad marriage.

After I broke it off with one woman, she told me, "I don't mind if you see other girls, too." Most women weren't so flexible. Far from it. I remember one who was clearly a one-night stand who'd call me up and tell me she'd told all her friends we were dating, that we were a couple, and that she was going to come down and see me. My thought was, *Excuse me? How does a one-night stand suddenly morph into a long-term relationship?*

One girl whom I didn't even know went on the radio to say she was very proud of me and that she couldn't wait until I came back home to Florida. That was like, *Whoa!* It is spooky, because I run into girls like her everywhere, in Miami, in Chicago.

What are they thinking?

One time I was propositioned by two girls at once, but I passed. Two girls might be able to handcuff me and kill me.

Mostly they just want more of your life than you can give them. I'm sure some of them wanted to get pregnant. I'm sure others wanted something else. I hoped I was always smart enough to know.

I love women, and as much of a dog that I can be, I do have

respect for them. I try to be as nice and civil as possible and never take advantage.

When we went cold against the National League teams in inter-league play, we dropped a half game behind the Yankees in the American League east, and the Boston press began to panic. This was 2002, my first year with the Red Sox, and I couldn't believe the negativism in the newspapers, because as far as I was concerned, we were still sitting in a great spot. We were in front for the wild card, and to be a half game back was nothing. But if you read Dan Shaughnessy and Gordon Edes and those other guys, you'd have thought we were the worst team in baseball.

We never discussed the journalistic naysayers, never spoke about the havoc their negativism could wreak. We didn't have play-ers who sat around much and talked anyway. In my case, since I de-liberately chose ignorance over current events, I didn't care what they wrote about me or the team. I only knew what they were saying about me when someone put it right in front of my face.

Early in my career at Kansas City, Jeff Montgomery, Greg Gagne, and Gary Gaetti taught me to never read or listen to the local stuff—no papers, no radio, no local sports on TV. They taught me always to read the national stuff, read *USA Today* or listen to ESPN radio, which has a lot more straightforward reporting of what's going on, the transactions, trades, and injuries. They mostly do pos-itive stories and leave out the negative opinions you find in the local papers.

When we went out to face the Toronto Blue Jays on July 2, Pedro had a lot of fire. He had a certain look in his eyes. It seems that when he has that certain look, the other team can sense it right away, and it just folds. They know they don't have a chance. When his stuff is great, it doesn't matter how well you're swinging the bat. You're not going to do well. If he's throwing his great change up, he makes you swing and miss by as much as three feet.

That night Pedro shut them out and struck out 14 batters.

The next day I did exactly what I was supposed to do as a lead-off hitter. I got on base five times. That's what's important to me, that and scoring runs. I feel like I've been the best at doing that over the last seven years. I've been pretty underrated, but that suits me fine. I'm happy to let the Mannys and the Pedros get all the recognition as long as we win.

The next day, July 5, 2002, Ted Williams passed away. We were in Detroit, and that day I hit a home run.

I never got to meet Ted, as much as I would have liked to. I never even laid eyes on him. Of course, I'm aware of how great a hitter he was and how he gave up a lot of time from his baseball career to serve our nation. I also heard he was a pretty awesome fisherman.

The day Ted died we arrived at Tiger Stadium and outside were a fleet of TV trucks and a crush of reporters.

What happened? we wondered. *Was there a big shakeup? Did something happen to one of our current players?* We had no clue. Ian Brown of the *Boston Herald* whispered the news to me.

When we returned to Fenway Park, the Sox held a memorial service for Ted that was a tribute to him as a ballplayer and a war hero. It was done with great class, another example of our new owners doing something very well. They showed highlights and passed out memorabilia and newspaper articles about Ted—Teddy Ballgame. People left that day with a great sense of what Ted Williams meant to the game and to our country. It was a moving experience.

The Yankees rivalry resumed in early July 2002, and what I discovered my first year with the Red Sox is that it's a rivalry that's never-ending. It goes on and on and on. And because we were playing .500 ball and continued to trail the Yankees, everyone (except the players) was getting more and more upset.

Around this time our manager, Grady Little, asked Jose Offerman to pinch hit late in a game, and he refused. I really felt for Jose. Whenever he went out and played, he put his body on the line, tried as hard as he could. He'd played some first base when I was with him in Kansas City, and the Red Sox actually signed him as a second baseman. I always knew him as a good fielder, but sometimes when a player gets a little older, his skills start to diminish. He was a super-nice guy, but his time in Boston was as miserable as any player could ever imagine. When he made a play, people said, "Oh, he was lucky." Whenever he didn't get to the ball on defense, or if he made an out hitting, the fans at Fenway would always let him hear it.

"I can't do anything right here," he'd say to me with a grin. "If I win the game tonight with a grand slam, tomorrow I'll be back in the doghouse."

I didn't know the Jose Offerman the fans didn't like. I'd liked him as a teammate in Kansas City, and I liked him in Boston.

Anyway, that day he said to Grady, "I'd rather not go in." Jose knew his time was coming to an end in Boston. The fans really didn't care for him, and he no longer cared for them. It was a situation where both sides wanted to be free of the other. This request not to play was the straw that broke the camel's back. When we acquired Cliff Floyd from Montreal, the Red Sox released Jose.

Cliff Floyd had been a big star with the Florida Marlins. He'd hit 30 home runs in 2001, but in early 2002 the Marlins traded him to the Montreal Expos, who were trying to improve. When Cliff didn't hit in Montreal, he was traded to Boston.

Cliff was supposed to pay big dividends for us. He was a great defensive outfielder, and he went to left field. Manny became our DH. Cliff had a lot of talent, had one of the most gifted bodies for a baseball player. But when you come to Boston, you better make a good impression, and fast, or you're going to have a lot of heartache.

When Cliff came over here, he was used to the Florida weather, used to having a set routine. In Boston, there were no cages in the clubhouse, and he wasn't used to that. Any time a player makes a change, it can be difficult. Once again with the Red Sox, it seemed like the best moves we could make didn't always pan out the way we wanted them to.

Cliff couldn't believe how intense Boston was, how the fans and press could remember every pitch, every swing, every out you made. He started off badly, and when we needed him for the stretch run, he couldn't get it together. In the final year of his contract, he struggled. He experienced the pressures of having to play in Boston.

"God bless you who can do it," he said to me. "This place is the toughest I've ever seen. There's no way I'm going to come back here next year." And he didn't.

In late August of 2002 we were still playing .500 ball. I can remember a game we played against the Texas Rangers. We were winning 2–0, and then Nomar made an error and our closer Ugie Urbina gave up a home run to Ivan Rodriguez. We lost when another of our relievers gave up another home run. Part of our problem in 2002 was that most of the Red Sox players were haunted by the memory of 2001, when the team fell under the pressure of the pennant race, gave up and folded down the stretch, and the players split off in 20 different directions.

Grady Little called a meeting of the players.

"I'm not going to have this," Grady said. "You guys need to go out there and play." And we did.

Sometime after that I remember telling the guys, "Don't worry about doing too much out there. I'm going to carry us into the playoffs. I'm going to be the one who takes us there."

I was back to being Johnny Damon, the guy who could make the difference. Everything I hit was hard. Everything I hit fell in. I was a man on a mission. My life was vibrant. I was enjoying myself. I was the happiest guy in the world. I thought, *You know what, we're going to do it this year—we're going to win it all in 2002.*

And sure enough, that day I went out and hit the crap out of the ball. In my mind—and I have a strong mind—I thought, *We* are *going to the playoffs.*

It was my first year with the Red Sox, and I didn't know anything about the "curse." Not knowing about how Boston really was, I was ready to take the team to the next level—to do something no one thought was possible.

I was giving the team what it lacked: intensity. There was only Carlos Baerga and me to lead. I thought Shea Hillenbrand was our best hitter, more clutch than even Nomar and Manny. The guys who had been with Boston for a while were filled with all of the negative energy that came with playing in Boston.

"It's tough," they'd say. "We're never going to win here." I was determined to change all that. I was looking forward to making the difference.

In baseball, you come to realize, your luck can turn on a dime. A couple days after I made my pronouncement about my taking the team to the next level, I was leading off first base. There was a left-handed pitcher on the mound, and I was told he didn't have a very good step-off move.

Sure enough, he stepped off, and I dove back into first base dislocating a finger on my right hand. My finger was pointed 90 degrees to the right.

They took me out of the game, and as I was walking to the dugout I could hear a Fenway fan mocking me, saying, "It's only a finger." I held up my hand so they could see it clearly was dislocated.

"Yeah, you're right," I said, "It's only a finger."

I went in and the trainer popped it back into place. I missed the next game. We didn't have much depth that year, and I figured we'd be better off with my playing with a dislocated finger than my sitting out. But I was also faced with the realization that with my injury I wouldn't be able to play with the skill I needed to take us to the playoffs.

In late summer of 2002 we had another distraction. We were faced with the possibility of another player strike. We were very fortunate to have Tony Clark with us. He was busy looking out for all of the players, trying to inform everyone how the negotiations were going. There were times we thought, *Yeah, we need to strike.* But we also looked back to the long strike of 1994–1995, and we realized it had taken a long time to get these fans back. Cal Ripken had broken Lou Gehrig's record for playing in the most consecutive games. Mark

McGwire and Sammy Sosa chased Roger Maris's one-season home run record in 1998. Barry Bonds beat Mark's record. And of course the Yankees–Red Sox rivalry helped. Our attitude was, *The game doesn't need another blow.*

We felt the owners were going to lock us out. I was ready to go home, buy some baseball equipment, and put together a team of big leaguers from Orlando, start a beer league, and have some fun.

The best strategy for the players would have been to set a strike date in early September, but we decided not to do that. Our feeling was that we should play out the season, even though striking after the season would give us no leverage whatsoever.

We did the right thing—and not for us, but for the fans. Young players didn't need to experience a strike, and guys who were at the tail ends of their careers didn't need to have their careers interrupted and perhaps ended.

Don Fehr and Gene Orza, the leaders of the Baseball Players Association, deserved a lot of credit. They told us if we struck, it would be for a long time, and if we didn't strike, there'd be a loss of some wages when guys became free agents and went to salary arbitration. We decided not to strike anyway. We knew what not striking meant to the game of baseball. Laying down our bats just wasn't the right thing to do.

The agreement called for any team that spent more than $117 million in salaries to pay a salary tax. Of course, we players aren't in favor of that. We'd love to see every team spend $250 million without penalties. We compromised, and to my mind, everything worked out for the best. Baseball is moving smoothly. Salaries are good, and players are happy.

By September of 2002, our team continued to trail behind the Yankees, and we couldn't catch the red-hot Angels for the wild-card spot. We won 93 games, which for any other team is a bucketload of games, but in Boston it didn't mean a thing.

We didn't have quite enough pitching that year. John Burkett had had some good years, but he and Frank Castillo were at the end of the road. Our team had been better when Tim Wakefield was in the bullpen earlier in the season, and when he returned to the rotation, the relief corps was weakened because no one was able to step up and take his place. We had Pedro and Derek Lowe, and on other days it was "hold on" even though our other starters still went out and competed. We just didn't have the bullets the Yankees had.

I can say that the team never quit, even after the Angels clinched the wild card.

The Angels were very scrappy, rebellike, with hard-nosed players. The team was led by David Eckstein, a little scrappy guy who's a lot like me—he can lead a team through sheer will. I've always said, you win with your heart, not with your body.

We battled right to the final days. The team morale under Grady was great. The team was vilified because it didn't make the playoffs, but we improved by 11 games over 2001, even though we had no depth in the outfield, our starting pitching was good at times but suspect at other times, and we were banged up.

We were expecting great things from Rich Garces, for example. He was supposed to be our main guy in the bullpen, and he didn't get the job done. Ugie Urbina pitched well in a lot of games, but he couldn't do it alone.

People don't remember it that way because we didn't make the playoffs, but we had a good team. I remember talking to Rich Dauer, who used to play on the great Baltimore Oriole teams during the years when the Yankees were always winning.

"Our teams would win ninety-five, ninety-six games, and we'd miss the playoffs," he said.

"Are you kidding me?"

But that's how it was. The wild card makes things so much more interesting now.

Who would guess that the wild-card team would win the World Series three years in a row?

Chapter 7

Theo Takes Over

In the fall of 2002 there was a lot of talk about who John Henry would hire to be the next Red Sox general manager. One of the candidates for the job was Billy Beane, my GM from Oakland. John Henry, who was an expert at statistics and probabilities, had made his money by studying what prices actually did, not what people predicted they were going to do. He wanted a guy like Billy, who did the same thing with baseball talent. One year Beane asked his old scouts which prospects they liked. Every player they named he dismissed. Then he asked his young assistant, who'd never played the game but who kept track of the stats of every college player on his computer, for a printout of those players with the highest on-base percentages. That year he only drafted players from that list, and he fired all the scouts. Numbers, not hunches, were what he relied on.

Since Billy Beane believed in on-base percentages more than

other statistics, his favorite player of all time is Barry Bonds, because of his walks. He also likes me.

I'd heard that if Beane had become the Boston GM, Boston would have had to give up a player to get him, and I'd heard that at first the player was going to be Trot Nixon, and then in the end the player was going to be me. I could be mistaken, but I'd also heard that when Billy finally turned down the Boston job after initially accepting, one of the reasons he said no was that he didn't want to go to a team that would be losing one of its key players. Also his wife and kids didn't want to leave Oakland, where he had a pretty good gig going. He had the big three—Hudson, Zito, and Mulder—and a bargain-basement team that keeps winning. The year I played in Oakland our fourth starter, Cory Lidle, who he had snookered from the Devil Rays, was 13–6, and Eric Hiljus went 5–0. He knew what he was doing.

The person John Henry ended up picking for the Boston GM job was a bright guy in the front office who the players would talk to every once in a while, but who to us didn't look like a candidate because at 28 he was so young. His name is Theo Epstein. We considered him just a cool guy who came around and talked.

When the Red Sox gave him the GM job, the newspapers and the radio guys poked fun at him. When the reporters came flocking around us, the big question they wanted us to answer was, "Will you be able to take criticism from a twenty-eight-year-old GM who's calling the shots?"

What a ridiculous question. If you're a ballplayer, you don't care who your general manager or your manager is. If you're a ballplayer, you step up, and you play. Could a 28-year-old have authority over us? Absolutely he does. We're working for him. He's working for the ownership. That's how it works.

I'd had a decent year in 2002. I hit .286 and scored 118 runs. We had a good year, won 93 games, but you play the game to make the play-offs, and that we didn't do. The Angels had won 99, and when you come up short, you look back and remember the games when you came to bat with runners on and you struck out, or you grounded out with two outs, and you point the finger at yourself and vow to do better. That's natural. All players do it.

I was curious what Theo was going to do to improve the team. The mark of all great general managers is that they are bold, not afraid to make moves. Theo began remaking the team by letting a bunch of players go—Jose Offerman, Tony Clark, Dustin Hermanson, Darren Oliver, and Ugie Urbina, our closer. Of that group, Ugie was the only one who'd done well for us.

I didn't know it then, but Theo is another proponent of the theories of sabermetrician Bill James, who's made a career analyzing baseball statistics and using them to come up with novel theories about how to play the game. One of his pet theories was that a team didn't have to spend big bucks on an established closer if it had a talented, deep bullpen. When Ugie was let go as closer, Theo didn't replace him. He did, however, hire Bill James as an advisor.

Theo then began adding players, the kind of unsexy, underrated players that Billy Beane loved to go after. His first sign was Todd Walker, a great move. The guy could hit. He had a perfect swing for Fenway. We picked up Kevin Millar, who'd been released by the Florida Marlins with intentions to sign with one of the Japanese teams. When Theo claimed Kevin, he killed that deal. The Marlins and the Japanese team were furious, but the Sox paid everyone off, another terrific move.

Then Theo signed Bill Mueller, who'd played third base for the Cubs. I knew he was an outstanding ballplayer. Then came relievers Mike Timlin and Chad Fox. I'd played against Chad in the minors and was impressed. I'd played against Timlin and knew he was a pitcher who didn't waste any time and went right at batters. He always wanted the ball, and he was good for 80 or 90 appearances a year.

Then came Theo's biggest coup. Minnesota waived first baseman David Ortiz. I knew Ortiz was well mannered, very nice, and cordial. He had a very scary swing, but he was playing behind Doug Mientkiewicz, so he hadn't played much. Why the Twins let him go rather than trade him is what I never understood.

Manny Ramirez was the person responsible for our getting

Ortiz. They both come from the Dominican Republic. Manny went to Theo.

"Is there any way we can give him a shot?" he asked.

Ortiz could have signed with any team, but he chose Boston because of Manny and Pedro.

While we were signing these players, the Yankees were also hard at work. We were supposed to be signing a Cuban pitcher by the name of Jose Contreras. His dream always was to play for the Red Sox. We felt for sure we had him, and then somehow, dreams got whisked away when George Steinbrenner started throwing around his money, and he ended up signing with the Yankees. Jose also knew that Steinbrenner would keep signing players until the team won. As a player, you have to love Steinbrenner. He's going to do what he wants. Of course, if you're a Yankee and you don't perform, you're gone as quickly as you arrive.

Normally it's the players' comments that end up in the papers, but when the Yankees signed Contreras, Larry Lucchino, our CEO, called the Yankees "the Evil Empire," a term that is sure to make him famous over the years. Steinbrenner responded by saying that Lucchino had ruined Baltimore and San Diego when he was running them. When you hear great slander like that, you just say to yourself, *This is just going to make the Red Sox–Yankees rivalry even bigger. These owners hate each other—this is perfect!*

The next big pitcher we tried to get was Bartolo Colon, but the Yankees again pulled a fast one, and they made a trade that didn't help them much but got Colon to the White Sox. The Yankees are always out there trying to make sure we don't get the guys we want. Colon had pitched well against the Yankees, and they weren't going to let him come here. That's one reason the Yankees are a great organization. They don't stand pat. They'd trade Derek Jeter if they could get five guys for him. Nobody's safe on the Yankees. When the Boston media saw what the Yankees were doing, they stirred it up even more, made things even crazier between the two teams. Of course, as ballplayers, if the Yankees are the only team we get up for, shame on us. There are a dozen other teams we have to go out and do well against. We play the Yankees 19 times a year. We play 143 games against the other teams. We need to prepare for *every* game. In 2003 we did that. In 2003 Theo put together an awesome offensive team.

We started with Manny, Nomar, and me, and added to that nucleus Ortiz, Bill Mueller, Todd Walker, and Kevin Millar and his big mouth. When we got to spring training and we heard Millar yelling across the locker room for the first time, we knew this was really going to be a special bunch.

"Man, you look so great getting ready to take a shower," he'd shout. "Look at the bod on that guy." Everyone would look, and the guy would get all embarrassed. Millar was such a character. He made you shower real fast. He was never short on words.

During the game Millar would constantly yell at the umpires, telling them to hurry up or pointing out how pathetic they were, but he'd never get thrown out, because they know him, know his sense of humor, and are used to hearing him complain about something that hasn't even happened yet.

"Get the game going," he'd yell, even though there were still 10 minutes to go before it was scheduled to start.

I thought I was the primary troublemaker and shit stirrer. Now I had a teammate who was even worse than me. I'm not a needler like Millar. He's the sort of guy who will go on *The Best Damn Sports Show Period* and chuckle it up with Tom Arnold and those guys. He's hilarious, knows what he's doing. In 2003 Kevin Millar became a very important person in our ballclub. No one could keep us loose the way he could.

We opened the 2003 season in St. Petersburg against Tampa Bay. Pedro pitched great, and so did Ramiro Mendoza. As I said, Theo decided he'd try Bill James's theory of building a bullpen without a dedicated closer. Our relievers were a group of setup guys. If the first does well, he stays in the game. If he doesn't, someone else gets up and goes in for him. I was one of those guys who thought the theory just might work, and then we played the first game of the season.

In the ninth inning with the Sox leading 4–1, Grady Little called in Alan Embree, who gave up a single and a home run. Grady then brought in Chad Fox, who got two outs, then gave up a walk and a home run to Carl Crawford to lose the game 5–4.

When the game ended, I looked at it like this was just one game. As players we didn't sweat the loss of a single game. We went back to the bar at the Vinoy Hotel, talked about it a minute, and got over it. We had 161 games to go. But the Boston writers wouldn't let it go. They obsessed about it like this was the thing that was going to kill our season. I must say, this time they may have been right.

It was two weeks before a Red Sox pitcher got a save. The problem with the no-closer theory, it turned out, is that when there are no defined roles in the bullpen, nobody knows when they're supposed to get up and get warm. And it's very important for guys like Timlin and Embree to know that.

The pitcher who got the first save in 2003 was a kid by the name of Brandon Lyon, who had come over from Toronto. He had good stuff, threw about 95 miles an hour, and had decent sink to his pitches. What made his life easier was that he had had no experience, so he had no idea what he was supposed to do, and he didn't care. He was also helped by the fact that the hitters around the league didn't know much about him, either. He was just happy to be on a pretty awesome team. We used him a lot. He was the one guy Grady called on to close out games. He kept us going—for two or three months, until he hurt his arm.

Grady Little knew my body had worn out by the end of the 2002 season, so in 2003 he decided to rest me after extra-inning games or against certain left-handers, even though I love hitting against lefties. In 2002, we really didn't have a backup center fielder, so I played in 154 games. In 2003 we had Damian Jackson to fill in, and Grady figured he was doing me a favor by giving me days off here and there.

"I'm going to give you a day off tomorrow," Grady would say.

I'd reply, "How come I'm getting the time off?"

When I was 13 and playing for the Mets, I thought I was good enough for the big leagues. (I am on the top row, second from the right.) (*Courtesy of the author*)

We couldn't afford a glove. This one, which was given to me, was for a right hander even though I was a lefty. (*Courtesy of the author*)

Mom, Dad, James (40), and me (41). I wanted to be a star receiver, but the coaches wanted me to be a safety. I ended up quitting to concentrate on baseball. (*Courtesy of the author*)

After my junior year in high school I was asked to play on an All Star team that included Todd Helton, middle row, far right; Alex Rodriguez, middle row, second from left; Danny Kanell, to the right of ARod, and me, top row, far right. I was 16, and it was the first time I was away from home. *(Courtesy of the author)*

Kansas City manager Tony Muser played me every day in 2000, and I led the league in stolen bases and runs scored. *(Getty Images/Jonathan Daniel)*

While with Kansas City I had the privilege of meeting former President Bill
Clinton. At right is Jay Henrich, the assistant general manager of the Royals.
(Courtesy of the author)

My first year with Boston I played on the same team as Ricky Henderson, the
best lead-off hitter ever. *(Courtesy of the author)*

On Family Day my twins, Madelyn and Jackson, show off their cuteness skills before a game at Fenway Park.
(Courtesy of the author)

Here I am with Ben Affleck, a Boston boy who lives and dies with the Red Sox.
(Julie Cordeiro/Boston Red Sox)

After Damian Jackson and I butted heads in the playoffs against the A's, I was in la-la land for weeks.
(Getty Images/Jeff Gross)

After scoring the winning run in Game 5 of the American League Championship Series against the Yankees, I'm mobbed. *(Getty Images/Al Bello)*

The bases were loaded. I knew Javier Vasquez was going to throw me a fastball. I looked for a fastball in. He threw a fastball in. I was lucky to get enough of it for it to go out.
(Getty Images/Doug Pensinger)

Circling the bases after hitting a home run against the St. Louis Cardinals in Game 4 of the World Series.
(Getty Images/Ezra Shaw)

Wake, Johnny Pesky, Kevin Millar, and I celebrate after winning Game 4 and sweeping the Cardinals in the World Series. Curse? What curse?
(Getty Images/Brad Mangin)

I love a parade. These girls know what they're talking about.
(Getty Images/Gil Talbot)

Red Sox game at Fenway: $320
World Series Champions t-shirt: $18
Posterboard, Markers, & Glitter: $11
Gas that got us here: $47
Parking and paying "T" fees: $15

...a KISS from Johnny Damon...
$ Priceless. $

Michelle and I cut the cake after our wedding. I am a *very* lucky guy.
(Courtesy of the author)

What would Johnny Damon do?
(Upper Class Collectibles/Bill Lopa)

"You'll thank me later on in the season," he'd say.

Grady was looking out for me, and for the Red Sox.

In mid-May of 2003, we suffered our first serious injury of the season when Pedro Martinez went on the DL. That was a good six starts that he missed, and with him in there we would have expected to win five of those games. Without him, who knew? The rest of the pitching staff knew it would have to step up.

In late May, Theo decided to shed the no-closer theory and acquire a pitcher who could close effectively. He traded third baseman Shea Hillenbrand to Arizona for pitcher Byung-Hyun Kim. Though I hated to see Shea go—he was a hard-nosed player, a great clutch hitter, and one of my best friends on the team—at the time I thought the trade was a pretty good one. I knew that Bill Mueller would do just fine at third, and I also knew the trade would allow Grady to play David Ortiz a lot more. Before the trade Ortiz, who was splitting time with Jeremy Giambi, didn't play much at all. In fact, in his first 50 games, David hit exactly three home runs. Ortiz badly needed a chance to play, and when Jeremy went on the DL right about this time, he got it. Grady started playing David every day against righties and when he started to hit, began playing him against lefties, too. It was a move that worked out for both Grady and Ortiz.

Also, Kim had awfully impressive numbers. He'd struck out far more batters than he had innings pitched in his career, and I heard he threw in the mid-90s. We were disappointed when Kim came over and from the start in Boston only threw 86, 87 miles an hour. He definitely wasn't the same pitcher he was in Arizona, and he never did help us as much as we thought he would.

In May of 2003, Grady began giving me days off without telling me the day before. I'd arrive at the ballpark, look at the lineup card, and my name wouldn't be on it. I was in my ninth year of playing ball, and no manager had ever done that to me before.

When I asked him why, Grady really didn't give me an answer. But then in early June Grady asked me, "If you knew you had the next day off, would you be partying?"

"No," I told him. "I have a good time. But I don't get drunk. I'm never out of control. I go out and do my thing."

Apparently, Grady was doing this because of my reputation as a partier. He was figuring if he told me I was going to get the day off, I'd go out and party hard, because I knew I wasn't playing the next day. We'd lost our lines of communication, but on this day we got them back.

"If I need a day off, I'll let you know," I said. "I've been around this league a long time, and I know my body better than anyone. Play me. Run me into the ground. That's why I get paid the big money by you guys."

Grady said he understood, and after that he played me every day, and it was never an issue again.

In early June of 2003, Casey Fossum, the young pitcher Theo Epstein had refused to trade to Montreal for Bartolo Colon, pitched one inning against Milwaukee, gave up five runs, and went on the DL. Inside the locker room some of the players voiced their opinions that Theo should have traded Fossum for Colon, even if he had to give up a kid with great potential. Fossum had a live fastball and a good curve, and he was cheap. Colon was a stocky veteran who'd always been able to throw and eat up innings. He'd been to the playoffs. Some of the guys were shocked Theo wouldn't make that trade, because guys don't want to win down the road; they want to win now.

We ended up winning that game 11–10 when Trot Nixon and Jason Varitek hit home runs late in the game. The next day, Kevin Millar hit two home runs to beat Milwaukee again. In 2003, we started the season not thinking we had the horses, but when Theo's acquisitions—Mueller, Millar, Ortiz—all started to hit along with me, Nomar, Manny, and Jason Varitek, all of a sudden we hit all the way down the lineup from one to nine. We never had that before, and we got hot, and when you're on a team that starts to win consistently, there's nothing quite like it.

In 2003 some of our hitters had the year of their lives. Every game we went out there expecting to win. We looked to the future, and we were expecting to go to the playoffs and the World Series.

We credited Theo for putting this team together, and for working to improve us. When I played for Oakland, I knew that Billy Beane would make the moves he needed to make, so that we would have one of the best winning records in August and September. I felt that way about Theo as well. We knew how sharp he was. We knew how much he studied and did his homework. I always said it was the bad GMs who'd ponder a situation until the opportunity passed. Theo would shoot from the hip and make a deal. If he wanted to get someone, he was smart enough to figure out a way to make it work.

On Father's Day, we played the Houston Astros and beat them in 14 innings. After Todd Walker singled, Nomar, who had three doubles and a single, on his own laid down a sacrifice bunt that got him to second, and Manny drove him home. By the fourteenth we were sitting on the bench tired, and when Nomar bunted, we were taken aback.

"What just happened?" we asked. Because we were not a bunting team. But Nomar was unselfish, and he sacrificed for the better of the team. What impressed us most about Nomar was that he was never satisfied with how he did. He thinks he can hit 1.000, and when he doesn't, he's pretty teed off. He actually expects to go 5 for 5 every day. If he's 4 for 4, and he makes an out, he's livid. His critics accused him of caring too much about his statistics, but they were missing the essential truth about Nomar: he was a perfectionist.

You have to love that. When you've been so good for so long, you have that kind of attitude and confidence. Nomar felt that every time he stepped to the plate he'd make a difference.

One of the highlights of the 2003 season came on June 17, 2003, when with a runner on base and down by a couple of runs, Trot Nixon caught a ball in right field and then tossed it in the stands to a fan. The only problem was that there was only one out. The media made a joke out of it, but to Trot, it was anything but a joke. He took it hard. When he came into the dugout, no one gave him grief, even though we were giggling under our hats, because we know how hard Trot goes out and plays, and he felt he'd lost the game.

Despite the addition of Byung-Hyun Kim, our bullpen kept blowing games. Pedro was beating Philly 2–1, when Mike Timlin gave up a long home run to Jim Thome. We took the lead, and then Thome hit another home run in the twelfth. We tied it again, and Todd Pratt hit a home run off Rudy Seanez to beat us. We had three blown saves in one game, which is tough to do, but we did it.

That game was nuts. Our pitchers knew better than to give Thome too good a pitch to hit. They could have just stood up and thrown him four balls. Once I can understand, but twice? That game went on forever. It seemed like there was no end to it.

Did the writers talk to us the next day about the game? No. All they wanted to know about was why Pedro had left the clubhouse early. The real reason: it was a long day, and we hadn't yet put out the spread, and he was hungry. Did any of us care that he left to go get something to eat? No.

I would have loved to tell Pedro to go back to the Dominican for four days, rest up, and come back to us and pitch. But if we had let him do that, the guys who lived in Florida would have wanted to go home between starts, and you couldn't do that, either. If too many guys did it, you wouldn't have a team anymore. On the Red Sox, Pedro got special treatment but he'd earned his special status. As long as he got his work in and went out there every five days and pitched, that was fine. We wanted him to be happy. We *needed* him to be happy. And we'd do *anything* to keep him that way because where there was a happy Pedro, there was a winning Pedro.

We mauled the Tigers three games in a row, and then on June 28, 2003, we hosted the Florida Marlins. What is so wonderful about the game of baseball is that you never know what's going to happen on any given day. Your pitcher might throw a no-hitter. You might make a triple play. You might see something you've never seen before on a ballfield.

Against Florida, we scored 2 touchdowns—14 runs—in the first inning. We scored 10 runs off Carl Pavano and 4 more off two relievers before they could even get an out! I had never seen anything like it. We didn't hit any home runs. We just kept getting on base, and we kept clearing the bases like you wouldn't believe. We had 14 runs, and we still had eight innings to go! It was pretty amazing. You have to have luck, because there are plenty of times when you hit the ball right on the screws, and the ball goes right at someone. In this game every ball we hit found a hole.

In that inning I got up three times, and I had three hits. I was told that that was only the second time that ever happened. I started off the game with a double. My second at-bat I hit a bases-loaded triple to right. My last at-bat I hit a slow roller through the shortstop hole. The ball went through to the outfield, and the left fielder threw out a runner at home for the third out. If that hadn't happened, Todd Walker also might have gotten three hits that inning, because he had two hits and was standing in the on deck circle when the third out was made.

That first inning I had a single, a double, and a triple, and so for the rest of the game I had a chance to hit for the cycle. I didn't get it, but I ended up 5 for 7 on that day.

We won that game 25–8, and the next game we again lost because of our bullpen—we gave up eight runs in the last two innings. We were up 9–6 in the ninth, then Brandon Lyon allowed three hits and a run, and then Mike Lowell homered to beat us.

I felt bad for Brandon. He'd started out so well, and we used him a lot, because he was effective at a time when not a lot of our relievers were. Then he started getting a twinge in his pitching arm, so he wasn't 100 percent. Our bullpen struggled for the whole year pretty much, which made it hard for us at times. Those losses were the toughest to take. You battle all game, through nine innings, and then all of a sudden, a couple of pitches seal your fate. You start questioning what's going on. How come the pitches that are supposed to be on the outside corner were on the inside corner?

Brandon was 23, young, and he had a strong arm, but when you're younger you want to challenge hitters. He didn't want to walk batters, and when that ball drifted toward the heart of the plate, the balls tended to disappear. Losing games late kills a team's morale.

I'd been part of tons of late-game blown saves when I played at Kansas City. But you also have to understand that you win—and lose—as a team. Unless it's a walkoff home run, you still have the opportunity to come back, and it's your responsibility to pick up the other guys and score more runs. It's also why you try to score a lot of runs early, so you don't go into the late innings down by a run.

In the next game we bombed Florida into submission. We hit six home runs, which showed people just how great a hitting team we could be. In 2003, everybody was having a career year, except me. You expect Nomar and Manny to be consistent, but we had Todd Walker and Kevin Millar and Jason Varitek and Billy Mueller and David Ortiz, and Trot Nixon—all having career years.

We traveled to Yankee Stadium over the July 4 holiday. The Yankees had won 16 of 19 games. They led by 4 games for the American League East, but we still felt we had the better team. We knew we didn't have the closer that they did. We knew they could be scary. The Yankees we feared the most were infielders Alfonso Soriano and Nick Johnson.

The thing about Soriano was that you didn't know how to pitch him, because he'd hit anything. He'd hit a fastball up at his eyes. He'd hit a slider down in the dirt. You couldn't make adjustments on him. You might strike him out on a certain pitch, but the next time if you threw him the same pitch, he might hit it out of the park.

Nick Johnson had great plate discipline. On any other team this guy would be good enough to hit anywhere from the two hole down to number six. He was hitting ninth on the Yankees, which was scary. I thought Johnson was pretty special.

I felt we had a team strong enough to match them. You expect the guys in the heart of your order, Nomar and Manny, to hit their home runs and drive in 100 runs. That's a given. When you start the season, the variable is what the other guys are going to do. Can the new guys hit at Fenway Park? How will the one and two guys hit in front of them? Well, Todd Walker, who hit behind me, and I got on base quite a bit, and the new guys adapted to Fenway Park just fine. If we kept on, we were on track to set new team records for home runs and slugging percentage.

In the opening game against the Yankees, Derek Lowe allowed a long home run to Soriano. But we turned around and lit David Wells up. When we were done with him, he walked toward the dugout and threw his glove and his cap into the stands. It was the perfect birthday present for George Steinbrenner. Not only did the Yankees lose, but he was going to have to go out and buy Wells a new ball cap.

Roger Clemens was our next opponent. Good teams are never surprised when they beat a talented pitcher. We didn't go into a game sweating whether we had to face a Roger Clemens. We went into it thinking we were going to win. When Ramiro Mendoza beat him, we expected it to happen. All we needed was for Ramiro to hold up his part, to get some outs, because we were planning to score some runs regardless.

In addition to winning those two games, the other important contribution that promised great things for us was the awakening of our sleeping giant, David Ortiz. Up until July 4, he had hit exactly five home runs. In the three games we played against the Yankees, David hit four home runs in nine at-bats! David was finally getting comfortable playing regularly, and Grady was starting to feel more comfortable playing him.

We'd been having some trouble finding a DH who would hit consistently. We started out using Jeremy Giambi, and though he got his walks, he didn't hit very much. Though his on-base percentage was .380, he was hitting .200. The fans got on him because he wasn't producing, and when he got hurt, David Ortiz took over the role.

When David started to hit, it changed the makeup of our team dramatically. That's when we started beating up teams.

Manny is such a good hitter, but until Ortiz started to hit, pitchers would pitch around Manny. When Ortiz started to hit, they couldn't do that anymore. If they did, they were playing with fire. Manny finally had someone behind him who could hit. And he knew that if the pitcher threw him four straight balls, it was okay, because David would say, "I'm going to hurt you now."

As much as we wanted to sweep the Yankees, we learned in 2003 that they never give up. They had pitchers who could dominate you, and after Andy Pettitte beat us in Game 3 of the Fourth of July holiday series on a four-hitter, in the finale Clemens beat Pedro 2–1 in a game marked by controversy.

Why what happened was controversial was beyond me, except that it involved Pedro, who made headlines whenever he went out there. In one inning, he hit Alfonso Soriano and Derek Jeter on the hands, and both had to leave the game. The Yankees were furious, but for the life of me, I couldn't understand why. I was standing in center field watching, and I could see quite clearly that both Soriano and Jeter were leaning over the plate. Pedro pitches inside. He was trying to pitch exclusively on the inside part of the plate. I actually thought the pitch to Soriano would have been called a strike if he hadn't been hit and the pitch to Jeter was close to it, a borderline strike.

It's odd to hit batters back to back, but neither batter made a big deal out of it because they knew they were hanging out over the plate. When it happened, though, I thought to myself, *We're going to be in for something this game.*

We knew how the Yankees felt, but we also knew we had Pedro's back. If someone charged the mound, we were going to get Pedro out of the ruckus. Jason Varitek had his assignment to protect him from the batter.

The game proceeded with no further incidents, because no one—except the New York writers who were looking to sell newspapers—really thought Pedro did it on purpose. We lost 2–1, a close game. We played well, so after the game we went into the locker room, and in no time we forgot about it.

After the game Steinbrenner ripped Pedro, but Pedro made sure he let Steinbrenner know he wouldn't be intimidated. "He's not going to put any fear in my heart," Pedro said. He also said Steinbrenner couldn't buy his heart, unless he "bought every player in the league."

We then ripped off five wins in a row, and at the All Star break we finished with a 55–38 record. We were two games out of first, and we were playing really great baseball.

Everything was clicking for us. Nomar, our leader, was having a great season. He was hitting .317, had 13 home runs, was tied with ARod with 60 RBIs, scored 73 runs, and was just playing great— amazing numbers considering that he hadn't hit much in July.

We felt very good about our team. We were doing it without an established closer, and for guys to step up and play as well as they were, well, it was a testament to how great our team was.

Chapter 8

Cowboy Up

July 2003—October 2003

I n mid-July 2003 the rumors returned that the Red Sox were going to trade for Carlos Beltran, and I was going to Kansas City. When I heard that, I called Scott Boras. I figured that since Scott was also Carlos's agent, he'd know what was going on. Scott said the rumors were baseless. The Royals had traded me in the first place because they didn't want to pay me.

Theo Epstein did make a trade, but it wasn't for Beltran. Rather it was yet another attempt to bolster our bullpen. He traded Brandon Lyon, who'd been struggling, to Pittsburgh for Scott Sauerbach, a left-handed relief specialist. We badly needed someone to complement Alan Embree. Any time a lefty batter came up, the other manager knew Embree was our only lefty in the pen.

When you have two lefties, it really helps your pen. You can use one lefty pitcher and still have another to face a lefty batter later in the game.

After sweeping the Tigers and beating the Rays two out of three, we returned to Fenway Park on July 28, 2003, to play three games against the Yankees.

The opener was another of those memorable Yankee games. Pedro pitched, and he lost in the ninth when Enrique Wilson singled, stole second, went to third on a grounder, and scored on a sacrifice fly.

Grady left Pedro in to finish the game, and after the game the reporters, who counted all 128 of his pitches, wondered whether Grady was trying to ruin his arm. Man, can these guys second-guess! Pedro was throwing great, and since our bullpen wasn't exactly getting the job done, Grady felt he didn't have much choice if he wanted to win the game. We were shooting to overtake the Yankees. We needed to win, and he thought Pedro was the best pitcher to do that. If he had to do it over again, I'm sure he would.

Grady took a lot of criticism in Boston. It was just unfortunate, because we as players loved playing for him. He went with his gut. Pedro wasn't the best pitcher in the league for nothing. You've got to go with your best.

We won the other two games and closed to within a game and a half of the Yankees. In the second game Byung-Hyun Kim held them at the end, and David Ortiz beat them in the ninth with an RBI single.

In the finale we were trailing 3–0 after six innings, and we came back and won it. Tek and I homered off Chris Hammond to make it 3–2, and then in the eighth with the score tied at Fenway, I walked. Ortiz came up, and he hit a line drive in the gap. I took off as soon as he hit it, never stopped, and when I scored, we were up by a run. In the top of the ninth Manny saved the day with a tremendous backhand catch of a ball hit by Jorge Posada.

People get on Manny so much about his defense, but he's actually pretty decent. People get on him because every once in a while, he makes a mistake and you wonder, *How did that happen?* He makes tough plays, but sometimes the easy plays have a sway over him.

Manny makes $20 million a year, so the focus is always on him.

Fans think that because you make $20 million a year, you better be the best at everything—hitting, fielding, being a great teammate. They feel the money warrants that.

As players we don't measure another player's talent by his salary. I can't blame a player if he's offered a ridiculous contract. You have to commend him. This is a tough game. I commend anyone who makes that kind of money, pat them on the back, and hope for their sake they can live up to it.

No one is ever going to remember you for the money you made. People are going to remember you for how much you put it all on the line, how hard you played the game. The never-say-die guys are the players I really admire.

Fans talk about the money because the owners use the salaries to sell their teams. The salaries are even printed in the game programs. *USA Today* publishes everyone's salaries every spring. When a player signs a contract, ESPN will run how many years and how much money on its ticker. It's pretty gross that everyone knows how much we make. If I go 0 for 4, and a fan sees I'm making $8 million a year, he says to himself, *How can that bum be making $8 million?*

Theo Epstein, who like the rest of us never gives up, on July 31, 2003, acquired Scott Williamson, a fireballing closer, from Cincinnati. Scott was rookie of the year when he came up. He has a great split-fingered fastball that he throws in the 90s. The ball tumbles like a knuckleball. He was getting too expensive for the Reds, and when he came to us, he was lights out.

He set up for us, closed for us. Unfortunately, he had elbow problems, and he couldn't go every day like he used to. In some games he would have pain radiating from his elbow down to his forearm. He would get up to get loose, and he wouldn't be able to go. It's just too bad he wasn't healthy.

Theo also acquired starting pitcher Jeff Suppan from Pittsburgh. He'd started with the Red Sox and spent some time in Kansas City. I loved him. He was a regular guy, didn't have anything spectacular, threw 87 or 88, but he was one of the guys who went out there and had pinpoint control, and just knew how to pitch. He helped eat up innings and gave us what we needed.

All season long Theo kept making the bullpen and the bench stronger and deeper. It's great when you have people on your bench who are just as good as your starters. The more good players a team has, the better it gets.

In early August 2003, we played the Angels, one of the teams we needed to beat to win the wild card, and after we won the opener 10–9 on home runs by Kevin Millar and Nomar, we beat them again in a game in which I made what was probably the best catch of my career. I've made plenty of good plays in Kansas City and Oakland, but no one was paying much attention when I was playing there. I remember the look on Adam Kennedy's face when I caught it.

Kennedy hit a ball that could have been a double or triple, a long ball hit so high and deep that when I leaped, I felt like I must have jumped 15 feet in the air. The ball would have been a home run if the wind hadn't been blowing. He hit it good, but I stayed with it, leaped, and caught it. The crowd went crazy. A lot of the fans in center field didn't get to see the catch until they showed it on the replay. Everybody just went nuts. I used to be able to dunk a basketball, but I've gained 15, 20 pounds since then. I couldn't believe I could jump that high.

When John Burkett beat the Angels the next day, our record was 38–16 at Fenway, the best home record in the major leagues. When people ask me how the fans at Fenway affect the way the team plays, all you have to do is look at our record at home. We don't need any more motivation than our fans.

As I've mentioned, John Burkett—aka "Sheets"—was a very interesting person to have on our team. He bowls on the PBA tour. He's like Suppan, another one of those pitchers you love because even though he doesn't have great stuff, he's very smart, knows how to change speeds, and he goes out and competes. He throws that ephus pitch which I once saw timed at 48 miles an hour. John keeps the game moving, keeps his fielders in the game. It's fun to watch.

• • •

Following the series against the Angels, we had lost two out of three to Baltimore, then lost the first two games to the A's in Oakland. In the third game Derek Lowe was pitching for us, and he had the bases loaded in the fifth, and Erubiel Durazo up. The game easily could have gotten out of hand. But Derek threw him a helacious fastball for strike three, and he thrust his fist up in the air and celebrated.

Derek's an emotional guy. He'd never want to come across as cocky, but he was beginning to realize how much the game of baseball meant to him. He was beginning to really *care* about the game, beginning to enjoy himself out there, really get into it. When Derek made that gesture, it showed to us how *much* he cared, and we were psyched by that.

We were losing the game 2–1 in the ninth, when the A's brought their star reliever Keith Foulke into the game. Manny came up. He fouled off a string of pitches, and then he hit a long home run to tie it. After Byung-Hyun Kim pitched two perfect innings, Billy Mueller, who was among the top hitters in the league, hit a sacrifice fly to win it. It was a *big* win for us because Foulke was pretty much lights out for Oakland. He hadn't blown a save all year until that game. The home run Manny hit was huge for us, and Mueller's hitting was just as huge.

You never see Billy Mueller give away at-bats. He goes out and battles, even when he's got nothing going for him. He goes out and tries to move the runner, tries to play the game of baseball right. I learned a lot from him. I doubt that Billy has twenty bad at-bats a year! Other guys in the majors have a hundred bad at-bats a year. I've told Billy how amazing I think he is.

We lost three games in a row to the Mariners in mid-August 2003 and then went home to Fenway and lost the opener of the series to the A's when Scott Williamson gave up a home run in the ninth to Ramon Hernandez. The next night Byung-Hyun Kim blew the save, as the Fenway crowd booed and booed, which was warranted, because our team never should lose that many games in a row. We were too good a team. The fans were remembering what had happened in 2001 and 2002, what happened in 1946, 1978, and 1986—they'd come to expect the losing, and when that didn't change, they grew more tired of it and less patient.

After the game Kevin Millar really let the press and the fans have it. Kevin was so good for our team. All year in private he'd say, "Somebody has to cowboy up." In Kevin talk, that meant somebody had to get behind the team and lead us. On this night, he told the reporters, "I want to see somebody cowboy up and stand behind this team and quit worrying about all the negative stuff and last year's team and 1986 and ten years ago." He said he didn't give a shit about the past, that the fans had to stop with all the negativity.

"I'm here to have fun," he told the reporters. "The past makes zero sense to me."

In other words, quit talking all that curse nonsense. But when you get down toward the end of the season, that's all you hear about from these guys. "Do you believe in the curse?" "Is the curse overtaking the team?" Since Dan Shaughnessy is the guy who invented this curse nonsense in the first place, I find it kind of odd that he keeps talking about it. He's a bright guy. I can't believe he actually believes in it. I guess the Curse of the Bambino has a better ring to it than the Curse of Dan Shaughnessy.

By August 20, 2003, the Yankees held a $7\frac{1}{2}$ game lead over us. When the Yankees came to town on August 30, we had to play them without Manny, who was sick. He'd been going out there, busting his butt every day, and he'd worn down. Then after one of those games, a game we lost, Manny was seen by somebody after the game sitting with the Yankees' Enrique Wilson in the bar of the Ritz-Carlton, where Manny was living. If you'd read the papers, you'd have thought Manny had committed a serious crime against the game of baseball.

I also live at the Ritz-Carlton, and what people don't realize is that if you want to eat something late at night, the bar is where you can do it. Many a night I ate dinner late at night at the bar. People assumed that just because it was a bar, Manny was sitting there drinking booze. But Manny doesn't drink very much at all. There are others of us who do, but Manny isn't one of them. He wanted some food, and that's why he was there, and from where I'm sitting, I didn't see anything at all wrong with that.

The writers wanted Theo to fine Grady for not being more of a disciplinarian, but that was a bunch of crap. We're older guys. We know what we have to do to play baseball, and not just play it but win. What would have happened if Grady had become a rigid disciplinarian? Imagine if Grady had started shouting at Manny or Pedro and made them unhappy? With veteran players, you don't have to do that. Maybe you get the team together and say, "We need to go harder. We need to start thinking more about the team and less about personal goals." Or if guys are pressing, you say, "Go out and have fun." That's all a manager needs to say with a team of veterans. And Grady would say exactly those things.

Manny returned, and on September 4 at Yankee Stadium, he made an amazing play when he robbed Bernie Williams of a home run to beat the Yankees. He ran a good distance down the left field line, jumped up, caught the ball, robbed Bernie, and sent the whole stadium into shock. It was perfect Manny, because he then threw the ball into the stands even though there was only one out. It was a good thing nobody was on base. On the bench we were dying laughing. But Manny, who is laid back and very cool, was a great sport. Manny could be mayor of Boston if he wanted to be, but he doesn't want to be. He's happy living his life, and there's a lot to be said for that.

We won that game, and the next game we beat Roger Clemens and the Yankees 11–0. Now, all of a sudden, the press and the fans were back on our side 100 percent. Yeah, we'd been losing ground to the Yankees, but we were in the playoff hunt, and that's what was most important to us. The press is very knowledgeable, but their mood swings can be a terrible distraction. One week we're getting it with both barrels, hearing about Bucky Dent and Bill Buckner, and the next week we're the darlings of the town and certain to win the World Series and avenge the curse.

The cheers we understand. We don't understand the boos. We relish the cheers. When you get the boos, you can't take it personally and you have to fight your way out of it. That's why there have been players wearing "Boston Red Sox" on their jerseys who couldn't take it and had to go elsewhere to survive.

We would have liked to have swept the Yankees, but winning three in a row against New York is always very difficult. David Wells beat us in the finale 3–1. Then on September 9, David Ortiz hit a home run, the two hundred and fourteenth home run of the year, beating the old record set by the 1977 Red Sox team with Yaz, Jim Rice, Fred Lynn, George Scott, and Dwight Evans. Theo had predicted we'd be a hard-hitting team, but I doubt if he guessed we'd be this good. If the Yankees hadn't been as exceptional as they were, there's no doubt the 2003 Red Sox would have gone down in the history as its greatest team.

As it stands, I'd have to say the 2003 Red Sox are among the top five Red Sox teams. The way we hit the ball, we ended up breaking the slugging record hit by the 1927 Yankees with Ruth and Gehrig. If we'd had a closer at the beginning of the year, 2003 might have turned out very differently.

We took the series from Baltimore and Chicago and beat Tampa Bay two of two. We had a $2\frac{1}{2}$ game lead over the Mariners for the wild-card spot with 12 games to go. We knew every game was important, and we kept up the pressure. We didn't play a single game all year that wasn't stressful. When you play in Boston, every game is the most important game of the season. It's amazing the emphasis the press and the fans put on every game. We knew the season was winding down. We knew we had to be better than everyone else. We hadn't gotten into the playoffs in 2001 and 2002. Everyone knew that we *had* to get there and that once we got there, anything can happen, including the chance to erase an 85-year-old curse.

Once we got there, we knew, we had as good a chance to be 2003 World Series champions as anyone.

On September 23, we were losing to the Orioles by three runs at Fenway Park. We had two runners on and two outs, and two strikes on Todd Walker in the bottom of the ninth. Todd homered to tie it up, and then David Ortiz homered to win it.

Todd Walker was one of the best hitters I've ever seen. He has an awesome approach, and he doesn't ever seem to have a bad at-bat. He came up through college at Louisiana State University. It took him a couple years to get adjusted to wooden bats, but he was always a great hitter. He drove the ball. He batted second in our order in 2003, and he did one of the best jobs ever batting behind me—he knew how to hit, had an idea what he was doing every time, and knew how to move the runners. It was so important to have me and Todd at one and two getting on in front of the three, four, and five guys. Todd was a two guy who drove in 80 runs and kept innings going so the big bats could come up behind him.

David Ortiz was the guy most responsible for getting us into the post-season in 2003. Though he only had 3 home runs in his first 50 games, he finished the 2003 season with 31 home runs and 101 RBIs. The guy was on fire. He had to pick up just about every base runner to reach that number. I would have liked to have seen his numbers if he'd been allowed to start coming right out of the box.

David is incredible. If you look at him, he's definitely someone you don't want to bump into in a dark alley. He looks intimidating, even though he's a very gentle person. He's very loving to his family, and he always has an entourage of friends around him. He's a very nice, humble guy who thanks God every day for the blessings he has.

We clinched the wild-card spot on September 26, 2003, when we beat the Orioles at Fenway 14–2. After the game, we went out and thanked the fans for the great year and for what was to come. Instead of showering and getting dressed, a few of the players, Bill Mueller, Todd Walker, Scott Sauerbach, and Kevin Millar, ran across the street to one of the local bars to celebrate. That's the kind of fun team we had. There we were, professional ballplayers, running down Boylston Street in our uniforms.

The fans were going nuts. It was pretty wild out there. It was like we'd just won the World Series. That night we started hearing it: "Is this the year?" We felt it was. The energy was incredible. It was awesome how Boston got very electrifying and prepared for the up-coming games.

We felt we had the best team. All we needed was for a few breaks to go our way, and we were going to be champions. We knew it wouldn't be easy, but we knew it was very possible.

We thought it was curious that the Sox hadn't bothered to extend Grady Little's contract. We knew he didn't see eye to eye with the front office, but we loved and respected Grady. In 2002 he won 93 games, and in 2003 he won 95. Of course he had the horses, but he'd taken us there, so we couldn't understand what the holdup was.

We met the Oakland A's in the first round of the playoffs. These were most of the guys I'd played with two years earlier. They were built around that great pitching staff with Hudson, Zito, and Mulder, and they still had Miguel Tejada, Jermaine Dye, Terrence Long, Eric Chavez, and a tough hitter, Scott Hatteberg, at first base.

The series opened in Oakland, and in the first game we were tied going into the bottom of the twelfth inning when the A's loaded up the bases. Derek Lowe was on the mound in relief. Their catcher, Ramon Hernandez, who was one of the very few guys on their team capable of bunting, laid down a perfect bunt to beat us, prompting Derek to wear a T-shirt that said, "I survived a walk-off bunt."

I'd never seen a walk-off bunt before, but it worked, and it put the A's up one game to none.

Barry Zito beat us in the second game, and though it looked like curtains for the Red Sox, we were never discouraged.

I couldn't forget that when I was with Oakland in 2001, we'd led the Yankees two games to none and lost three in a row. If it could happen to the A's once, I felt it could easily happen again.

"I was in the same spot with that same team with those same guys," I told the guys after the game. "They're thinking about getting past the first round, something they've never done. We've got nothing to lose. There's no pressure on us. Let's go out and give it our all."

We returned to Fenway, which always gave us a lift. We were hard to beat when we played at home. We loved playing there. Our fans are the best in the world. Teams coming in hated to play there, and for good reason.

Before the game Kevin Millar, being as superstitious as he was, went and shaved his head completely. Since he didn't want to be the only one looking like Travis Bickle from *Taxi Driver*, he went to the other guys who'd shaved their heads in the past—Gabe Kapler, Jason Varitek, and Trot Nixon—because he knew they'd go along.

After he cut their hair off, he had four baldies. Then he started going around to the other guys saying, "The whole team's doing it. We'll cut all our hair off, and maybe we'll change our luck."

He got more and more of the players to go along. Todd Walker even crumbled. Todd had told Kevin, "I won't do it unless Johnny does it." But Kevin kept in his ear, working on him for about six hours straight until Todd finally gave in just to shut Kevin up.

I told Kevin I had to look good for the girls going into the off-season.

"If I cut my hair off," I said, "it might never grow back."

Nomar's excuse was that he was getting married, and Mia wouldn't like it.

Millar got John Burkett, Scott Sauerbach, and Bill Mueller to go along. Kevin Millar has a little peanut head, and he looked terrible without his hair. Only Derek Lowe looked worse.

That night Derek went out and pitched a beautiful ball game. The score was tied 1–1 in the eleventh inning when Trot Nixon pinch hit a long home run to win the game and put us back in it. We thought that was one of the greatest home runs in Red Sox history. He hit it long and far over the center field wall. It kept our dreams alive. Granted, we hadn't scored much, but the win was huge.

In Game 4, we trailed the A's 4–3 in the eighth with runners on first and third and two outs and David Ortiz at bat. Keith Foulke, their unhittable closer, was on the mound for the A's. David, who hit so often in the clutch that year, then lined a double into the right field corner to win the game and tie up the series. That was another amazing, amazing game, and it must have seemed like déjà vu for the A's players, who couldn't believe what was happening.

After the game John Henry burst into tears, and I thought I

knew why. I don't think John knew what he was getting into when he bought the team. He didn't realize that he'd be on the edge of his seat every game, knowing our team could do something pretty amazing every night.

After that win, we were very, very excited, of course. We were still alive. We had to get back on the plane to Oakland. It was a game the A's desperately didn't want to play. The A's had been so sure they were going to win that fourth game that they didn't bother to bring their bags to the ballpark. They left them at the hotel, figuring they'd win and then fly directly to New York to play the Yankees. That's one of those things you just don't do. And because they didn't pack their bags, we beat them into Oakland by a good two hours.

The fifth game, is, of course, a blur, owing to my collision with Damian Jackson. We were tied 1–1 in the sixth inning when Manny for a final time showed what a great hitter he is, hitting a three-run home run to give us the lead. That was a huge home run. I later watched the highlights of the game on tape, and you could see that Manny hit a hanging curveball—he tattooed it—and that gave us the life we needed.

The next inning was when Damian and I smacked into each other, and as I was on the way to the hospital in an ambulance, the Red Sox were on their way to a date with destiny and the New York Yankees.

Chapter 9

America's Team

Not long after our 2003 season ended, courtesy of Aaron Boone, the Red Sox put Manny Ramirez on waivers. I didn't know it at the time, but any team could have picked up his salary for the $20,000 waiver price. We could have lost him for nothing. It was kind of shocking. Manny had joked about wanting to play for the Yankees, and I guess Theo Epstein felt that if Manny wasn't happy in Boston, he'd do him a favor and give him a chance to go elsewhere. If he wanted to play for the Yankees badly enough, Theo felt, here was his chance. If the Yankees took him, Theo was going to use the $20 million a year he'd save to buy other players.

My feeling was that they were taking Manny's jabbering about wanting to play for the Yankees way too seriously. Manny walked around the clubhouse joking all the time. Sure, he may have dreamed of playing for the Yankees when he was a kid growing up on those playgrounds in the Bronx, but as far as we were concerned, every time we played the Yankees, Manny was a main contributor, fighting against them as hard as any of us.

If Manny had a reason not to want to play in Boston, it was because of the way he was treated by the media. Manny sometimes did things that got misinterpreted. Also, if someone else did something, no one noticed. If Manny did it, it was an issue. For instance, Manny might show up late, and the writers would always make a big deal about it.

Sometimes Manny had good reasons to be late. Sometimes something is going on at home, and it's nobody's business. Or maybe his wife or kid was sick. We deal with it. Sometimes there was no good reason, but we didn't care about that, either.

We'd get to the ballpark, and we'd hear stories about Manny as the reporters tried to stir things up. The media in Boston is always a danger zone. We tried staying out of the way, so our first answer was always the same, "Who cares?" Or we might say, "Oh, that's just Manny being Manny."

When I arrived in Boston in 2002, I decided to try to change that. I'm the type of guy who can handle media pressure. It just falls off my shoulder. When I was with Kansas City and then with Oakland, I always stood in front of the media and talked. I always spoke what was on my mind. I gave the truth—good and bad.

After a while I got sick of the writers picking on Manny, and instead of just saying, "That's just Manny being Manny," I—and other teammates—began to step up and say, "That's a bunch of hogwash. Manny's a great teammate. Manny comes to play every day." Major league baseball is a very high-pressure game, and Boston is a very tough city to play in, and we needed for Manny to be able to relax, so our team started taking a stand whenever the media would talk to us about him. We would defend Manny as hard as we could.

When the Yankees left Manny unclaimed, the next thing we heard was that the Sox were going to trade him to the Texas Rangers for Alex Rodriguez. When I heard that, my first reaction was, *That doesn't make a lot of sense. We have the greatest athlete in Red Sox history still playing shortstop for us.*

As a player you have no say whatsoever in what the club is trying to do. We are their property. When a team brings in a new general manager or manager, the writers ask, "Will you play for him?"

Damn right I will. These guys pay our salaries. The managers put us in the lineup. That's the least we can do. We make a lot of money playing this game. It doesn't matter who we play for—what manager, what GM, what owner—we're going to go out there and do our best.

At the same time, when I heard what Theo was trying to do, my admiration for him grew, because he wasn't standing pat, wasn't standing still, like most general managers who are afraid to make a mistake. Here he was trying to make the biggest trade in the history of the game, and I liked that. You've got to have balls to be in that position. You've got to have that fire that allows you to make any trade that will help the ballclub. That's the way Theo goes after it. I dug it.

A lot of the guys hadn't wanted to play in Boston because of some of the things General Manager Dan Duquette had done. But as soon as Theo came, that all changed. Everyone felt he'd treat us fairly, and as a player, that's all you can really ask for. It didn't take long for the players to trust Theo's decisions. Sometimes when he did something, the end result wasn't always obvious, but before long you'd figure out what he was doing, and you'd be impressed. Like with the hiring of Terry Francona, who was bench coach with Oakland under manager Ken Macha the year before. I didn't know him, but his name struck a chord because I remember when I was a kid collecting baseball cards, he played for the Expos. Also I knew he'd managed Philly. The writers talked about how the Philadelphia fans had run him out of town, but at the time I didn't know or care what happened to him in Philly. Things happen in this game of baseball, and I wasn't going to judge him by anything that had happened in the past.

After Terry was named manager, he called a bunch of the players on the phone. He called me at home, and he said he was happy to be my manager because I'd made him sick the year before when I was beating up on the A's. He said he was glad to finally have me on his team. I don't know whether he was bullshitting or not. So be it. But he called me a couple more times during the off-season. He asked me about batting leadoff or maybe batting second. I told him, "Whatever you want to do—whatever will make our team better—that's where I'll be." He kept me at leadoff, and it worked out.

Theo hired Terry because he wanted a manager who did a lot more computer work and statistical analysis than Grady Little. He wanted someone with the same statistical-minded philosophy as Billy Beane in Oakland or Bill James. Theo wanted a manager who studied the charts, who knew who hits what average against whom. Art Howe, the Oakland manager, did a lot of paperwork and review before a game. Theo wanted that, and Terry Francona was the guy who did the statistical work for manager Ken Macha.

As a player, I can go along with that, but for the most part, athletes trust in ability, because statistics can lie. As an example, I believe I'm 0 for 7 against Danny Miceli, a high school friend of mine who also ended up in the big leagues. Most of the outs were fly balls to the warning track. You're not going to be mad with those at-bats. You're just not successful. With a little luck, you're looking at a completely different outcome.

I believe I was 3 for 30 against pitcher Eddie Guardado, but 15 of those outs were hard line drives to the shortstop. So you can't say I swung that bad against him.

There was a situation against Steady Eddie in Seattle in 2004 when Terry said to me, "I may pinch hit for you."

"Why's that?" I asked.

"Well, your numbers really stink against this guy." He showed me the chart.

I told him I saw the ball really well against him, that typically I hit hard line drives to short against him. He let me hit. On the second pitch I hit a hard line drive to short. I got back to the dugout, and he said, "All right, I'm never going to pinch hit for you."

There are some pitchers you just hit very well, but if you're not swinging the bat well that day, you're not going to hit them. So it's a give-and-take situation.

I've been around the league. I've seen a lot of pitchers. Terry gives me the benefit of the doubt.

We hired Terry in early November 2003, and at the end of the month it was announced that Theo had signed Curt Schilling and that one of the key reasons Curt signed with the Sox was that he and Terry had been close when he was pitching for Terry on the Phillies. I'd faced Curt in 2001 when Oakland went to Arizona. I wasn't blown away, but I saw that the guy was hitting every spot possible, that when he was on, he was tough to hit. When I faced him in 2003 when Arizona came to Boston, he was lights out.

Kevin Millar was the one who told me about the ARod deal. We were going to trade Manny to Texas for ARod, and Nomar was supposed to go to the Chicago White Sox for Magglio Ordonez. With all the trade rumors, I just kept hoping I wasn't one of the guys involved in any of those deals. As I've mentioned, I know John Hart, who became the general manager of the Texas Rangers after he left Cleveland. I went to Hart's baseball camps when I was in high school, and I knew he liked me. I knew Texas needed a center fielder, so I was hoping I wasn't going to be part of the ARod deal.

For me, baseball is so much more enjoyable when you can stay in one place. I was feeling so insecure about remaining a Red Sox player that I had sold my house during the 2003 season and moved into the Ritz-Carlton. I figured if I got traded, selling my house in advance would make the move that much easier. I could leave with my clothes.

Besides not wanting to see Nomar leave, I had one other reservation about the ARod deal. We knew what a great player he was. But things hadn't worked out for him in Seattle, and things didn't work out for him in Texas. He signed that huge contract with the Rangers, and then when Texas didn't win, he wanted out of it. Well, you signed that contract. Honor it. Yeah, ARod wants to win, but so does everyone else. When I was in Kansas City we wanted to win. We wanted to win in Oakland. What would happen if every player decided to get out of his contract just because his team wasn't winning?

When I got home to Orlando in the off-season after the 2003

season, I was really concerned, because my name was being thrown around everywhere. I was still very banged up from my collision with Damian Jackson, still getting migraines. I didn't even know we'd acquired Curt Schilling until a week after it happened when I ran into my brother and he told me. I tend not to focus on baseball when the off-season rolls around. I tend to change my cell phone number a lot so the newspaper guys can't find me. And if they do, I always give them the response, "I don't know what you're talking about." One, because I really *don't* know, and two, because the season is so draining and stressful on your mind and body and family, once you get to the off-season, you become a fan yourself. I start watching football and hockey and NASCAR.

I'm a guy who needs to be doing something all the time. That's probably why I've lived in five homes in the last three years. I keep buying properties. I buy different toys—Jet Skis, wave runners, an ocean boat, a lake boat, a motorcycle, a '71 Bronco, all the fun that baseball affords you the privilege to buy. I stay busy. I live on a lake, and normally I go out and fish a bit, ride the Jet Ski, knee board, pull people on tubes. Every night I watch the Disney fireworks and swim. I just can't stay still. I'm always going.

I can relax again once spring training comes around. I can concentrate on my body, on my swing, on my mind. I'm all about baseball then. Being a baseball player is so great. You never know how long a game is going to be. When my friends go to work, they know how long they're going to be there. They always know. They know they'll punch in at eight and punch out at five. For me, it's never like that. I don't even wear a watch, even though I've started collecting watches.

When the ARod deal fell through, it just seemed like another example of things not going the Sox's way—to the fans, at least. Gene Orza, the lawyer for the players union, refused to allow the trade. The Red Sox were trying to cut Alex Rodriguez's pay, and Orza felt he had to protect the money ARod had signed for. I'm a big part of the union, and not making that deal was great with me. Number one, because we got to keep Manny, and we got to keep Nomar. They were my teammates. You always want what's best for them. Even though Boston wasn't making life too easy for Nomar, I still thought his place was with the Sox. If I'd believed otherwise, I'd have supported his leaving. It's a short life, and it's hard to play the game of baseball and be miserable where you are.

Through the off-season, I kept getting reports of the moves the Red Sox and the Yankees were making. We'd desperately needed a closer in 2003. If there was one reason we lost in 2003, that was it. The Yankees have had a big advantage for years because they have Mariano Rivera, who's been the best in the game. When he pitches, you know what's coming: shutout innings and a lot of victories. You know what he's going to keep throwing, and you still can't hit it.

As I've mentioned, when you use relief by committee, it's hard on the guys in the pen who don't know their roles. They don't know when they need to get up and start stretching. They have to wait for the phone call. We had a whole bunch of good guys, Scott Williamson, Mike Timlin, and Tim Wakefield, in 2003, but no one knew whether they were closing from one day to the next.

Closers are expensive, of course. Good ones cost $5 million a year or more. In December of 2003, Theo addressed the problem when he signed Keith Foulke, who that year was 9–1 with Oakland with 43 saves to lead the league. Whenever I hit against Foulke, I had decent at-bats, but nothing too great. He's a fastball, change up pitcher. His change up is one of the best in the game, so his 87-mile-an-hour fastball looks like it's 95. That's what makes him so tough. And he has pinpoint control. He doesn't walk very many. With Schilling and Foulke, I was very confident we'd be able to beat the Yankees in 2004. When I heard that Andy Pettitte and Roger Clemens were going to Houston, David Wells was going to San Diego, and third baseman Aaron Boone had torn up his knee playing basketball, I was sure of it. We'd been five outs away from going to the World Series against them. I was very optimistic.

My thoughts were, *This is great. We should run away with it.*

When the Yankees signed Tom "Flash" Gordon, that was a huge sign for them. Then right at the start of spring training it was announced that the Yankees had traded Alfonso Soriano to Texas and that they themselves had acquired Alex Rodriguez. I couldn't believe it. The Boston press went bananas, and rightfully so. When that happened, our feeling was that it was like having your best girl marry the guy you hate the most in the world.

The Yankees, of course, replaced Clemens, Pettitte, and Wells. They signed veteran pitcher Kevin Brown, Jon Lieber, and Jose Contreras. And they still had Mike Mussina.

When we arrived for spring training, Manny was as happy-go-lucky as ever. He wasn't bothered that Theo had put him on waivers or that he'd tried to trade him. Manny was getting paid and he was back in Boston, and he was fine with it.

Nomar, on the other hand, had been hurt when Kevin Millar went on ESPN and told everyone how happy he was that ARod was going to be playing shortstop for the Red Sox in 2004. Nomar, who like I said is very sensitive, didn't know who else felt that way. I think he really didn't know who to trust or who on the team to believe in anymore. He was also still looking over his shoulder, wondering, *Are they still trying to trade me?*

All through spring training Nomar acted like a gentleman. I can remember having a day off and coming back the next day and being told, "Nomar's hurt." At that point I felt our team was going backwards, though we still had plenty of confidence. We told ourselves, *Okay, if Nomar is down, we'll throw Pokey Reese in. We know offensively he won't be the same, but we all need to step up until Nomar gets healthy.* Reese had been signed to play second, and now he'd have to move to short, but we had the perfect person to play second in Mark Bellhorn. We were ready to play, and all through spring training we beat up people.

We got to see Curt Schilling pitch for us for the first time. Here was Schilling, the big superstar, wearing those throwback baseball or football jerseys to the ballpark. We'd rag him about the shirts, telling him how ugly they were.

Kevin Millar, who can rib pretty good, let him have it every day during spring training. One day he told him, "I never knew Johnny Unitas was that fat." If Mark Bellhorn doesn't talk, Kevin doesn't shut up. There was such unity on our team, we felt we could say anything, do anything. In spring training Alan Embree, Keith Foulke, Kevin Millar, Gabe Kapler, and I all bought motorcycles. Kevin had a friend in Beaumont, Texas, who drove down to Fort Myers with about 20 Thunder Mountain motorcycles, and we picked out the ones we liked best and bought them.

The night I picked mine out, I learned to ride. It was the first time Gabe Kapler had ridden a bike, too. And what's so great about playing for the Red Sox, whatever we did was okay with Theo, who shared our Generation X perspective. He knows the importance of having an identity, of being yourself and not caring what anyone thinks. Of course, Theo probably stayed awake nights, worrying he'd get a phone call telling him something terrible had happened to us on our bikes. With our team being as rowdy as it was, I'm sure he didn't sleep well. He probably hoped we didn't get thrown in jail. He knew we weren't going to get invited to the White House—except for Schilling.

Theo also let me keep the long hair and beard I'd brought with me to spring training. Ordinarily during the off-season I liked to grow my hair long because on days when I'm skiing or doing any of the things I'm not supposed to be doing, I don't want to devote time to shaving or visiting the local barber.

I was skiing at Aspen with Michelle Mangan, my then girl-friend—now wife—in the winter of 2002. She had moved to Miami, and after the 2002 season I went down and saw her, and we started dating. During the week, I hadn't shaved, and so I had a full face of hair. We'd been there three days, and one day we got back early and the concierge on duty didn't see us walk into our room.

I shaved and got ready for a nice dinner, and when we walked out, the concierge looked at me, but she didn't recognize me because I'd shaved. She said to Michelle, "What happened to the guy you had here earlier?" Michelle, being as crazy as she is, said, "He was driving me nuts. He was whining and complaining, so I shipped his ass back to Orlando."

"How did you find this guy?" the concierge asked her.

"I saw him skiing and he looked cute, and I was alone, and he was alone, so I just said, 'Why not?'"

"What do *you* think about it?" the concierge asked me.

"I don't care," I said, "it's just a piece of ass for a couple of days."

After about 30 minutes, we told the concierge the truth, because it wasn't making Michelle feel too good, and it definitely wasn't making that clean-cut guy, me, feel too good. That's the power of the beard. You can disguise yourself.

After my concussion, I would have a migraine headache every day around two in the afternoon. It made me feel so bad that I didn't shave during that whole time. When I shave, I'm thorough. I spend a lot of time, and I just didn't feel like spending 30 or so minutes shaving. So that was another reason for my full beard when I arrived in camp. The migraines also made it harder for me to work out during the off-season. I started going to a chiropractor in Orlando, and then they began to diminish.

At the outset of the 2004 season Pedro Martinez went into the clubhouse and decided to claim one of the trainer's lockers, located in an area not accessible to the media. He put a Sony TV and a DVD player in there, and brought in a massage chair that he let the players use when he wasn't sitting in it.

It was also the first year that Pedro showed up for Photo Day. Every other year the Red Sox had to superimpose his face on the photo. He wasn't pitching that day, and I guess he was bored at home and just happened to be at the ballpark, and he got caught off guard.

"Oh, we have picture day?"

Pedro joked about it.

"I'm here," he said. "This is the first and only picture I'm going to take, and I guess that means we're going to win the World Series."

I don't know why it is, but we always seem to lose on opening day. We were in Baltimore, and Pedro started, went six innings, and then he left the clubhouse without telling anyone to get a bite to eat. It was a superlong game, and he was hungry, so he left.

You think, *Who cares?* But the next day in the papers the reporters got hold of it and made headlines with it. It was almost an exact replay of that game against Philly in 2003 when Pedro left the clubhouse early. You'd have thought Pedro had committed murder.

"Is Pedro disrespecting the manger?"

"Is Francona weak because he isn't going to punish Pedro?"

It was pretty crazy—déjà vu all over again. All he did was go out to get something to eat.

The next day Curt Schilling did his thing against the Orioles, and the Pedro incident was forgotten. Keith Foulke got his first save, which was pretty impressive considering that he'd had such a bad spring. But one of the reasons he began slowly was that every day Keith would take pitchers' fielding practice, what we call PFPs. A coach would hit him hard ground balls, and he isn't that great a fielder, so the ball would hit him in the leg, in the ankle, on the calf, and his leg would be black and blue. He was one of those bad-luck guys who had bull's-eyes all over his body.

Terry told everyone to be patient with Keith, even though he hadn't been pitching that well. Terry knew we had a good team. What Terry didn't know was that he had a bunch of idiots who loved to play the game, guys who once they stepped out onto the field, played baseball. Keith was one of those idiots. Once the season started, he played ball.

After going 0 for 9 in the first two games, I surprised everyone in the rubber game against the Orioles when I got five hits in another win. A leadoff hitter is supposed to have a high average, but personally, I didn't care. In Oakland one year, I'd hit .256, but all I cared about was that our team was winning, our morale was good, and we were going in the right direction.

I don't sacrifice bunt. If a runner is on second with nobody out, I try to hit a ground ball to the right side. That's one of those at-bats where you get a nice pat on the back when you return to the dugout. Its effect is the same as a sacrifice, but it counts as an out in the scorebook. If I really cared about my batting average, I'd bunt and hit 20 points higher every year. What I care about is driving in runs and scoring runs.

In that same game against the Orioles I made a leaping catch to rob David Segui of a home run. People remembered my collision with Damian Jackson, and they wondered whether I'd be able to move and if I'd be afraid to run into walls. In spring training there were four or five balls I should have caught, balls I didn't go hard after because I was gun-shy. Of course, it makes the other players around me look bad. In the game before, a ball fell between Gabe Kapler and me, which didn't look too good, and later in the game Kevin Millar in right field called for a pop up that he had to race over to get, and I didn't hear him, and just as he caught it, I ran into him, slamming my shoulder into his face and knocking him down. We were both lucky no one was hurt. Even though I made that catch to rob Segui, the question about my ability to chase the ball against the wall would not go away until June or July.

Baseball has a long season, and part of any player's success is whether he can avoid injury, big or small. The injury bug can bite you at any moment. In the opening day loss at Fenway, Ted Lilly of the Blue Jays threw me a running fastball, and I fouled it off against the back of my left knee. I stayed in the game a couple of innings, and then I had to leave. I kind of walked for a couple of days, and I couldn't move as well as I would have liked for the next couple months.

On Easter, Michelle and I were engaged over at Martha's Vineyard. Time had flown by since we had met. I had a boil taken off my knee, and was forced to take a couple days off. So on April 11, 2004,

Michelle and I flew down to Martha's Vineyard and spent the night. Someone must have seen me, because "What's Johnny Damon doing?" became a headline in the tabloids. The year before I'd flown to Las Vegas after a game to meet Michelle and gamble for a couple of hours. When I came up, players did that all the time, so to me it was no big deal. But I got into a lot of trouble, because the alternative newspaper *The Inside Track* said, "Johnny doesn't care about the game. He goes to Vegas gambling and stays out." The Sox management heard about it, and they told me not to do it again. So when I went to Martha's Vineyard, people immediately thought, *He's down there partying.* In actuality, everybody connected with the team knew I was going down there to get engaged.

My going to the Vineyard was no big deal, but if you play in Boston, you just have to accept the fact that people will call in to the radio stations and say, "We have a Johnny Damon sighting here."

I took a room at a hotel that had a spa. It was while I was sitting in the spa naked that I asked Michelle if she'd marry me.

She thought I was kidding.

"You can't look at the ring until you give me an answer," I said. Because that ring was a doozy! I didn't want the ring to influence her or make her go blind!

She said "Yes," and then of course being naked, the rest is history! Then this tough girl from Missouri got teary eyed and called her parents.

We returned to Boston, and the next day I hobbled to a charity luncheon hosted by Ben Affleck and one of the actors from *Saturday Night Live,* Seth Meyers, both big Red Sox fans. During the dinner Seth was making fun of my Jesus-like appearance. He asked me whether I could turn clubhouse wine into water. Trying to give him a smart answer, I said, "No, we haven't gathered for the Last Supper." It got a nice laugh.

After we split the series with the Blue Jays, the Yankees came to Fenway for the first time. There was so much hype. Hundreds of reporters, dozens of cameras. It was the first time Alex Rodriguez was playing against Boston in the Yankees uniform.

The clubhouses were full of people. Those are the days when you just want to run and hide. On those days I tend to work out more. You try to do whatever you can to achieve some peace.

It was a series where we made a statement—we won three of four. Everybody was on a high. Everyone was ecstatic about the way we played. ARod didn't swing the bat very well. He was getting a lot of grief, and we were absolutely ecstatic about that.

My most vivid memory about that series was watching Curt Schilling on the day he pitched. This guy is kinda sick. It makes you want to throw up, because he prepares so much. The day before he pitches he goes through all of his charts. He's got suitcases full of them. He has information on every hitter he's ever faced. In fact, he even has footage on DVDs of most of them. Curt has gone high tech.

I'm sure he has someone who works with him on the side. He figures this is his career and he owes it to the game to be very prepared. I wish I could be that dedicated, but I know I'd drive myself nuts. I need a different routine night in, night out. He has his set routine. He spends hours and hours going over his charts with Dave Wallace, our pitching coach, and Jason Varitek, our catcher. Without Jason, our pitchers' ERAs would be two points higher. Jason is that good at knowing batters and calling a game. He's the absolute best in the game by far.

The day after Schilling pitches, Curt will take a day off to free his mind. The next day he's a maniac in the bullpen, throwing a lot of pitches. And on the day he starts, the guy is down in the bullpen throwing for 20 or 30 minutes to get ready for the game. He throws a ton of pitches. Any other person would be worn out, but he just keeps going, and he isn't done until he's ready. The guy is a little psycho when it comes to that.

And on the day he pitches, don't talk to him. There has to be something wrong for him to talk to you, so nobody even attempts to say a word to him.

And after an inning, he'll come in, sit down in the middle of the dugout, and fill out his notebook on what he just did to the hitters. Then he looks at what he's going to do to the hitters the next inning.

On days he's not pitching, you try to pick his brain about the pitcher you're going to face that day. He's a power pitcher, and he knows what they're thinking. I'm not going to reveal any secrets, but he's pretty much right with his information.

These days pitchers don't pitch many complete games. The pitching coach counts pitches, and usually a manager won't let a pitcher throw more than 100, 110 pitches in a game before taking him out. In Schilling's first 2004 start against the Yankees he threw his 100 pitches by the seventh inning, and Terry Francona went to take him out. Curt looked like he wanted to kill him.

Francona, who'd managed Schilling in Philadelphia, well knew how much Schilling hated to be taken out of a game. In fact, in spring training I was standing nearby when Terry came over to Curt and said, "When I come to take you out of the game, you better not give me any smack like you used to do in Philadelphia."

Sure enough, Terry went out to get him, and Schilling was walking up the mound and back, just mad.

"Do what I tell you," Terry said to him. "Don't give me any lip. It's for your own good." Schilling handed him the ball and walked back to the dugout.

I've already said a lot about Pedro. The third member of our pitching rotation, Derek Lowe, was one of the funnest pitchers you can ever have on your team. The guy was amazing. He had a sinkerball, and when he was on, he also had a change up. This was one guy I really wanted on the mound. When you went to the ballpark, you always knew this guy was going to give you his best stuff. And if it wasn't there, he wasn't going to cry about it. He'd say, "I wasn't right today. I'll get them the next time."

Unlike Schilling, Derek would talk to you on the day he pitched. He didn't get bent out of shape. I remember a game when Mark Bellhorn made two errors behind him, and Derek just looked back and put his hand under his chin and lifted it, as if to say, "Keep your chin up."

We started the first two weeks playing .500 ball. Then the Yankees came to Boston, and we swept the three games. The key play in the

series was a running catch made by Manny Ramirez on a long fly hit
by Bernie Williams just before crashing into the left field wall. You
never know with Manny. He'll make a catch like that, and then he'll
make an error on a ball, and you wonder how it happens. But I'll
take Manny any time. He gets after it.

We flew to New York after taking two of three from Toronto. We
were never going to forget what had happened in Game 7 in the
playoffs against the Yankees in 2003. And we were never going to be
intimidated by them. Aaron Boone, the hero from the year before,
was gone, and Alex Rodriguez was on third in front of the sold-out
Yankee Stadium crowd. We loved going there. We didn't let their
rowdy fans intimidate us. We discovered that the stands were filled
with plenty of Red Sox fans, and we'd get pumped up when we
heard from them.

In 2004 the Red Sox had more fans than ever before. We were
bringing people to this game who'd never cared about baseball before. It was because we were individuals having fun. They looked at
us and saw me with my beard and long hair, Pedro and Manny with
their nappy hair, and Bronson Arroyo with his cornrows. They knew
something different was going on.

We were never cocky. We weren't hooting and hollering, saying
the other team stinks. We weren't fist pumpers. We respected the
game. In 2004 every park we went to had Red Sox fans, and sometimes, like in Tampa Bay, there were more Red Sox fans in the park
than home-team fans.

You could even say that in 2004 we became America's team. We
boosted attendance at every stadium we went to. We knew we weren't
the greatest players assembled, but no one franchise played as a team
like we did. We had a couple of has-beens, a couple of never wuzes, a
couple of superstars, but a lot of guys who were pluggers, who hustled and played hard. The fans couldn't get enough of us.

In the opener at Yankee Stadium, Derek Lowe again was outstanding, beating Jose Contreras, the guy Steinbrenner had paid
$10 million to so we couldn't get him. In the first inning Gary
Sheffield, another of Steinbrenner's high-profile acquisitions, hit a

shot to left center that I ran after, slid, and caught. It seems like Gary can hit anything, a fastball up at his eyes, a fastball away at his eyes, down at his shoelaces. The guy hits everything hard, and he usually hits it to left. When Sheffield is hitting, I'll take 15 steps over into left center field. That's what Terry Francona's paperwork told me to do. With Terry as manager and John Henry as owner, all our coaches are very alert to the scouting reports. We play based on the odds. And the odds of Gary Sheffield hitting it where he did were very good. I was playing him just right. I still had to go a long way, but I was able to catch the ball, and it kind of got the team going, perhaps for that series. I know it got Derek going. He's one of those guys you try to do your best for.

We then beat the Yankees in the twelfth inning on a Mark Bellhorn sacrifice fly. The key was our bullpen: Scott Williamson, Alan Embree, Keith Foulke, and Mike Timlin held the Yankees scoreless from the sixth inning on. Our team in 2004 was always very appreciative of those guys. We couldn't have won without them. Timlin, especially. Wow, this guy, every day he was ready to go. He made sure everyone in the bullpen also was ready to go. He's a religious guy, and if someone cried about having a sore arm, he'd say, "Hey, have a little faith in God. He'll get you through it." He was always telling guys to suck it up.

"You're not hurting that bad. Get yourself going. Get yourself ready to pitch every game."

Timlin has been around the game for what seems like 50 years. He understands the psychology. And for anyone who's watching, pay attention. I want you to notice when someone hits a home run into the Red Sox bullpen; it's always Mike Timlin who catches it with a towel in his hands. Always.

When Pedro and Manny combined to win the Yankee finale 2–0, the Sox had swept the Yankees in the stadium for the first time since 1999.

Pedro Martinez is a superstar. So is Manny Ramirez. Those guys are pretty amazing. Neither of them are ever given a break because they make so much money. If you're a superstar, you can't afford to be bad, not for one game, one inning. If you slump for 10 at-bats, you hear about it, especially in the press.

As I've mentioned, in 2004 Kevin Millar and I decided that if Pedro had a bad game, or if Manny did something the writers didn't like, we wouldn't just sit back and let them take a pounding in the papers. Instead, we stuck up for them. That's what our team does. We have to deal with each other for eight months. If we have a problem, like if someone doesn't hustle and he gets thrown out, we discuss it behind closed doors. We'll go up to him and say, "You're better than that. Give it your all." And in 2004 no player ever didn't respond. Our team left our egos at the door. As a result, there was never any talking behind a player's back. Before, when it used to be discussed in the media, the player was left hanging out to dry. No longer.

Manny always starts slowly, and at the season's beginning we were teasing him. We joked that he was swinging like Pokey Reese, who's certainly not a home run hitter. Manny, who was in great spirits, joked back.

"I've been working on my Pokey Reese swing," he said, "but it's not working out."

We were rolling along. We were looking real good.

Chapter 10

Nomar Returns

In late April of 2004 we played host to the Devil Rays. The press talks about how bad they are, but that team scares me. They have a great leadoff hitter, Carl Crawford. All he has to do is make contact, and he can beat the ball to first base. That team is so close to being real good. Those young players, led by Aubrey Huff, are learning to hit. Rocco Baldelli will get better. And their bullpen is always pretty decent. The team spends no money, and it never has decent starters. They either have guys who are over the hill, or young guys with no experience. Every time we play the Devil Rays, we wonder, *What are we going to get today?*

What we ended up getting was a sweep. Curt Schilling shut them out, and then Byung-Hyun Kim shut them out, and then we won our ninth game in 10 tries that evening to win it for Derek Lowe.

We went to Texas. They were expecting rain, so we sat around for two hours and twenty minutes before it started raining. We could have played the whole game. That kind of started a little downturn for us. First of all, we were exhausted from flying in to Texas. Everyone woke up early, and we were ready to play. We felt that Texas knew all along they were going to call the game, because they needed to rest their pitching staff. After selling a lot of hot dogs and beer, they finally called the game at 10:30.

Texas knew we were pretty hot at the time. And after their young pitchers finished with us, we thought we were playing the best team in the league. Those guys played great ball. Their hitters were on fire. RA Dickey pitched a great game. This Rangers team is going to be a team to be reckoned with in years to come. They have Michael Young, Hank Blalock, Mark Teixeira, and Carl Everett, in addition to Alfonso Soriano, whom they got from the Yankees for Alex Rodriguez.

After we lost three to Texas, Cleveland beat Curt Schilling 2–1 at Jacobs Field. We'd gone on this road trip thinking we'd come home 7–0, and all of a sudden, we were starting out 0–4. In that Cleveland game I was standing on third base with two outs when the game ended.

The next night, even though the Indians were beating us 7–1 going into the ninth, Terry Francona was walking around the clubhouse, telling everyone to "stay positive. We'll get out of this."

What was funny, their pitcher Kazuhito Tadano is Korean. The catcher, Victor Martinez, is Spanish. I went up to hit with two runners on base, and just as Tadano was delivering the ball, their manager, Eric Wedge, tried to call time out. He wanted to talk to the pitcher, so he could stall while another pitcher was warming up, but it was too late. Tadano threw me his bloop ball, I hit the ball into the stands, and then we scored two more runs, and though we lost, 7–6, the late comeback gave us momentum.

Terry, whose demeanor is very much like that of Grady Little, was the perfect manager for this team, because if he'd been cursing and screaming at us, we would have resented him. We would have thought, *You don't have to do that. We're a veteran team. We know what we have to do.*

With a younger team, if there's a lack of hustle, yeah, you have to kick butt a little. Terry knew he didn't have to do that with us, and we appreciated that. And we won the final two games against the Indians.

Kansas City came to town. The Royals haven't had much luck with the guys they draft lately. When Oakland drafted Hudson, Zito, and Mulder, they didn't keep them in the farm system too long, and all three turned out to be stars. Once Billy Beane thought they were ready to go, he brought them up with confidence. Kansas City also drafted good young arms, but management, afraid to bring talent up too soon and have to part with it, tends to keep their top guys in the farm system too long.

Once the KC pitchers struggled, they had it in their heads they couldn't pitch in the big leagues. There's talent there. The question remains whether the Royals will ever derive the benefits of their talent.

We beat the Royals in the first game of the series on Manny's hustle. We were losing by four runs in the ninth when, incredibly, we caught up. With the score tied and Manny on first, Jason Varitek hit a pinch hit double down into the right field corner. Manny hot-footed it all the way around and then as the throw came home, he made a tippy-toe run onto home plate to win the game. Manny makes this game so much fun because you never know what he's going to do next. Baseball can get pretty repetitious, but when you have a guy like Manny around. . . . Manny didn't slide. He just tippy-toed it across the plate, beating the tag by a hair.

The next day Schilling pitched his first complete game, allowing just one run. This time Schilling talked Terry out of taking him out before he could finish. Schilling got his way when he told Francona he'd always dreamed of standing on the mound at Fenway Park with two outs in the ninth. Didn't he do that when as a Diamondback he beat us a couple years before?

What a workhorse! What a competitor! He said when he came to Boston that he was going to help the Red Sox win the World Series. The last time an athlete went out on a limb like that was back in 1969 when Joe Namath promised that the Jets would beat the Colts in the Super Bowl. There are not a lot of people who can offer an assurance like that and then back it up.

After we swept the Royals, we played Cleveland, and pitcher Byung-Hyun Kim, who came to the Red Sox with a reputation for being a stud, started and was bombed. I remember when I was with Oakland, I faced Kim. He threw 94 miles an hour with a wicked sidearm pitch that came from down below. His stuff was nasty. But in 2004 he'd lost at least 7 miles an hour off his heat, which made him a lot easier to hit. Did he hurt his arm? I don't know. And you can't ask him.

It's tough when you have a guy on the team who doesn't speak English. We try to make Kim part of the team, try to talk to him, pat him on the back. What's unusual about this guy is that he stands in front of a mirror for three or four hours a day working on his form. He holds the ball, but he doesn't let it go. We don't judge him. That's just what he does. He just doesn't communicate with the team. We do have a Korean trainer, Chang Lee, so he can translate for him. The downside of getting Kim was that we traded away a guy I thought was our best young clutch hitter, Shea Hillenbrand. That guy can hit.

Manny didn't play in that game because he was in Miami being sworn in as an American citizen. Nobody knew why he'd left, and of course in the media you read, "Where's Manny? Is he taking a hiatus?"

Manny came back and told the reporters, "Now they can't kick me out of the country."

Before the next game Manny ran out on the field, and he saw a fan with a little American flag, and he grabbed it, and as the PA system played "Proud to Be an American," he ran around waving the flag as the Fenway fans went nuts.

As much abuse as America gets, everybody wants to be part of it. I think that's what makes our country special. I was so happy for Manny. I have a picture of him waving that flag that sits on top of my locker. Some things are very precious, and that was a special time in his life, a special time for America.

It was around this time that rumors flared again about the Red Sox trying to acquire Carlos Beltran from Kansas City. I'd played with Carlos and knew he could do some things I couldn't. Also, that I could do some things *he* couldn't. But Carlos is a center fielder, and if he came to Boston, that was going to affect me, and I was feeling a little insecure.

In 2003 I'd only hit for a .273 average, so even though I'd scored 103 runs that year and even though everyone knew the team wouldn't have been where it was without me, there was talk I might be moved. I would have scored a lot more runs, but Nomar went from hitting .330 to ending up at .301, and in September I was on base 50 percent of the time. If Nomar had been up to par, I would have scored 120 runs. So when 2004 rolled around, everyone was saying that Billy Mueller, Manny, and David Ortiz were the key players on the team, and I was wondering, *What about me?* They had me talking to myself. Players would tell me I was the Most Valuable Player on the team, and year after year I would be left off the All Star team. In 2002 I was hitting .320 and leading in runs scored. I had to be voted in as the thirtieth man. Outfield is a tough position. It's hard to leave Manny off. Or Vladimir Guerrero. Or Ichiro. Unfortunately for me, Ichiro, who definitely deserves being on the team, has the entire country of Japan voting for him on the Internet. At a certain point you run out of room.

In 2001, the year Ichiro won the MVP, he had 60 RBIs and 127 runs scored. The year before I had 88 RBIs and 136 runs scored, and I was lucky to get a single point in the voting because the Royals finished last. When you look at my numbers, you wonder how seven guys can beat you out for MVP. One reason, I suspect, is because in this game, it pays to be controversial. But if you have a certain personality, if you've determined you're going to be a good guy, you're going to be a team player, you're going to move runners and do all those things the manager wants you to do, you can't look at the MVP voting and complain about it. You can't have it both ways.

Here I was taking pitches for the team, rather than swinging at the first hittable pitch, and that causes your batting average to go down. You do it to wear out the other team's pitcher, and you'd be amazed how many games you win because of it. But I felt I wasn't getting any credit for doing that, that I was going to be traded anyway, and I was beginning to question whether I should stick to this same style of play if I wasn't going to get any credit for it. All of this was preying on my mind. Baseball is a game where you need to be positive to succeed, and doubts were eating away at my confidence.

In mid-May 2004 Theo Epstein, being the classy guy he is, came to see me. Almost every day he comes down to the clubhouse. On that day, he said, "I know you're hearing about us trying to get Carlos Beltran. Don't be worried. You're not going to be traded. What I want to know is, if we do get him, will you move to left field for the remainder of the season to make Carlos happy and more comfortable?"

"You know what," I said, "I did it before, and I'd do it again."

I knew that if we got him, we'd be a better team, so I said, "Theo, do what you need to do. Thank you for being honest with me."

All I ask of a GM is a little advance notice that he's going to trade me, so it doesn't hit me quite so hard. I've been in the league 10 years, and I think I've earned that kind of respect. Not all the GMs communicate as well as Theo. He's one of the reasons Boston has become the best place to play.

We went on the road and took two out of three from both Toronto and Tampa Bay before returning home in late May. All spring all everyone talked about was my beard, and I kept getting calls from companies that wanted me to cut off my beard and hair for charity and publicity. My beard had gotten grossly thick and nasty, and when Gillette approached Peter Caparis, my representative, and asked if

I'd help launch a Gillette shaving system in exchange for giving "Read Boston" $15,000, we said yes.

"Read Boston" has two parts to it. One part is a reading program that makes sure kids are able to read by the time they get out of the second grade. The other part brings tutors into the Boston Public Library to help kids with their homework. We raised awareness of this latter part of the program. Hopefully, the kids of Boston will benefit, becoming smarter and more educated.

I went to the Prudential Center, on Boylston Street, and a very nice and attractive woman shaved my beard. The local news and ESPN covered it. I couldn't believe how many media people I had to talk to after that. This town truly is Red Sox crazy.

The Blue Jays came into Boston, and we swept them three games. Bronson Arroyo, the skinny, rubber-armed pitcher from Brooksville, Florida, won the opener. I'd heard about Bronson when he was pitching for Pawtucket. He threw a perfect game there, and that opened the Red Sox's eyes. Jim Mann, a friend of mine, would call me a lot when Bronson was at Pawtucket, telling me about this kid and asking, "When are they going to call up Bronson?" When the 2004 season started Bronson relied a lot on his slider, but as we went along, Jason Varitek taught him to vary his pitches a bit more, and he became awesome for us all year. We liked the way he took the ball. He's a young guy who has a real spark on the mound. That's the kind of pitcher you like to play behind.

Nomar Garciaparra was still out in late May, and the reporters were starting to wonder why. Bill Mueller also went on the DL around that time, and when that happened, we thought we were in *big* trouble.

We brought up a young kid by the name of Kevin Youkilis to take his place. We didn't know what kind of player he'd be. We just knew he was the best prospect in the Red Sox farm system, and he turned out to be awesome. He was given his own chapter in the book *Moneyball*, which praised him for having a high on-base percentage.

He was called The Greek God of Walks. I remember Terry Francona calling him that when he came up. Youkilis arrived and filled in nicely for Mueller.

The A's came to town, and we beat them up in the first two games, and Youkilis reached base four times in the opener. He was putting the *Moneyball* theory to work. I think his approach at the plate may be too good. He lays off pitches that are close and should be balls, but he gets penalized for it. The umps call them strikes—because he's young. He's going to play a big part in the team's future success unless he's trade bait.

Curt Schilling dominated in the second A's game, and in that game the A's young shortstop Bobby Crosby made a bad error, and we scored four unearned runs to beat them. You can't make mistakes against our team. If you do, you pay.

A season is a living, breathing thing, and every season is different. You can be going along, winning regularly, playing great, and then all of a sudden, you stop winning. On May 27, 2004, we faced Mark Mulder, and we lost 15–2. Then we stopped winning.

When I was with Oakland in 2001, Mulder was hands down the best pitcher in the league. He should have won the Cy Young. He dominated every game against the Angels, Texas, and Seattle, who won 116 games that year. The guy was incredible. Mulder throws a fastball that runs in, hard, on lefties. He can run it away. He can cut it to righties. He has a good change up. And he has presence. The guy is strong and very confident, and that takes him a long way. Even though he broke his hip two years ago, the guy is very special.

I don't know exactly what happened that day, but for the next two months—the entire month of June and into July—we played under .500 ball. Then the doom-and-gloom talk in the press started up: "We need Nomar to come back. We need Trot Nixon to return." Our problem was that during this period, only four hitters in the lineup were producing—myself, Mark Bellhorn, David Ortiz, and Manny—and it was impossible for the four of us to score every time. The whole bottom part of our lineup was in a slump. The pitchers weren't doing a bad job. We were. We couldn't score runs. The pitchers were getting abused because we weren't winning, but it wasn't the pitchers' fault at all.

I felt pressed to contribute even more. I get up four or five times every game, so I have a chance to score four or five runs. If we're not scoring enough runs, the blame, as I see it, is mine.

I tried as best I could to take the pressure off the other guys. They were feeling it. We had a lot of guys on the edge. And the trade rumors didn't help, because we knew trades were going to change the lives of a couple of players.

As I've said, it's never fun when you have a chance to lose your job. We'd been through the battles. We'd all experienced the loss to the Yankees in the 2003 playoffs. You want to contribute. You want to be the man. That's how Kevin Millar felt. When Kevin was confident, he felt every time he held the bat in his hand, he could play pepper with the outfield wall. A lot of guys think that way. But now Kevin was feeling a loss of confidence. He was our first baseman, and he was losing playing time to David Ortiz, who was really starting to hit. Kevin was able to play right field when Trot Nixon was out, but that affected Gabe Kapler, who would be benched.

While all this was going on, we were struggling. The media kept asking, "Do you guys think you can turn this around?" My answer always was, "Yeah, we've got time." But when you hear this—"When are you going to turn this around?"—day after day for a couple of months, it gets old. Every time I'd say, "We're fine." The trick is to continue to believe it.

Though we were still leading in the wild-card race, the press and fans were completely focused on the Yankees, who were leading in the East and playing .750 ball. I'd say, "We're fine. We're fine." But the media just didn't get it. All they wanted to do was talk about the lead the Yankees had over us.

I'd say, "What part of being three games up in the wild-card race don't you get?"

"But Anaheim is really going to get going," the writers would say. "Oakland is going to win a lot of games in the stretch. You guys need to win this division."

"Not necessarily," I'd say.

We knew how good a team we had. Unfortunately, we didn't really get going until the middle of August.

Nomar returned to the team on June 9 at Fenway Park. The fans really love Nomar, and they cheered him loud and long, and when he came to the plate he acknowledged them by putting his hand over his heart. I was moved by how the fans stood up and cheered like that. It was special, and to me that's what baseball is all about. Also, I believe a lot of fans were wondering if this might well be Nomar's last year with the Red Sox.

There'd been talk that Nomar had been unhappy that the Red Sox hadn't come back to him after he turned down their initial contract offer. Also, every reporter was bashing him, and the fans had to be wondering why they were bashing their Golden Boy, wondering out loud whether he was really hurt or whether he was faking it. They questioned why he hadn't signed the contract extension that was offered him. Nomar just couldn't do anything right, it seemed.

I thought Nomar *was* Mr. Boston, that they'd have to rip the jersey off his back when the time came. Every year Nomar holds a bowling tournament to raise money for charity. He gets movie stars like Ben Affleck, a few of the Patriot players, and a bunch of us to come, and they mix with the fans and raise a lot of money. Nomar has been to Boston what George Brett was to Kansas City or Derek Jeter is to the Yankees. You could never picture Jeter in another uniform. Just as you never thought you'd see Nomar wearing anything but a Red Sox uniform.

So Nomar returned, and on his first at-bat, he hit a single through the shortstop hole. We sat there on the bench looking at each other in awe, thinking, *Wow, it's that easy for him. He can wake up and get base hits.*

That day Nomar started a double play, and he also made a bad throw. With his style of play, he'd get caught off balance a lot. He's always in motion, always throwing his body around, swinging his arm. The press made a big deal about the error, but no matter what Nomar does, they make a big deal out of it. It's the same way with Pedro and Manny, two guys who aren't allowed to ever fail. We expect them to be good *all the time.*

The next day the fans continued to cheer Nomar like a long-lost son, which he was. He meant so much to Red Sox Nation that Nomar was leading Jeter in the All Star balloting even though he hadn't played a game!

Even after Nomar came back, we continued playing .500 ball. We were doing too much reacting to what our opponents were doing. We weren't able to put teams away. There were a lot of close games, and we lost some of them in the late innings. It wasn't Nomar's fault. It was our whole team's fault. Our pitchers were so much better than what they were showing. We didn't give them any cushion. We had chances, but we just weren't producing.

We just weren't able to mesh. Nomar coming in meant changes. Nomar was placed in the five hole in the batting order. Varitek and Kevin Millar had to adjust. Trot Nixon came back from his injury, so he caused more shifting. It was like we were back in spring training as Nomar and Trot tried to get the feel for the team, tried to get back into the swing of things.

Moreover, when Nomar returned, he wasn't healthy, so he couldn't play every day. He'd play one game, take off the next, play two games, take off the next. Our team didn't have a flow to it. Players didn't know when they were playing or where. That's why injuries can tear up a team's chemistry. It's the not-knowing part. Every day we'd wonder whether Nomar would get traded, whether Trot was going to be able to play. Bill Mueller had a bad knee, and we never knew about him. Nothing was jelling.

Making it harder on all of us was the press and talk radio. The focus on the Red Sox is unbearably intense, especially when we're not doing well. They talk so much smack. The radio hosts were ripping Nomar a new one, and Nomar's problem is that he loves to listen to sports talk on the radio. He reads all the newspapers. He wants to know who's saying bad things about him, so when a guy comes to him and asks for a radio or press interview, he can say, "Why in the hell should I do this for a two-faced mother-f'er."

The problem with reading the papers is that if you're in a slump and a writer like Tony Mazarati, who writes for the *Herald*, tells the truth: "The guy is in a slump," you don't want to hear about it. Nomar has been in Boston seven years, reading the papers, listening to the crap on the radio, and all that adds to the pressure. Remember I mentioned that Ted Williams once said that Nomar is the greatest athlete ever to play for the Red Sox. That's a lot of pressure to face. The fans loved him from the very first day, but things seemed to be turning against him.

The writers have been great to me. Through the good and bad, I talk to them. For me, it's part of the game. I only hide when they hang around too much.

There was a time during the American League Championship Series when the radio talk guys were even talking about benching Bellhorn and me. Anything to get the fans going. It's something they do. It's their job to start controversy, and they do it all day long. And it affects us. You have to have a thick skin to play in Boston. The guys who play in other cities have it so easy. Some guys are afraid to even come to play in Boston, because they hear about the everyday pressures.

Guys on other teams, like the Devil Rays, Kansas City, or Detroit, know going in that their team is not going to earn a playoff spot. Some teams know they have an outside shot. Texas, say, if it gets off to a good start, it might keep that momentum up all year. Kansas City might have had a chance had they not been bitten by the injury bug from the start. Once the injuries piled up, you knew they weren't going to be around. In Boston, the fans don't worry whether the team will make the playoffs. It's expected. You have to make the playoffs or else.

Our goal, of course, is always to win the World Series. It's also to beat the Yankees. At times the pressure on us is greater to beat the Yankees than it is to win the World Series, though "the Curse of the

Bambino" pressure, which started a few years ago, becomes greater and greater every year.

We understand what's expected of us. We'd love to beat the Yankees and win the American League East, but things sometimes don't go right. Sometimes you have injuries. Sometimes shit happens.

Every game we played in 2004 we expected to win. On the other hand, there was not one game in 2004 that we went into saying, "Oh, this is going to be easy."

We don't play to get by. We don't play to develop players. We play to *win*. When we brought Kevin Youkilis up, it wasn't to get him experience in the big leagues. He was expected to come up and help us win right away. We threw him into the fire. That's how it is in Boston.

The expectations are that we're going to win, and when we don't, you can be sure we'll hear about it.

Chapter 11

Heating Up

Toward the end of June of 2004, Nomar hit a grand slam home run against the Twins to win a game for Curt Schilling, but in the next game Pokey Reese, who'd been filling in at shortstop for Nomar, suffered a badly injured left thumb.

Pokey's loss would be felt.

Pokey had come to the Red Sox and immediately turned into a fan favorite. In his first few games he had two home runs, including an inside-the-parker and a home run over the left field wall. Fans could also see what a great fielder he is by the way he flashed his glove.

Pokey is probably the best athlete on the team. When you look at him, you see an athlete, a football player. He wanted to be a college quarterback, loves the Florida State Seminoles. I'm sure he was a decent point guard in basketball. He has great range in baseball, whether he's playing second or short. He's a classy teammate, one of those players who understands what it is to be a team player. He came over here to be the starting second baseman or shortstop, and when Nomar returned, he was benched, but he never complained. He accepted his role and did whatever he was asked. He sat on the bench and cheered for his team. He scoped out the team environment in Boston, and he thrived in it. Every time he was in the lineup, the fans would get up and cheer, "Po-key. Po-key."

I started worrying less about the Red Sox trading me when on June 24 Carlos Beltran was traded from the Royals to the Houston Astros. Houston was a half dozen games behind in the wild-card hunt, but they decided to improve their team and acquire Carlos, who immediately turned them into a contender. The A's got closer Octavio Dotel from Houston, which improved the A's considerably, because they'd lost so many games in the last part of the game. Arthur Rhodes, a set-up man, had been brought in to be the A's closer, but it didn't work out, so Billy Beane decided to change things up. The Royals ended up with prospects.

As June moved into July, we continued to play .500 ball, but no one was blowing up, no one was panicking, saying, "We need to win. We *have* to win." We had an inner confidence that told us we were going to be fine. The problem we had was that our critics in the media were doing what they could to shake that confidence. They were looking at how far behind the Yankees we were, and they were panicking. And that caused some of our guys to start telling themselves, *We need to stay close to the Yankees.* Quite frankly, every time we thought about the Yankees, we just stunk. When we relaxed and just played our game, that's when things started to turn around for us.

We went to New York for three games.

I have a rule that I learned from Jason Giambi when I was with Oakland. On a plane ride less than two hours, no one is allowed to sleep. That was our rule in Oakland, even if we had played a night game and it was one o'clock in the morning.

Since the teams charter planes and the players are the only ones on board, the way Jason saw it, a plane ride is one of the few times the whole team is together, so it's a chance to relax in each other's company. Typically, there is no media on board. We could play cards. We could blast our music.

You've got to enjoy yourself as a big leaguer. Your life in the big leagues is supposed to be glamorous.

The only players we allowed to sleep were Curt Schilling and Bronson Arroyo, who slept all the time. The card players were Millar, Kapler, Varitek, Doug Mirabelli, and me. Later in the year I began playing Boo Ray, a game similar to Hearts, with the coaches.

Mark Bellhorn and I are pretty good card players. Gabe Kapler is the best at Texas Hold 'Em. Mark was pretty good at that, too.

When we play poker, each player buys $200 worth of chips. If you lose your money, you're gone from the game. The one guy who shouldn't ever play is David Ortiz, who sometimes wins, but when he loses, he loses big.

Card playing today is nothing compared to what went on back in the 1980s. I've heard stories about guys losing $10,000 to $20,000 during one flight. The most I ever lost was $900. The most I've ever won is $1,200.

It was a lot more fun flying before the FAA cracked down and changed its rules. When I came into the league with Kansas City, one of our infielders, Jeff Reboulet, used to stand on a tray cart near the cockpit, and as the plane was lifting off the ground, he would roll all the way down the aisle to the tail section. I've heard stories of players joining the Mile High Club with stewardesses. In this age of sexual harassment, that doesn't happen much anymore.

I started the first game against the Yankees by hitting a home run, and later I hit another, but those guys pounded us. They were on a nice streak. We pretty much had no chance. They were just firing on all cylinders. ARod was starting to hit, Sheffield was doing his thing, Matsui was playing well. It seemed like all their pitchers were throwing great, their starters and relievers. They couldn't lose. And anybody they plugged into the game—Tony Clark, Kenny Lofton— did well.

We lost the next night. Nomar, who had made two errors in the first game, made another. It had nothing to do with pressure. You come up against tough plays sometimes, and he was having trouble with his ankle, so he had trouble making a strong throw. Because he was hurt, no doubt his range was awful. But nobody was giving him any credit for playing hurt. He was so beat up, he probably shouldn't have played all year long. The doctors wanted him to sit still and not move. They didn't want him to risk hurting the ankle some way. Before some games he was told, "Don't even *think* you're going into the game." When he played, it took him a long time to get his ankle loose. But when he played, he got criticized, and whenever he was hurt and couldn't play, people would say, "Nomar's just sitting and doesn't even want to pinch hit." He couldn't win either way.

He was hurting and sitting out on the day we played the Yankees in a game in which Derek Jeter, who seems to get better and better every year, made a play that amazed all of us.

There was a short fly ball down the left field line. His job was to make the catch and beat the Boston Red Sox, and without worrying or caring whether he was going to get hurt, he ran toward the stands, put his glove up, stretched out, and somehow caught the ball. That play impressed me, yeah, but I was even more impressed the next day, when I saw his face. It was all bruised and scarred from colliding with a railing or the seats, or whatever he ran into making that catch.

The next time I got to speak to Derek, I told him, "Hey, that was absolutely an amazing catch and it's even more amazing you considered playing the next day." I give the guy a lot of respect.

In that game, when Jeter made his sensational play, we kept taking the lead, and they kept taking it back, until the game went into extra innings. We were so close to winning a couple of times, but we lost and fell $8\frac{1}{2}$ games behind the Yankees, and all the press and the radio could talk about was how Nomar wasn't hitting and wasn't making the plays. It got so bad, Terry Francona even went on local Boston radio to defend him.

That's what a manager has to do: defend his players at all costs. A manager has to put his butt on the line so his players stay happy, so they respect him and understand he'll go to bat for them under any circumstances. That's the kind of manager Terry Francona is.

Dan Shaughnessy wrote an article in the *Globe* saying it was time for the Red Sox to trade Nomar. The two had their run-ins over the years. I heard later that Shaughnessy had warned Nomar what he'd be writing about. Anyway, Nomar was really disappointed that his years in Boston had come to this. If, like me, you'd seen the adulation Nomar received whenever the fans spotted him, you'd figure he'd be the one untouchable—the guy who'd get cut some slack by the writers. But in Boston the desire to win is fierce, and I guess Shaughnessy and the fans who agreed with him figured all options had to be put on the table.

Right before the All Star break, we won five out of six games, including three in a row against the A's, one of the teams we had to beat out for the wild-card spot. I had five hits in a game against Oakland at Fenway. Then Nomar and Mark Bellhorn hit home runs to help Pedro win. In the A's finale, I scored the winning run in the bottom of the ninth, running all the way from first on a double hit by Bill Mueller. It was a great win for us, with a big contribution from Bill Mueller, who'd led the league in hitting the year before, but who struggled with injuries in 2004. That's the thing about career years. A player who has one can't expect to follow immediately—if ever—with another. Before that game Billy had been struggling. And when he stepped into the batters' box in the ninth, he was still upset from a previous at-bat when I went to steal second, had it cold, and he swung at the first pitch and lined out, and I was doubled off at first. Well, big deal. This time he swung at the first pitch, and he hit it in the gap, and I was trucking. Both times he swung at the first pitch and hit line drives into left field. One just happened to be caught. The other was in the gap.

The A's made a nice relay, but our third base coach Dale Sveum knows I'm one of those guys he can send whenever he wants. He knows I'll go hard and that I can run, and he always sends me on the close play. Turns out, I barely beat the throw, we won, and the crowd went wild.

We were getting back on a streak, and beating the A's was huge. After the game I told the reporters, "We got written off, but this team is much better than we've been playing, and we're going to show the world that we are." I knew we would. I'd decided I'd be the one to carry the team on my back. And in the next game against Texas, I went 5 for 6 with a home run. In four games, I had 14 hits. I've never had a hot streak like that. The ball looked like a grapefruit, and I was hitting everything hard and in the gaps. Bronson Arroyo pitched a shutout, and we won again.

Once again I was hoping Joe Torre would pick me for the All Star game. He never has. I knew he was going to take care of his Yankee players. When he didn't pick me again, it was more motivation for me to help win the pennant. If Torre wouldn't select me, I knew Terry Francona would.

We scored 15 runs against Texas in the next game, and Mark Bellhorn, Nomar, and Manny went wild at the plate. Nomar was starting to feel comfortable again, and I can't say enough about what Mark Bellhorn did for us all season long. To me, Mark Bellhorn was our MVP in 2004. No one expected him to do anything. All he did was score 90 runs and drive in 80. He was the guy hitting behind me who could drive the ball, came up with big hits, and understood the game. He strikes out a lot, but he takes his walks, and he gets on base. He takes the inning further. It made the combination of Bellhorn and me pretty special.

We lost the last game before the All Star break. We saw on the TV monitor that before the game Manny was standing out in the outfield, and Curt Schilling was lecturing him. Manny was banged up, had taken a couple of days off, and Schilling was saying, "Manny, even if you have a broken arm, just the fact that you're standing there makes our team better. You don't even have to swing the bat to make us better. You change the way our team is pitched to."

But Manny was having hamstring problems all year long. Manny knew what Curt was saying, but he also understood that Gabe Kapler was a guy capable of going out there and catching balls Manny couldn't because his legs were hurting. Manny didn't want to risk hurting himself worse and missing even more games. He and Curt had different points of view, and who's to say which was right.

At the All Star break, we led the A's by a game in the wild-card race. I felt I'd done great, that our team was getting ready to turn things around. We couldn't have been happier. After playing badly for a long time, we were in the driver's seat. Though we'd been on a roller coaster for most of the season, we were in a great spot.

When Joe Torre didn't pick me for the All Star team—again—Michelle and I decided to spend the break at Cabo San Lucas, Mexico. We had a great time, went fishing, caught yellow-fin tuna. We took our catch back to the Esperanza Hotel, where the chef prepared it for us. I had no idea what had happened in the game. I came back from dinner, and I saw on the TV that the score was pretty high.

We had to stop in Houston, where the All Star game had been played, for our connecting flight. Tons of fans and autograph seekers were there wanting my autograph. They brought over All Star balls, but I wouldn't sign them.

"Save that for the guys who made the team," I told them.

Chapter 12

A Shove in the Face

As soon as the second half of the 2004 season began, the Nomar trade rumors started up again. This time the talk was that Nomar was going to the Chicago Cubs. The big reason was that Grady Little was there, and he knew what kind of player Nomar was. Another rumor was that Arizona Diamondbacks pitcher Randy Johnson was coming to Boston. Curt Schilling was saying how Randy really wanted to come here.

Oh wow! Randy Johnson? Really? Things were looking great for us. But soon enough, that died. I'm not really sure what happened. You never know what goes on between agents and general managers, but that was squashed in a hurry, and then we heard the Yankees might get him.

We went into Seattle thinking we were going to have a pretty solid road trip, but they beat us in the first two games. All year the Mariners didn't play up to their capabilities, but this time they showed up and played very well. We were shaking our heads. "How in the heck are those guys so far back?"

Bret Boone beat us in one game with a grand slam home run off Keith Foulke, but the next night, with the winning run on base, Foulke struck out Boone, Edgar Martinez, and a big kid named Bucky Jacobson. This is why you need a guy with a closer's mentality to win. You have to know that if your closer gets beat one night, he can come back the next night and have a fresh outlook. He can't be pouting all the time. He has to be able to get over a game like that as quickly as possible. Quintessential closers—like Keith—forget easily.

Over the past couple of years Keith has been just a notch below Mariano Rivera. In 2004 Keith had a comparable year, maybe even a better one. He's been durable. It's outstanding that we have him for at least two more years.

Nothing was easy in 2004. It was a struggle every day. After sweeping Oakland, we went home to Fenway to play Baltimore, and we lost two out of three games. We were nine full games behind the Yankees, who came to town. By this time the rivalry had really heated up. To Boston fans, the Yankees really *were* the Evil Empire. As players, we didn't feel that way. But in this town, the press creates its own reality, and the fans react to it.

Unfortunately, even though Kevin Millar hit three home runs, we lost the opening game of the series. At that point our record for the last three months was 37–38. The next game was one that seemed to get us going. It was a game I didn't think we were going to play. There was a long delay, and I wondered whether management wanted the game to be played. We ended up playing. The players walked in and said, "We want to play. We're not scared of the Yankees. We don't care what kind of lead they have and how wet the field is. Let's go." And sure enough, the Yankees started the game by building a big lead.

Then Bronson Arroyo, who wasn't pitching particularly well at that time, started some fireworks by hitting Alex Rodriguez in the arm with a pitch. When Alex started to say something, Jason Varitek got between him and Bronson and told him to get to first base. Alex told him to shut up, to get out of his face. Varitek wasn't the right guy to say that to. Varitek shoved Alex, and the fight was on. Here we go. Tanyon Sturtze grabbed Gabe Kapler from behind. David Ortiz and Trot Nixon got involved. I knew there'd be spats here and there, but I didn't expect the haymakers. There was a group of five or six guys going at each other.

It was one of those brawls where you get to see what kind of people your teammates are. In our case, we got to see great things—great camaraderie, great togetherness.

By the bottom of the ninth inning we were losing 10–8. Mariano Rivera was on the mound. He'd almost never, ever blown a save. He'd allowed exactly one home run all year.

Nomar got up and doubled. With one out, Kevin Millar hit a double to score him. Now it was 10–9. Bill Mueller got up and hit a home run that shocked everyone. We knew how tough Mariano was, especially against left-handers. But he didn't get the ball in enough on him, and Mueller, who had yet another great at-bat, got a pitch he was able to drive, and he really hit it. The whole Red Sox bench erupted. The Fenway crowd erupted. They'd witnessed one of the best games they'd ever seen.

As Billy crossed home plate, the entire team was out there to meet him. Jason Varitek and Gabe Kapler, who'd been thrown out of the game for fighting, ran out of the clubhouse onto the field. Terry Francona, who also had been thrown out of the game, ran out there in his socks. It's how our team is. We root intensely for each other to do well. With everything we've got we stand up for guys like Bill Mueller—guys who lay it on the line every night and give their heart and soul.

Billy had been hurt all year long, and I was so happy for him. He'd stepped up, and we felt like that was going to be a huge turning point for us, because the next night the Red Sox won the rubber match in a game that saw Alex Rodriguez get booed loudly in Fenway every time he came to bat. It certainly hadn't been ARod's fault that he wasn't traded to the Red Sox, but after the brawl the night before, ARod would never be welcome in Boston. He wasn't going to be liked here ever again.

I was pretty fired up after what happened. When I came to bat in the fourth inning of that third game, I hit a ball down the right field line. I felt it was a double, but it was called foul. I was cursing, upset, because I knew we had to win that game. I kept fouling off Jose Contreras's pitches, and I ended up getting a pitch I could drive, hitting the Pesky pole in right for a three-run home run. The crowd went nuts, and it ended up being a great night for us. In that game I made a leaping catch to rob Hideki Matsui. All year in the outfield I'd struggled. I don't know if my perception wasn't quite right because of my concussion, but I just wasn't myself out there. I just didn't feel right. So any time I could do something decent with my glove, I felt great.

The trading deadline of July 31 was coming up, and some of the players were on edge. Derek Lowe kept thinking he was going to be gone. The Phillies were in love with him because Joe Kerrigan was there. Derek wanted so badly to stay with the Red Sox. But he wasn't throwing very well, and the writers had all but traded him. When you're being run out of town, you know that's not a good thing. So Derek thought he was definitely gone. The day of the trade deadline Derek may have overstated his trade value when he predicted he was going to be traded to Atlanta for Chipper Jones, Andruw Jones, and Jarrett Wright.

But it wasn't Derek who was traded. It was Nomar. In return we got Orlando Cabrera, the shortstop from Montreal, first baseman Doug Mientkiewicz from Minnesota, and outfielder Dave Roberts from the Dodgers. I was very sorry to see Nomar go. All of us liked and respected him. But Nomar wasn't happy, his contract was running out at the end of the season, and it just seemed he'd become so bitter about his treatment in Boston that the chances of his returning were slim to none.

There was also concern about his physical condition. He was

playing one game, and sitting the next, and we didn't know if that was going to continue the rest of the season. Theo was able to get Cabrera, who'd been an All Star for Montreal, Mientkiewicz, an excellent-fielding first baseman whom I had known in high school growing up in Florida, and Roberts, who was decent with the bat but an outstanding fielder and one of the best base runners in the game. Theo knew that late in the season I tended to get beat up because I played every day, and Roberts was going to be able to give me a breather when I needed one. Having Dave Roberts on the team really helped me out.

One of the interesting things about the trade was that while David Ortiz had been Mientkiewicz's backup in Minnesota, in Boston Ortiz was the starter, and Mientkiewicz was coming in as *his* backup. It's pretty amazing how this game works sometimes. The Twins had released David, given him away, and I thank them every day. I'm not going to complain one bit about what the Twins did.

Things felt different when we showed up for a game and Nomar wasn't there. Before, if we were playing, say, Oakland, the game would be billed as "Nomar Garciaparra and the Boston Red Sox playing the Oakland A's." Everything about the Boston Red Sox was Nomar, Nomar, Nomar. He was Mr. Boston, the guy who'd meant so much to the team. And we liked it. He was the one who always got the scrutiny—the other players pretty much were left alone. We couldn't imagine what it was like not to be able to go out in public. Nomar was so huge, he'd be swamped by fans. And yet he was always considerate and nice to them.

Then he was gone.

Pedro said we'd miss him, and we did.

But we also were realistic: we knew we weren't going to be able to sign him. We knew that in his half-healthy state he'd continue to have trouble moving on the field. He couldn't be relied on every day. We also knew he wasn't very happy in Boston anymore. So it made sense for Theo to trade him.

The *Boston Globe* really let Theo have it. They said the trade was "horrible." But they were wrong about that. They underestimated

Theo Epstein. The trade turned out to be the most important in Boston Red Sox history.

In the end it was Dan Shaughnessy, Nomar's biggest critic, and the radio jocks who'd attacked Nomar's credibility as a ballplayer who convinced Red Sox fans it was a great trade. Shaughnessy wrote that Theo had made exactly the right move.

We knew how great Nomar was. If only he had been healthy. When a team wants to get rid of you, it's better for management if the player leaves on bad terms. If the player is getting bashed, that makes it a lot easier for the fans. And that's what happened. The bad press actually made it a lot easier for the Sox to get rid of Nomar.

Myself, I learned a long time ago not to read the papers or listen to the radio. That way, the criticism doesn't bother you either in your everyday life or on the field. If I read every negative comment about me and my teammates, I couldn't play the game. I'd be paralyzed. Of course, it's almost impossible to screen out all of it. I remember when people were making all those negative comments about my hair. Some fans called me "Sissy," because it was long. They dubbed my look "mullet cut." Fortunately, though, enough fans saw me out and about, with my hair flowing, chicks digging it, and the tide turned. Hey, what can I say? I'm just blessed with good hair. It's turned into a Samson thing. My hair is my strength.

The day of the trading deadline we were in Minnesota. Derek Lowe sat in the visitor's clubhouse in his street clothes waiting for the word. We were waiting with him. We knew he was being shopped heavily. There were a lot of teams with some pretty good players we thought we might get for him. We assumed he was gone.

Then the 4 p.m. trading deadline passed, and Derek was still sitting there, still a Red Sox. The next day Theo Epstein predicted that the primary beneficiary of the Nomar trade would be Derek, a ground ball pitcher who needed a little more defense behind him. I don't think Theo had any idea how right he'd turn out to be.

Any time you make a trade, the makeup of the team changes, and it takes a little while for everyone to adjust. It takes the manager some time to figure out how to use all the new players. We went to St. Petersburg to play the Devil Rays. Tim Wakefield won the opener, and then Bronson Arroyo gave up a grand slam home run to Toby Hall. We could have tied it in the ninth. There was no one out. Dave Roberts was on second, when Kevin Millar doubled to center field. Dale Sveum, our third base coach, is aggressive. He lets us score if the play is close, and as Roberts flew around the bases, Sveum sent him home. Rocco Baldelli, the Rays young center fielder, threw a pea, an amazing throw, that just did get Roberts. He was out, but all of us were real impressed with his speed.

I was the last batter in the game, and I popped up with the bases loaded to end the game. From the reporters' view, it was a bad at-bat, a pop up. But from my point of view, I had a great swing. If I'd laid the bat an eighth of an inch higher on the ball, it would have been a grand slam. I was very happy with my swing. I definitely wasn't happy about the result, but once the game ends, you don't look back.

If I can convey one thing to young ballplayers, it's never to look back and dwell on your mistakes. The guys on the Red Sox go out and have fun. And if you don't get the job done, you have to keep yourself from getting mad or discouraged. If you muff, guess what? You'll get them the next game. It's the only way to play the game and stay sane.

It took Orlando Cabrera a little while to get started. He came to Boston and replaced one of the best-hitting shortstops in the history of the game. He tried to do a little too much. He saw that short left field wall, and he tried to hit the ball over it. He just wasn't playing his game. He was trying to be Nomar, a bigger hitter. Cabrera isn't a home run hitter like Nomar. He's a line drive hitter, and he was pressing and trying to lift the ball. After a couple of weeks, he was hitting .095.

Cabrera had played in Montreal, where there is no pressure at all. It was tough at first going from Montreal to Boston to replace a legend. We all talked to Orlando, told him to relax and be himself, but he's human, and it was hard.

Terry Francona was still trying to figure out a way to incorporate Cabrera, Mientkiewicz, and Roberts while keeping everyone else happy. Roberts got to play some because Trot Nixon was injured. Or he played late-inning defense for Manny.

Cabrera was always going to be in the lineup. Terry just didn't know where to bat him in the lineup, especially with the other heavy hitters. One day he hit nine, the next day one, or two, or even three.

For the first week after the trade, Terry played Doug Mientkiewicz at first base. Kevin Millar, who had started there most of the season, hadn't played at all, and he was angry and feeling betrayed. Kevin had gotten a taste of what Red Sox baseball was like, and he wanted to be part of it. He didn't want to sit and watch. He's the kind of guy who would rather go to another team than sit on the bench. When you have a player with the passion for the game Kevin has, you want him out on the field. Heck, he hadn't even been drafted. He was signed after playing for the St. Paul Saints. He'd gone through a lot, and after he made the Red Sox and became one of the team's mainstays, he didn't want anyone taking away what he earned.

When Doug came over, he was hitting .240. Kevin was hitting .270 and was taking his walks and getting on base, and his attitude was, *Why should I be replaced by a guy hitting .240?* It wasn't that he was mad at Mientkiewicz, more that he wanted to be a part of something.

We were playing the Tigers, and right before the game Manny announced he had a sore throat and couldn't play. The reporters tried to make it out that Manny was sacrificing his position for Millar, but I'm not so sure. I wish I could tell you a great story and say, "Yeah, Manny did that," but I think Manny was really sick, because he went back to his hotel room so he wouldn't infect the rest of us. And Kevin got to play.

One of the things Kevin said when he was railing at Terry for not playing him was that he thought the Red Sox weren't playing as well as they could because every night Terry had a different lineup. Kevin had a point. The reason Terry had different lineups goes back

to the computers he uses. How does a given player hit off the opposing pitcher? If you don't hit the guy so well, Terry moves you down in
the lineup. If you hit him well, he moves you up. That's one of the
bad aspects of computers—there's never a set lineup. In 2004 I even
hit third a couple of times, especially after David Ortiz was sus-
pended for a few days after yelling at an umpire. But it bothers players when they go from hitting fifth behind Ortiz one night to hitting
seventh the next. Kevin wanted to be penciled into the fifth spot and
left there. He wanted to be the guy protecting Ortiz in the lineup.
Kevin is one hitter who never gets cheated. He takes his hacks. Kevin
doesn't mind if teams pitch around Ortiz.

On the night Manny got sick and went home, Kevin took
Manny's spot in left, got on base three times, and drove in a run.
Pedro pitched beautifully, and we won. And the next day, Terry
again put Kevin in the lineup, and we won again.

Mientkiewicz was the one who ended up not being able to get
his game going. He never could get comfortable and kept struggling
at the plate. He ended up playing for Millar defensively late in the
game. By the end of the season he began to adapt to Fenway. His
swing started getting more loft to it. I'd love to see him play a full
year at Fenway to see what he can do.

Kevin speaks what comes into his mind, and he went and apologized to Terry. I can't say enough about how great Terry is. He
never got angry, just listened to what Kevin had to say. Terry's been
around. He was a kid when his father, Tito, was playing. The guy,
and I'll say it again, is the perfect manager.

In early August we returned home to Fenway to play the pain-in-the-
butt Devil Rays, who hit three home runs to beat Curt Schilling. Sox
fans were beginning to lose hope that the team would get better.
The guy who was under the most pressure was Orlando Cabrera,
who was playing in front of the Fenway Faithful for the first time. At
this point Orlando was 3 for 25, not hitting much at all, and it
seemed that every personnel move the Red Sox had made during
the run had failed. The sentiment was, nothing goes right for us,

whereas anybody the Yankees pick up does well and helps them win the World Series.

But Cabrera wasn't the only one who was struggling, even though all of Boston was pinning it on him. The guys around him have to be consistent for us to win, and we weren't. Blaming Cabrera was extremely unfair. I'd talk to him, but he always seemed positive. No matter how he did the night before, he always came into the clubhouse with a "hi," or handshakes, or a big hug. I never once saw the negativity of the press and the fans affect him. He was a good fit with the rest of us, ignorant idiots who didn't pay any attention to the peanut gallery. Nomar had been the one addicted to reading the papers and listening to the radio, and he was no longer around.

It was against the Devil Rays that Orlando Cabrera became a Red Sox hero when on August 10 he, David Ortiz, and Kevin Millar combined to score five runs in an inning against the Devil Rays in a rousing win. Cabrera drove in a run early in the game, and then in the sixth his single knocked out reliever Jorge Sosa. He then hustled to third from first on a single, and scored easily on a double by Kevin Youkilis. When Cabrera ran into the dugout, he got a high-five from all of us, and a huge ovation from the fans.

Kevin Millar went 4 for 4 with a three-run home run to win the next game for Derek Lowe, and Pedro then pitched a shutout, walked nobody, and struck out 10. With Cabrera and Millar back on track, our whole team caught fire. And Terry made it easier for us by making things simple. He left the lineup alone, and he finally realized we were a bunch of guys who wanted to hit the ball, who didn't like to bunt. He gave us the green light to swing away. Myself, I didn't have one sacrifice bunt in 2004, and I was the leadoff hitter. I'm a swinger now. I want to hit.

We played two sloppy games against the White Sox at home. In one of the games Orlando made a pretty bad error. He talked to David Ortiz and Pedro, two great guys, Latin guys playing in Boston who knew it wasn't easy playing here. They were perfect to talk to because one was having a great career and the other was having a great year, and they tried to make Orlando understand how the fans of Boston react.

It used to be that black and Latin players had a hard time in Boston. Not anymore. Pedro, who is very well educated and very smart, knocked down a lot of the old barriers. The fans love him. Manny had it tough at first because he hadn't completely mastered English. Sometimes he didn't say what he intended, and it got turned around, at which point he might get blasted for it. It was one reason Manny stopped talking to the press for a while. For the Spanish-speaking players, it's real difficult in Boston, where most of the writers don't speak Spanish and the media market is so huge. The players want to say the right things.

Pedro and David Ortiz told Orlando to relax. We knew how good he was out in the field, and so did he. We were seeing his range, his good hands, certain things the shortstop he replaced wasn't able to do. All a player can do is make sure you are prepared every day. It makes you try hard every day. And if you get booed, you pick yourself up, and you get them the next time.

Cabrera's welcome-home party came on August 17 against the Toronto Blue Jays at Fenway. We were losing 4–3 in the ninth. Dave Roberts worked a walk from Justin Speier, the Jays' closer. I grounded out, forcing him at second. Then Cabrera came up, and we got to see what Orlando was made of when he hit a pitch high over the Monster in left for a game-winning walk-off home run. I jumped high in the air, and everybody on the team was so happy for him. It was like we'd won the World Series.

Everybody on our team was just in awe. That was something the fans of Boston needed to see. For one night, Cabrera had made the fans forget about Nomar. As I watched Orlando round the bases, I felt he'd given us the spark we needed to go all the way to the playoffs.

Chapter 13

A Bunch of Idiots

AUGUST–SEPTEMBER 2004

O ne of the side benefits of being a member of the Boston Red Sox is that I get to meet a lot of the rock bands I like to listen to. When we were in Toronto in late August 2004 playing the Blue Jays, I went to see a couple of Toronto friends who are band members from the group Our Lady Peace. I met them at their recording studio and got to jam with them. I'm a guitarist, a very bad one, but they still let me sit in with them. The band's lead singer wasn't there, so I got to do most of the singing.

I know a lot of the Our Lady Peace songs, but they were also playing songs of other groups like AC/DC and Creed. I had such a great evening, and I was relaxed because the team was finally starting to jell. We knew that every time we took the field we were going to do something great.

By the late summer of 2004 we had the loosest clubhouse around. Kevin Youkilis would help me stretch by setting up chairs for me to knock over and get loose. Kevin Millar, the team clown, could be heard over the din. He liked to sing, but he never bothered to learn a song's words. Rather, he made up his own. Kevin, who was nonstop, would crack a joke, and if no one laughed, he'd keep making something else up until someone did. I wondered how much coffee Kevin drank. David Ortiz also could get pretty loud.

"You guys are a bunch of bitches," he'd yell at us. We had no idea what he was talking about.

Trot Nixon, whose real name is Christopher, also could be very funny. He was big into the WWF and NASCAR. He loved the wrestler Triple X, and when he came up to bat at Fenway, the PA guy played the theme song of the wrestler "The Rock."

Trot would come up to me and say, "Nice hair, Johnny. When you gonna get that shit cut?" Or, "Hey Millar, when are you going to get that pump for your penis?"

Curtis Leskanic rolled around the locker room naked. I liked to do my pull-ups naked, though I was never able to recruit a spotter. Gabe Kapler and Trot Nixon threw a football around, and you had to pay attention if you didn't want to get smoked with it. Sometimes when you entered the locker room just before (or during) a game, one of our bat boys, Andrew Crosby, would deck himself out in hockey goalie gear, and Keith Foulke would grab his hockey stick and try to shoot pucks past him. During the game, if Andrew was still wearing his equipment, you could go in the clubhouse and take some shots at him.

Around this time we played a practical joke on Kevin Youkilis. It's called the Three Man Lift. Three people lie on the floor, and they lock arms. You brag to everyone that you're so strong you can lift all three of them off the ground at once. The victim is the guy in the middle, in this case Youkilis.

Lucas, one of our clubhouse boys, held him down on one side, and Gabe Kapler, the strongest guy on the team, held him down on the other. To sell the thing to Youkilis, the guys were all taking bets as to whether I'd be able to lift them all up or not. Jason Varitek kept on saying, "John, your knee is all banged up. I don't think you ought to do this. You're going to hurt yourself." Youkilis was sure this was on the level.

Then all at once, the rest of the guys started pouring on him everything they could get their hands on, ketchup, mustard, mayonnaise, Coca-Cola, All Sport, and anything else available. This was about a half an hour before the game and Kevin was wearing his Red Sox home whites; he was a mess.

All of this relieves the tension. If we had to concentrate on baseball 24 hours a day, we'd go insane.

If batting practice starts at 4:00, I usually get to the clubhouse around 3:15. That gives me enough time to say a few words to the media if they need something, and it gives me enough time to relax and get my bearings straight.

In Boston you tend to get a lot of fan mail. There are a million autograph requests, and I feel that signing autographs is one of the ballplayer's responsibilities. I try to accommodate everyone, but it's hard. First, I take care of the bulkier items, because they take up so much room in the locker. The letters I throw in a big box; when my brother comes and visits, he goes through it, and one day he lines them up, and I try to knock them out.

Not all ballplayers are as accommodating. I remember when I was playing in Kansas City, one of my teammates was Dean Palmer. He had a big box of fan mail, and he stared at it for about 15 minutes.

"What am I going to do?" he asked. He was agonizing, and then finally he said, "Who am I kidding? Oh, to hell with it. There is no way I'm going to sign all this."

The next thing I knew, he dumped the whole box of letters in the trash and said, "Sorry folks."

We came home to Fenway in late August, and we swept four games from the Tigers. We were getting great performances from everybody, especially Bronson, Wakefield, Cabrera, and Pedro, who was pitching like his old self. We wanted the playoffs to start right then and there. We knew teams would have to play really well to beat us. Some teams didn't have a chance, and that's a darn good feeling.

"Can we start the playoffs now?" everyone in Boston was saying. The guys on the team were saying, "We're firing on all cylinders now, from one through nine, to our bench, our starters, and our bullpen. We are unbeatable." Bob Hohler, a very fair guy who writes for the *Globe*, wrote, "No one is safe, not even the Yankees."

The Angels came to town the final days of August. Curt pitched beautifully, and Manny hit a three-run home run, then he hit another home run. The year before, Manny had been talking about wanting to play for the Yankees, but in 2004 his personality changed. I think, finally, Manny felt welcome in Boston. He had great support from the other Latin players. Orlando Cabrera came in, and he and Pedro and David Ortiz always were great friends to him. But I have to say that Manny got along great with everyone else on the team. Surrounded by his Latin buddies, Manny felt like a kid again. He had fun. Instead of refusing to talk to the media, he decided not to worry about them and just spoke his mind, and that helped everyone out, because it was no longer just Millar and me the reporters were going to.

Manny became very comfortable with his teammates. He began to loosen up, to crack jokes. One time I was in the clubhouse with my Puma rep, and he was with his Reebok rep, and he said to me, "You have some cool stuff. Maybe next year I'll go with Puma." In front of his Reebok guy. That's the kind of joking Manny does. He has a great sense of humor.

Manny hit another home run to beat the Angels again, on a day when the Fenway scoreboard sent our fans into a frenzy because the Yankees were playing Cleveland, and when they put the Cleveland score up, first it was a "6," and then a "9" and then a "16" and before it was over, the Indians had defeated the Yankees 22–0. We were aware of it, because each time a new number was put up, you could hear the "ooooooh" from the crowd.

We were definitely cutting into the Yankees' lead. We were only $3\frac{1}{2}$ back, but I knew the next night the Yankees would win. They have too much pride. They're a very professional team, but it was great to see them get stomped 22–0 because it doesn't happen too often.

Meanwhile, I was in a groove. I had four hits in the next Angels game. I started a four-run rally in the first inning. When you're in a groove, you feel like you can get a hit any time up. It doesn't matter who the pitcher is. In 2004 I felt that way the entire season, which was a gift. I'd hurt my knee, but in a funny way that helped, because when I was healthy, I was supposed to be the speed guy, so sometimes I'd start running even before I hit the ball. In 2004, I waited, and I became a better hitter. During this streak I could put a check-swing on the ball and I'd still get a base hit. When you can hit Ichiro-style, keeping the ball on the ground, it's very hard for them to get you out.

Unfortunately, in that last Angels game, I dislocated my finger. Bartolo Colon is so quick to first you can't take a big lead. It was the first inning, and I was intending to steal, and when he threw back, I dove and dislocated my finger. If this had been the year before, I would have kept playing. But since we had Dave Roberts, I didn't worry about sitting out a game. Dave is an excellent defensive player and a great base stealer. He'd get the job done. I was comfortable taking off a day to let my finger heal. I was able to get my bearings straight and get ready for the post-season run.

At that point we were looking pretty solid for the wild-card spot. The Rangers came to town, and Pedro shut them out, our tenth straight win, our sixteenth win in 17 games, our eightieth win of the season with almost the entire month of September to go.

We moved to within $2\frac{1}{2}$ games of the Yankees, and even "better," we heard that Kevin Brown had gotten hit hard, and that when he went into the dugout he punched the wall and broke his hand. Bad luck for him; good luck for us. Guys who've played with Kevin know how fiery he is. We were saying, "Wow, things are starting to unravel for the Yankees." Not only that, but it was clear something was wrong with Jason Giambi, who'd contracted a parasite in Japan, and who'd been sick all season long.

Jason remains a close friend. He's the nicest guy, the best teammate I've ever had. While with the A's he took guys out, was in control all the time, and he played great. He wore his hair long, and he had rock star status.

I don't know what the Yankees intend to do with him, but I'd take him as a teammate in a heartbeat. One thing is for sure: without Jason, the Yankees aren't going to be as good. The character assassination he's undergoing because he's admitted using steroids hurts me, because he's the kind of guy who'd never do anything to hurt anyone.

My feeling is, Jason has conceded that what he did was wrong, and going forward he's going to do whatever it takes to make things better and help ensure others avoid these banned substances. He's a great guy, and I hope he gets through all this. I love him like a brother.

I've never taken a steroid—ever. When I was 13, they were offered to me. I was working out with a 19-year-old, the neighbor of a friend. I was six foot one, weighed 185 pounds, and he said, "Man, if you take this stuff, you'll be six foot one, two hundred twenty."

I felt the pressure but then I thought, *I'm 13. I've got time to grow.* I passed, and to this day I'm glad I did. When I was growing up I remember seeing Lyle Alzado on TV talking about how he was dying from taking steroids. He was the reason I never took them. Lenny Bias was the reason I never took cocaine.

I'm glad Major League Baseball is going to test for steroids. We've learned a lot from the passing of Ken Caminiti. We need to control these performance-enhancement drugs and make sure they don't get in the hands of younger kids.

"You can make a lot of money by doing steroids," a lot of high school and college kids are saying, but that is not the right way to look at this issue. Hopefully we can clean this up.

I'm not one of those people, though, who looks at guys who

take steroids as cheaters. You still have to go out and hit the ball. The unfair advantage you get is that you're a lot stronger at the end of the season from taking these drugs. I know many a September I'm just worn out.

"Cheating" is a pretty harsh word. Baseball is these guys' livelihood. I'm not ever going to tell another player what to do. If a player is in the minor leagues on the edge of making a ton of money, the temptation is understandable. I would recommend he not take steroids, but if it's his only chance to make the majors, who am I to influence him? He has to make up his own mind. I just know the reasons I won't take these drugs.

We kept winning. Tim Wakefield and Curt Schilling beat the Rangers, and after the game Curt announced to everyone that "my splitter is back." It was the first time I'd known his splitter had been missing.

We finished the home stand 9–1, and headed to Oakland to finish off the A's, who seemed to fight for the wild card every year. With those pitchers—Hudson, Zito, and Mulder—you could never count out those guys.

It was the first time I'd been back in Oakland since running into Damian Jackson in the playoffs. I didn't play in the opener, but we were strengthened by the return of Trot Nixon, who came back wearing a Mohawk hairdo. That's Trot. We don't judge by hair alone. We embrace whatever a guy wants to do, even if it looks bad.

Trot grew up in North Carolina playing a lot of football. He signed to play quarterback at North Carolina State, though he looks more like a linebacker than a quarterback. He played during the same era as Brian Bosworth, who to many college football fans was the coolest guy we ever saw. Trot's from that same mold. The Mohawk fit him perfectly.

He blended right in. I had my long "What Would Johnny Damon Do?" hair. Pedro had his Dan Shaughnessy–like jerry curl. Mark Bellhorn, who looks like someone out of *West Side Story,* has some pretty good hair. He has what Kevin Millar calls "show hair."

And Bronson Arroyo, who had decent hair to start with, braided his hair into cornrows, which was kind of crazy. None of us were too sure about that, but after he did it, he started pitching well, so we told him, "Guess what? You're keeping it."

The funny thing about this array of unconventional hairstyles, no one orchestrated it. Each guy did his own thing. And no one was judgmental about it.

When I arrived for spring training, Theo Epstein saw me, and he said, "Hey, just as long as you play well."

Which went a long way in our minds. He was treating us as adults. We're not the Yankees. We don't want to be the Yankees, with their short hair and their suits and ties on the road. So what if we're sloppy. We don't care.

About halfway through the season I can remember Curt Schilling's coming up to me in the trainer's room. He said, "When I came here, I didn't think you were professional and hard-nosed. You had long hair. You were in the hot tub five minutes before the game. But, dude, you don't know how amazing you really are."

He said I reminded him of Lenny Dykstra. "You come out and expect to beat the other team every day," he said. "You hustle all the time, and the way you carry yourself, you know you're going to make a difference. You're one of the best players I've ever watched."

I was thinking, *Wow!*

"You deserve to win the MVP," he said. "You've got my vote." But Curt studies the statistics and he's a realist. He added, "Of course, you're not going to win, even though you deserve it. In the worst case, you should finish in the top seven."

After that it didn't matter where I finished. I had Curt Schilling's respect, and to me that's all that mattered.

While I sat on the bench for a week out with my bad finger, I drove myself crazy. I didn't know what to do. While I rode the pine, I told Terry, "If you need me, play me." I knew I could deal with it. I wouldn't be at my best, but, "Hey, if you need me, just put me in there."

My fill-in, Dave Roberts, drove in the winning run in that first game in Oakland. Having him on the team is one of the best luxuries in the world. He can play left, center, right, leadoff, he can hit ninth, he can hit second, he can bunt—he's just a good all-around player.

The next day Terry put me back in, and I hit a home run to lead off the game against Mark Redman. When I crossed home plate and came into the dugout, I told Terry, "Good day to put me back in." And then the guys started teasing me.

"Oh yeah, your pinky is *really* hurting," they said. But it was hurting. Months after the World Series, I still couldn't shake people's hands. The base got me good. I tore a ligament, and it took a *long* time to heal.

We ended up winning that game when Alan Embree, Mike Myers, and Curtis Leskanic came in and pitched shutout ball over the last three innings. I was so happy for those guys.

I'd heard a lot about Leskanic, heard he was a free spirit. Someone said to me, "He doesn't have all his marbles." I figured he'd be perfect for our team.

I'm always looking to improve. If I knew there was an available outfielder better than me to get, I'd tell Theo to get him. We're trying to win here. The day Kansas City released Leskanic, I went to Theo Epstein and asked, "Why did Kansas City release him? What's the deal?" We were in Colorado, and we were scuffling. I told Theo that Leskanic was a gamer, that he had a lot of heart, that he could help our team.

"I'll see what happened in Kansas City," Theo replied. "Do you really think this guy can help us?"

"Oh yeah," I said.

We knew he had stuff. He gave everything he had. Unfortunately, by the end of the season he had a separated shoulder.

Theo looked into it, checked into Leskanic's character, and he made the move to get him.

After Curtis joined the team, I figured out what people were referring to when they said he was a little odd. He's another guy who loves to talk, especially about the Pittsburgh Steelers. And like me, he likes to jump in the hot tub right before the game. When he jumps in, he tries to create the biggest splash he can. He tries to get everyone else wet.

The first time he jumped in there, it was five minutes before the game, when we were supposed to get ready. I told him, "You're going to have to get in there earlier, or share it with me, because I'm on the program, too."

Leskanic was another guy who kept our clubhouse loose. I was glad we had him.

We swept Oakland, as Pedro pitched another great game. The opposing starter had been Tim Hudson, who was close on his pitches, but wasn't getting them called strikes.

Everyone was saying how Pedro was having a bad year, but his record turned out to be 16–5. What do they want from the guy? Do they expect Pedro to go 25–0?

After the game Hudson, who is the best pitcher I've ever seen, told reporters, "I didn't want to show them what they're going to get in the playoffs."

Our win was our twentieth in 22 games, the greatest stretch run in Red Sox history. We wanted to show everybody we were for real, and we had. We took on Anaheim, Texas, and Oakland, and you're just not expected to win all those games. But we went 9 and 1 against them, which was very impressive.

In 2004, as the Sox began to win, and all of northern New England began to go crazy about us, we became known as the idiots. And I was head idiot.

Before a game normally we sit around the clubhouse and watch a good TV show, a comedy, or perhaps a football game if one is on. Then the guy in charge of putting together the video of the day's pitcher comes in and puts his tape in, and some of us start to boo. Most of us don't care to watch it. We'd rather do something else. Fortunately, there's another TV so I can compete in Play Station 2 while some of the other hitters watch the video of the opposing pitcher.

Grady Little was the one who said to us, "If you use your head, you're only going to hurt the team." It was his theory that we should react, not think. Grady is a very smart man.

I play better when I *don't know* the other pitcher's tendencies. When I don't know, I'm better able to react. A lot of times you remember what that pitcher threw you the last time, and then he'll have a totally different style. Everything is different, which is why I take more of a "see ball, hit ball" kind of approach.

When I go to bat, I'm looking to get a pitch around the heart of the plate early in the count. As the count goes deeper, you expand what you're looking for to both sides of the plate. That's why it's very important to get a good hack at that first strike. That's why Nomar swung at the first pitch so many times. Once the pitcher gets ahead by throwing that first strike, he expands and you begin chasing.

That's why when you take a lot of pitches, as I was trained to do in Oakland, you are sacrificing your personal records for the team. Since coming to Boston, I have learned to be more analytical about when I take pitches. Before I was taking just for the sake of taking. Against the better pitchers, I'm now swinging more often at the first pitch.

Just as I don't want to know what the pitcher threw in his last start, I also hate it when a teammate on second base signals what the pitcher is throwing.

"You better not look," I tell myself. It's tougher for me to hit when I have knowledge in advance of what's coming.

A lot of my teammates feel the same way about playing the game by sheer instinct, which is why I called us a gang of idiots. Another reason for the term is that we don't know how to steal signs. We try to be worry-free, and we do that by being oblivious to anything that's going on around us.

Some of the other guys and I had talked among ourselves about being "idiots," but I guess I was the only one to mention it to the press, so the term has been credited to me.

It started when a reporter asked, "How are you going to beat the Yankees?"

"I don't know," I said. "We're not going to try to figure it out. We're just a bunch of idiots. We're just going to throw the ball, hit the ball, catch the ball. We want to keep the thinking process out of it."

After my words were printed in the paper, the term "idiots" took off.

When he saw us being referred to that way, Trot Nixon said, "We're not idiots," but the label took on a life of its own. Hey, the idiot label should be taken lightly. We know we're all smart enough guys. But we also know that to beat the Yankees and win a championship we can't worry about playing baseball, stressing about it, not enjoying it. To do well in this game, you have to *enjoy* playing it, love it so much that the powers that be would have to rip the shirt off your back to stop you from playing.

There's no reason why you shouldn't have fun playing this game. There's certainly a time to be serious, but there's plenty of time to enjoy yourself. That's what Kevin Millar does. That's what Curtis Leskanic does. That's what Orlando Cabrera does. That's what Pedro and Manny do. That's what I do. That's what our team does.

We knew the curse was there, but we were guys who refused to worry about all those years of heartache. We stuck to just worrying about ourselves. We had the belief "We can party. We can have fun. We can win."

After we beat Anaheim in the third game of the series, we all went across the street and saw our friends from the band Alterbridge, which was kicking off their tour. The group used to be called Creed, but they have a new lead singer, Miles Kennedy. Anyway, they invited us, and we had a great time. If we'd lost, we still would have gone and jumped on stage and sang. That's what we do.

We're on the go every night. Some nights we get crazy, but we know how to control ourselves. There's no relaxing playing for the Red Sox. We enjoy being out there, being around the fans, being a little like rock stars. People worship the Red Sox. And we were the perfect team for them to worship.

Chapter 14

"The Yankees Are My Daddy"

SEPTEMBER 2004

By mid-September 2004, we knew we had the wild-card spot sewn up. We were on a hot streak, and we were playing the Texas Rangers at home. The crowd was chanting my name, "Johnny, Johnny." We were down by a run, and I got a high fastball—about 96 miles an hour—and I hit it over the right field fence.

After I returned to the dugout, Curt Schilling, who was quick with praise, walked up to me and said, "That's pretty amazing. The minute they chanted your name, you knew you were going to do something special."

He added, "Any other year you would be MVP."

As I said, Schill's encouragement was more important to me than the award itself.

We beat the A's into submission, and when we went into Seattle, the Mariners were out of it. We split the four games because we lost to two of their talented young pitchers. A lefty kid pitcher by the name of Bobby Madritsch ate us up. And Gil Meche, a pretty good little pitcher, beat us. When Bronson Arroyo pitched a shutout against the Mariners to even the series, the Red Sox completed a stretch of going 30–9 since August 1. We were six games ahead of both the Angels and the Mariners.

Bronson is a kid from Brooksville, Florida, and he still lives there. He spent some time in the Pittsburgh organization, and then one year when he was left off the roster, the Red Sox claimed him. As I mentioned earlier, at Triple A Pawtucket he threw a perfect game. Bronson will tell you that that game was what probably opened their eyes—he was pitching lights out.

I really admire Bronson. He's carefree. He's a great musician, a guy who could probably play in a band. He has a good voice. He could make some mad money playing in college bars. Every time I have my band member friends come to the hotel, we go to someone's room, and Bronson watches and studies them. He knows he's good, and he picks things up very easily. And he's the same way with his pitching. He has one of the best sliders I've ever seen. As the 2004 season went on, he began mixing up his pitches, throwing his fastball a lot more.

Bronson has been helped by Jason Varitek, the best pitch caller in the league, and by our pitching coach, Dave Wallace, a little, funny, witty guy. Wallace loves it when Bronson pitches. A lot of people thought of the Red Sox as underdogs when Bronson took the mound. We were never favored when he'd pitch. The irony was, a lot of times he was our number one. We had Pedro and Schilling, but Bronson was as steady as they came. Any time we needed him to pitch a big game, he came through. He was one of the reasons we went from being a .500 club to 30–9.

If you look at the history of the game, your one and two starters are going to win you games. Your three and four hitters are going to drive in the runs. To win, the other guys have to be consistent. You have to get your three, four, and five starters pitching well, and get your other hitters hitting. The secret is for a couple players to have career years, and for the other guys to be consistent. In Boston in 2004, we gained consistency all at once.

As the regular season wound down, our opponents were the Orioles and the Devil Rays. These teams scare me more than the Yankees. We know what we're going to get from the Yankees. We're always going to play well against them. Against teams like the Orioles and Rays, one night they can go out and score 15 runs—or you can shut them out. In the case of the Devil Rays, we faced a 21-year-old kid by the name of Scott Kazmir. He'd been in the Mets organization, but the Mets panicked, deciding they needed another veteran starter to help them in 2004, and they traded him for Victor Zambrano, the Rays' best pitcher. Zambrano ended up pitching two innings, hurt his arm, and didn't pitch again the rest of the year. When the Mets fired the GM for making that trade, no one was surprised.

Against us, Kazmir showed everyone why he was the Mets' top prospect. The guy was incredible. He had good, good stuff. He gave up three singles and no runs in six innings, and we lost. He reminded me of a young Andy Pettitte, only better. He runs that fastball in on left-handers like Pettitte. Pettitte throws 90. This kid threw 95. His curve ball was never in the heart of the plate. This kid was absolutely unhittable. I could tell what he was throwing, and I broke three bats against him. This kid was making *me* look like a kid.

After Kazmir, though, the Devil Rays didn't show us much on the mound. Tim Wakefield won, and then Curt Schilling won his twentieth game, his seventh win in a row. In that game I hit a home run off Jorge Sosa. It was a great at-bat, a 10-pitch at-bat. I felt right going into the game, felt like some time during the game I'd hit a home run to put us into the lead. Sure enough, I hit it, and the ball soared out in about two seconds. The team went wild because a win meant that we were a game closer to clinching the wild-card berth and going to the playoffs. People began to say, "John has a chance to drive in eighty runs from the leadoff spot." I was hot, and I kept on hitting.

We flew to New York for a three-game series against the Yankees. It was our one chance to take the pennant away from them. The series opener was on September 17, and the game was acknowledged to be the most memorable of the 2004 season. Bronson Arroyo started against Orlando Hernandez. After a rain delay, the

Yankees led 2–1 going into the ninth. Joe Torre brought Mariano Rivera in to close it out. Trot Nixon opened the inning by drawing a walk. Terry Francona sent Dave Roberts to run for him. As Jason Varitek swung and struck out, Dave stole second easily. Rivera then hit Kevin Millar with a pitch. Gabe Kapler ran for him.

Orlando Cabrera, continuing his heroics, singled to tie the game. It was the second game in a row Rivera had blown a save against us—the other one was back in July. There were two outs, Kapler was on second, and I was up.

I knew Mariano was going to come at me hard. The speed gun says he throws 94, but I'm telling you, he's 5 miles an hour faster than that. I did get jammed, but fortunately, he didn't break my bat even though I hit the ball on the handle. I hit a flare into right center—when I hit it I was sure it was going to drop, but then I saw Kenny Lofton in center closing quickly on it, and I thought, *You've got to be kidding me, not here, because we need this one.* But Lofton had to pull up, to make sure the ball didn't get by him, Kapler scored, and I ended up on second. That was a huge hit for me, coming in the clutch against the game's best closer.

Winning that game pulled us closer as a team. It confirmed that we could come back against Rivera. Twice we'd beaten him in the ninth inning. We now knew for sure that when we faced him down by a run, we could beat him. Down by two runs? Ah, that's a little tougher.

The win was important for us. We were happy. We were getting closer yet to the playoffs. And by winning, we closed to within a half a game of the Yankees.

Remember, with respect to the Yankees, what I said about being an idiot and not thinking too much? After our win in the opener, we started doing a lot of planning, started to . . . ugh, *think.* We didn't just go out, use our talent, and play. There is no reason to overanalyze. And the next two games we got clobbered. We lost 14–4 and 11–0.

After we lost those two games, the Boston papers really let us have it. All that Bambino curse crap that Nomar used to read and that Schilling keeps track of. It crept into the clubhouse, even though we all tried not to pay any attention to it. Mostly, we succeeded. That's because what's important to us is enjoying life and doing what makes us happy. Yes, we're good baseball players, but we were other things before we became good baseball players, before we became Red Sox.

It's funny how, for the most part, our team just didn't care about what everyone was predicting would happen to us. We knew Theo had put together a good enough team to win it all. We knew that once you got to the playoffs, you had to have some luck. I've experienced playoffs when the better team didn't win. I thought we were the best team in 2003. The team I was on in Oakland in 2001 should have won the World Series, and we lost to the Yankees in the playoffs.

Guys don't need to read newspapers when they're playing ball. That's when they start feeling the pressure of the curse.

I know what I'm going to read when I'm sitting in the club-house—*Playboy*. And even then, all I'm doing is looking at the pictures.

After those two losses to the Yankees, we returned home to Fenway to play 4 games against the Orioles. When we lost the opener, we were $4\frac{1}{2}$ games behind the Yankees with 14 to play. Dan Shaughnessy moaned and groaned that our chance to catch the Yankees had disappeared, that we'd have to settle for being the wild-card team. Well, what's wrong with that? Who won the World Series in 2002 and 2003? It was the wild-card team. And we intended to make it three in a row.

The reporters made a big deal out of our finishing second, but we didn't mind. Of course we wanted to beat the Yankees, but if things don't go right at certain times during the season, you're not going to win the division. As far as how good we were compared to the Yankees, our team matched up. But we'd been more beat up most of the year.

I wish the writers had talked to players around the league. If they had, they would have found many who believed we were the best team they'd ever seen. Darren Erstad told me that. Our feeling was that if everything went right, if we didn't run into any bad luck, like a blown call by the umpires, we could do something remarkable.

After losing that first game to the Orioles, Curt pitched and came within one pitch of winning his twenty-first game, but Javy Lopez hit a two-out home run off Keith Foulke in the top of the ninth. When we got up, Kevin Youkilis, "The Greek God of Walks," walked, Bill Mueller doubled, and after I got up and popped out for the second out—a lousy out—Mark Bellhorn, one of the Red Sox's most underappreciated players, hit a line shot into the gap to win the game.

I've known Mark since I was 15. We started playing against each other a lot in high school and in the summer leagues. In the fall of our senior year we played on a Central Florida All Star team on Thursday nights. When we graduated, we went to Oklahoma to represent Team Florida. Mark was the shortstop. Doug Mientkiewicz was the first baseman. Mickey Lopez, who finally made the big leagues this year, was our second baseman. I was also a teammate of Mark's for a short time when I was with Oakland. Mark came up in the A's organization, but nobody knew much about him. He was a backup infielder, a guy who had to fight to make the team. He had a chance to win a starting spot, but fell short. Fortunately, when he went to the Cubs in 2002, he hit 27 home runs. In 2003 he hit only 2 homers total for Chicago and Colorado, but attracted the interest of Theo, who was smart enough to sign him as a free agent. In 2004, Mark was booed more than any other player because he struck out a lot. He scored 93 runs and drove in 82, but the reporters didn't write about the runs scored or the RBIs. Instead, their mantra was, "He struck out again." I'd ask myself, *Don't they realize how big he has been for our team?*

The next night it was Orlando Cabrera's turn to be a hero. He'd flown home to Colombia to be with his wife, who was sick. She'd begged him to stay an extra day, but he felt he owed it to the team to return. I don't know why she wasn't living with him here in Boston. Some things you just don't ask. Usually it's because the kids are in school. Billy Mueller's wife stayed back in Arizona because she was pregnant and she and Bill had other kids. He was miserable at times because he wasn't with her. It's a tough lifestyle.

When Orlando arrived at Logan airport, he called Terry Francona and left a message that he was back and wanted to play. Terry started him at short against the Orioles, and the game went into the twelfth inning. In our half of the twelfth Orlando led off against Rick Bauer, and he hit a fastball over the Monster to win the game. When he crossed the plate, we all ran out there and mobbed him. By this time we knew that Cabrera was the answer the Red Sox were looking for. As I've said, getting Orlando Cabrera would turn out to be the biggest trade in Red Sox history.

Derek Lowe got beat up by the Orioles right before a big three-game series against the Yankees at Fenway. In the opener against the Yankees, Pedro was pitching beautifully, and we led 4–3 in the eighth inning after I hit a home run off Tom Gordon. Pedro had thrown 100 pitches, but Terry left him out there to pitch the eighth. When Hideki Matsui hit a long home run to tie the game, Terry left him in. After Bernie Williams doubled, and Ruben Sierra singled him home, we were losers.

Pedro took that defeat very hard. After the game he told reporters, "The Yankees are my daddy." He was in disbelief we'd lost. He didn't know what else he could do. He'd pitched so well against this tough team, given it everything he had, and in the end they'd taken it from him.

Pedro wanted to win so badly that night. The intensity of the Red Sox–Yankees rivalry had grown that season with every game, and it was excruciating for him to be in the spotlight's glare and lose like that. I found out about that "daddy" quote the next day from the reporters.

Personally, I didn't care that he'd said it. It was a comment made out of frustration, and the media blew it up, especially the

New York media. My teammates and I told anyone who asked that he was talking out of emotion, that if there was one guy we wanted on the mound, it was Pedro.

We find out so much about what our teammates have said or done from the media. Usually the next day, when the reporters come to you, the questions are mostly negative. The press tends to have bad things to say. This goes back to the days of Ted Williams, whom the press tried to run out of town. I remember reading an interview Ted gave. He said his first year he didn't run full out on a hit, and the press really got on him.

We know when and how to handle the media when we're asked negative questions. If they ask me something negative about a teammate, the answer is, "I have no idea." Or, "I'm sorry. I have no clue." Or, "I don't care."

Anyway, when the reporters asked me about Pedro's "The Yankees are my daddy" quote, I told them, "Pedro is very frustrated because he's pitched great games, but against the Yankees, they always seem to get to him. Pedro takes it hard. He doesn't want it to happen that way."

Every time we play in Yankee Stadium, as soon as the game ends, we walk through the tunnel to get back to the clubhouse. The game is barely over, and all the reporters are standing there at the clubhouse door waiting to talk. We don't even have a chance to catch our breath, to compose ourselves, before we're bombarded with questions. The New York herd is even bigger than the Boston herd. The Yankees have a lot more newspapers not to read than we do.

The biggest negative slant on the Pedro-pitched game was directed at Terry Francona. The Boston writers were saying that Francona had left Pedro in too long exactly as Grady Little had the year before in the playoffs. Grady had gotten fired for it, they pointed out. I don't really think that was the case. Rather, I think Grady was fired because when Theo Epstein came in, he wanted to pick his own man. *His* man was Terry. Major League players know all too well that few managers last very long. When a guy is hired, it's just a matter of time before he's fired. Terry runs a good ship, as Grady did.

They were two guys who were about the team and not themselves, and I've been proud to play under both of them.

The next two games—big wins at Fenway—would prove very important for the Red Sox in 2004. One of the great things about the wins was that we prevented the Yankees from being able to go out onto our mound to celebrate their winning the division title. We also showed them that if—when—we met in the playoffs, we wouldn't be afraid of them and we had the horses to beat them.

Mark Bellhorn and I had a hand in winning the middle game of the series. We were tied 5–5 in the eighth when I singled—I did my job, got on base. That's what I am supposed to do. If you don't beat them early on, you keep plugging away. Mark walked, and Manny drove me in with the winning run. Tek and Doug Mirabelli then drove in two more runs each, and we won the game 12–5.

In the next game we had to face Kevin Brown, a great pitcher. But with our team it doesn't matter how great the pitcher is. We can face Cy Young or Walter Johnson, and guess what, we still feel we can beat them. So when we face great pitchers like Kevin Brown, we feel like we can win. It doesn't matter. And we boxed Kevin Brown around and won 11–4. He pitched two thirds of an inning and gave up four runs before Joe Torre took him out.

It was the final home game, and for me the highlight came when the Red Sox fans began chanting, "Ellis, Ellis, Ellis." Ellis Burks had begun his career with the Red Sox in 1987, played great for the Sox for six seasons, and then played 11 more years before returning to Boston for his swan song. Ellis was retiring, and the fans wanted to see him out on the field one more time. Unfortunately, his knees were banged up so badly, he couldn't play. I got goose bumps when he walked out of the dugout, took a bow, and walked off to a rousing, loving ovation. It's wonderful to be beloved and to be a Red Sox.

About a week before the end of the season the veteran Red Sox players who'd been there the whole year voted to distribute playoff and

World Series shares. The meeting was pretty intense because we were voting to pay out large sums of money not only to ourselves but also to guys who, because of a trade or because they'd been sent down or released, had only been on the team a limited amount of time.

I was team rep, speaking for the players, and my feeling was that we should be as generous as possible. I got up and said, "We're not playing this game to get a big share of playoff or World Series money. We're playing to fulfill a dream, to win a championship."

Some of the guys agreed, though most didn't want to be as generous as I did. Some players took the position that if a player was on the World Series roster, he'd get a full share, but if he wasn't, the most he deserved was a one-third share. What made that stance tricky was that at the time we had no idea who was going to make the post-season roster.

"Terry Adams deserves to be on the team in the post-season," I said, "but he may be left off because he's not left-handed. Or because of something else."

One of the players argued that players who were with us half the season ought to get half a share. Others thought that less than fair. Curtis Leskanic had been a Red Sox for only half the season, and his arm was hurting, so there was also the possibility he might not be on the post-season roster. To me neither mattered.

"Curtis has been instrumental in our getting to the post-season," I said, "and he deserves a full share."

Some guys didn't want to give a full share to Kevin Youkilis, who'd spent most of the year in the minor leagues. Again, I said, "No. He helped get us here. He did well. He's as important as anybody else on this team and he deserves a full share."

Orlando Cabrera, who'd been traded over in the Nomar deal with only a third of the year to go, deserved a full share. Yet a lot of teams would have awarded him a one-third share.

"Look what he did for us," I reminded. "Consider where we would have been without him. How could anyone in good conscience not give him a full share?"

Here I am looking thoughtful in the photo that *People Magazine* used in their "Sexiest Man Alive" issue. I was named "Sexiest Hit Man." Sorry, Trot, maybe next year. *(Perry Hagopian/Contour Photos)*

Sometimes, it just feels great to get out on the field.
(Getty Images/Layne Murdoch)

With all the craziness of the past couple years, sometimes you've got to remember to stop and smell the flowers.
(Sports Illustrated/ *Tom DiPace*)

I love David Ortiz. He's got a great work ethic, he's one of the best hitters in the game, *and* I can always beat him at poker—what more could you ask for in a teammate? (*Getty Images/Ezra Shaw*)

I was looking pretty scraggly for the first few weeks of 2005 spring training. (*Associated Press/Robert F. Bukaty*)

Alan Embree and I relax in the locker room with a quick game of poker. That's Manny behind us, getting ready for the game.
(*MLB via Getty Images/Michael Zagaris*)

Here I am hitting against the Yankees on April 5, 2005, the second game of the season for us. We were tied going into the ninth inning, but Derek Jeter hit a clutch home run to steal the game. *(MLB via Getty Images/Rich Pilling)*

This is the media blitz before our April 11 home opener against the Yankees. At moments like this, you've gotta keep reminding yourself that whatever the history, it's just another game. *(Getty Images/Ezra Shaw)*

I'll never forget this moment, receiving my World Series ring before the home opener. Here I am shaking hands with Curt Schilling, and that's Alan Embree next to me. *(Getty Images/Jim McIsaac)*

Another great moment that day was meeting Boston sports legends Richard Seymour, Teddy Bruschi, Bill Russell, and Bobby Orr, who came for the ring ceremony and to throw out the first pitches.
(Corbis/Rick Friedman)

Chucking it to the infield, during game 3 of that series against the Yankees. We won 8 to 5, and I had a pretty good game, scoring twice on a hit, a walk, and a steal. *(Reuters/Brian Snyder)*

Here I am signing baseballs at the Ronald McDonald House in New York. One of the best things about being a pro athlete is getting the chance to give these kids some happiness.
(New York Daily News/*Susan Watts*)

I had a great time on Regis and Kelly's show at the start of the 2005 season. Regis is a die-hard Yankees fan, so we had some fun ribbing each other. (*Buena Vista Television*)

Me with Ashton Kutcher, Matthew McConaughey, driver Mike Wallace, and Jessica Lynch, before the start of the Daytona 500. It was fun meeting those guys, and we had great seats for the race. (*Associated Press/Glenn Smith*)

This is a shot of me on my book tour for the hardcover edition of *Idiot*. The young woman whose back is visible was so overwhelmed she couldn't even speak—she just stood in front of me and cried tears of excitement. Fans like her make me want to play that much harder. *(Associated Press/Bebeto Matthews)*

Michelle and me as Hollywood royalty, at the premiere of *Fever Pitch*, which was held—where else?—at Fenway Park. *(Getty Images/Darren McCollester)*

It was quite an experience getting style tips from Carson and the guys from *Queer Eye*. At least I didn't get my back waxed like Kevin Millar.
(*EPA/Eliot J. Schechter*)

I had an argument with the center field wall running down a fly ball against the Orioles on May 31, 2005. I needed a few stitches afterwards and was a little banged up, and when I came in for practice the next day, I found this chalk outline there as a reminder. Yeah guys, very funny.
(*EPA/Matt Campbell*)

The biggest fight was over what to give Nomar. Billy Mueller wanted to give him a full share, and so did I. He had been a pivotal member of the Red Sox, the go-to guy for years. The only reason we didn't give him a full share was that the Cubs were still in the wild-card race, and someone asked what would happen if Nomar and the Cubs made the playoffs and he got a full share from the Cubs, and then faced the Red Sox in the World Series? Nomar would have stood to have made close to 600 grand. We gave him a three-quarter share, and I must admit that some players didn't think he deserved that.

"Hey, this guy was Mr. Boston," we said.

The arguing continued.

"We don't know if Theo is going to put Dave Roberts on the post-season roster," I said. "How can we not give him a full share? The guy is a professional. He's been in battles. He's certainly good enough to be on our team in the playoffs, whether he is picked or not."

I made my closing argument. "If he's good enough to be on the team and good enough to help us, why are we giving him the shaft?" I told them, "Every one of you in this room has enough money. We need to take care of these people."

I was so disgusted with their attitude, I was about to walk out of the meeting.

"Hey, you guys take care of it," I said. "I'm not going to be part of us not giving Kevin Youkilis a full share. I'm not going to be part of your giving Mike Myers a one-third share or giving Curtis Leskanic a half or Terry Adams a third."

When I said, "You guys take care of it, I'm leaving," they knew I was angry and ashamed, and after that they agreed to go along. We even took care of guys like Adam Hyzdu and Andy Dominique, who was in the big leagues for 15 days.

Trot Nixon was one of the players who spoke in favor of what I was saying. In the end, I think everybody felt happy because they understood what I advocated was right. The post-season shares weren't just for us and our pockets. They were for everyone who contributed to the fight, including the guys who helped fix the field, who helped in the front office, who helped keep us healthy, who helped with the video reporters, who helped with our scouting—in short, anyone who helped make the Boston Red Sox a success.

The season ended with four hurricanes in Florida and two games against the Devil Rays. I have a home in Orlando, and I was hit with about $25,000 worth of damage. I was lucky. A lot of people were hurt a lot worse.

When we arrived in St. Petersburg to play the Devil Rays, I got a big kick out of a group of fans with hair that looked a lot like mine getting together in the left field bleachers to carry on and cheer for me and the Sox. One of them carried a big banner that read, "What would Johnny Damon do?"

Party, dude. That's what I'd do.

Once again we had to face that kid Scott Kazmir. Bronson Arroyo started for us, and with Tampa Bay leading, he hit Aubrey Huff with a pitch. The score was 2–0 Rays in the fourth, and Kazmir had a no-hitter. We didn't even have a sniff against the guy.

Well, Kazmir hit Manny with a pitch. He didn't mean to do it, but Bronson had hit Huff, so the umpires had no choice but to give both teams a warning. Then the kid hit Kevin Millar, and the umpire had no choice but to throw him and Lou Piniella, the Rays' manager, out of the game. As soon as Millar got hit, all of us on the bench jumped up and cheered. "All right. The guy's out of the game!" We didn't want to see him anymore.

Of course, once they got Kazmir out of there, the Devil Rays were goners. The Rays brought in Jorge Sosa, and after David McCarty singled, Kevin Youkilis walked. After an out, I got up, and Sosa threw me a pitch I could turn on, and I hit it into the right field stands to put us ahead 3–2. Mark Bellhorn doubled, and my home run was forgotten after the one Manny Ramirez hit. Manny crushed a pitch, hitting it over the center field fence about three quarters of the way off the roof of the restaurant in center field. It was Manny's forty-third home run.

When you see Manny taking batting practice, he works on hitting to right field. He'll hit balls to the second baseman, and you say to yourself, *I can hit better than that.*

When I take batting practice, I try to hit the ball over the moon. For me, batting practice is to show your balls, to try to show how much of a man you are.

Though I'm six foot one and 220 pounds, I'm still considered a little guy, and when I first came up to the majors, I just worked on hitting the ball to the shortstop hole between third and short. That was fine, but when it was time for me to hit a home run, I didn't know how to do it. I had that short swing with no power. I needed to know how to hit home runs. I needed to know how to tie the game in certain situations, and I began working on that. In the off-season I went and played home run derby, one of the no-nos of hitting. Normally, if you swing for the fences, you're going to struggle. But as I got older, I got smarter. I also got stronger, and so even though I'm the leadoff hitter, I'm good for 15 to 20 home runs a year. And as I did against Sosa, I can pick my spots and hit one out.

After we knocked out Kasmir and beat Tampa Bay, we clinched the wild-card berth. We were ecstatic to be in the playoffs again, and we ran out onto the field under the Tropicana Dome and had a great celebration. We did it, because you never know how far you're going to go into the post-season. And for some players, it was the first time they'd ever made the playoffs. For others, it might be their last time, so it was important to enjoy what was out there to be enjoyed, just as if you'd won the World Series.

When we returned to the clubhouse, the newspaper guys wanted to know why we were celebrating since all we'd won was the wild-card spot. Guess what? We do what we do, and they can do what they want to do. It's not about them and the way they think. It's about the Red Sox and how the Red Sox go about their business. It's just us being us. Who knows? This could be my last time in the playoffs. Because of injuries, it could always be your last year.

I think back to the day Damian Jackson and I collided in Oakland. Before that I appreciated the game. I'd said I was going to retire if I won a World Series. But now, after having had that experience and almost having the game taken away from me, when I think about it, I cry, because I don't ever want to leave this game. I know the day will come, and I know I won't be ready. This game is so precious and meaningful to me.

I finished the 2004 season batting .304 with 20 home runs, 94 RBIs, and 123 runs scored. I was only the fourth leadoff batter in major league history ever to drive in more than 90 runs.

A lot of guys I've played with have told me they've enjoyed the style of play I bring, but the fans tend to focus on the final stats. If you hit .300, conventional wisdom says you've had a good year. But that's not necessarily so. I've seen so many players hit .300 who were awful. It was a meaningless .300 because they put themselves first and not the team.

If you're not a player who's willing to give himself up and move the runner over, what's the point of playing? For me, nothing is more important than earning my teammates' praise.

When I retire, what I want most out of this game is for teammates to call me up wanting to get together and do things. I've always wanted to be the go-to guy. My friends know if they need tickets to a concert, I can get them. If they want to go on a fishing trip, I can arrange it. If they need a plane to see their family, I can hook them up. If they need a house to stay in, they can stay with me. If they need money, my wallet's open. That's what I'm about. Everything I've made in this game is great, but what's most important is for me to keep the respect of the brethren I've gone to war with.

The hell with stats. I want to be able to sit with my old ballplayer buddies, and play poker and reminisce about how great it was to wear a major league uniform and be a ballplayer.

Chapter 15

The Playoffs—One Year Later

OCTOBER 2004

The matchups for the first round of the 2004 American League playoffs pitted the Yankees against the Minnesota Twins, and the Red Sox playing against the Anaheim Angels. Going into the series, I felt the Angels might be the best team. Their offense started with David Eckstein, the smallest of players, a guy with no huge talent but all heart who will beat you in any way possible. It's thrilling for me to see that kind of player, the little guy who always gets the shaft but who works his way to stardom.

Eckstein had started out with the Red Sox, but in 2002 he led the Angels in winning the World Series.

The first two games were played in Anaheim, an amazing town where the weather is perfect every day. Before the first game, Dave Roberts set it up so my fiancée and I, Gabe, Kevin, and Trot could come into Quicksilver, the clothing store, shop and pick out whatever we wanted. I picked surfboard shorts, T-shirts, and pants, and I also got my kids clothes and bathing suits, just some very cool stuff. Quicksilver didn't want anything in exchange. I guess they just liked having ballplayers around. It was a very generous gesture.

That night I went to dinner with Mike O'Malley, the star of *Yes, Dear*. He's a big Red Sox fan. Earlier that year he had been sitting right behind our dugout at Fenway, and after a thrilling win, I grabbed him and brought him down into our clubhouse. He thought that was the coolest thing. Actors and rock stars had always shown me special treatment, so I decided to return the favor. He was beside himself.

All I was looking for was "Thanks," but as a token of his appreciation, Mike sent me two Harley jackets. It's incredible how people love the Red Sox. Anyway, I can truthfully say I loved his show even before I met him and was the recipient of his generosity. I would do anything for this guy.

Curt Schilling pitched the opener and made it look easy. Why not? He hadn't lost a playoff game since 1993! Theo had gotten Curt to take us to a world championship. Who was to say he couldn't?

"We're not the cowboys anymore," I announced after the game. "This year we're the idiots." Once again I explained that our approach was just to go out and have fun, and I ventured my opinion that this was the reason we were so popular with the fans.

When Bob Hohler of the *Boston Globe* asked Angels manager Mike Scioscia about our being idiots, Scioscia said, "If they are, they're idiots who can play ball."

Terry Francona didn't think we were idiots, either. Instead, he referred to us as "idiot savants."

I knew better. We'd be "idiots" to the end.

Bartolo Colon was the Angels pitcher in the second playoff game. Bartolo was a big, robust guy, but that didn't matter. Maybe his gut gave him more balance. Pedro came into the game with a 117–37 record as a Red Sox, which doesn't seem possible, but he'd been hit hard the last few times out, and the press was on his butt, talking about whether he was washed up. Only in Boston! Pedro went out and kept us close, and we didn't score until Tek hit a two-run home run in the sixth. Then in the seventh, I grounded into a fielder's choice, a play I should have been out on. But I outhustled the throw, and it helped us win the game.

I stole second, and scored the go-ahead run on a sacrifice fly. That's what I mean about statistics. I got up and made an out, but I ended up scoring the winning run, and as far as I was concerned, nothing else mattered. When we scored four in the ninth, it was all over.

We'd felt more pressure before the playoff series against the Angels than ever before. We were now up two games to none, but as I said, we couldn't relax, because we knew if the Angels won just one game, they possessed the talent to sweep us. If they took one game from us, we felt we were done. We knew the Angels had a lot of weapons, that their pitchers could be lights out. The stress was almost unbearable.

I own a 47-foot boat that is docked over in the Boston Harbor. It's the best party boat in Boston, and during the 2004 season I went out on it at least twice a week. Whenever we had a day off, I tried to get a couple of players to come out with me, and we stayed out for eight or nine hours. Kevin Millar normally went, and Kevin Youkilis and Doug Mientkiewicz, who is a big fisherman. My Puma rep, Arden Czyzewski, went too. Arden is one of the main reasons why my life is so enjoyable in Boston. He has a no-care attitude, like I do, and we grab our girls and take them out. We have the Jet Skis ready and jump in the wake, and it's thrilling to cruise behind the boat and jump 30 feet.

We returned to Boston after the first two playoff games. The day of Game 3 against the Angels, I took the boat out. It was low tide and my anchor didn't catch, so we ran aground. We didn't panic. We weren't worried. We just sat back and drank beer. When I take the boat out, we draw a crowd, and an armada of boats came over asking if I wanted some help. I told everyone we'd be fine, that we'd wait for the tide to rise. It's crazy how when it comes to Red Sox players, word spreads so fast in Boston. My grounding even made the papers.

That night at Fenway it looked like Bronson Arroyo would

pitch us to a Division Series title, then the roof caved in. He was ahead 6–1 in the seventh when Anaheim tied it up. Vladimir Guerrero—when I see him, I see Roberto Clemente—decided to come and play. He stands about six five, and he's massive. The thing about Vladimir is that he's all around. There aren't that many all-around players. There are Barry Bonds, Ken Griffey Jr., ARod, and Nomar, though Nomar has stopped running. No one is as all around as Barry Bonds, but Vladimir certainly belongs in this group.

We didn't quit just because the Angels tied it up. Our pitchers didn't allow them to go ahead. With the score tied, Keith Foulke pitched the ninth. The Angels had runners on first and third and two outs, and again coming through in the clutch, he got Chone Figgins, a small guy who can drive the ball, one of those pesky players you just can't figure out, to ground out to shortstop. The game continued.

Derek Lowe, who always seemed to be the odd man out, was given a long-relief role for the playoffs. Why was he given the shaft? Who knows, though I have to admit that Schilling, Pedro, and Bronson had been pretty awesome. So after Terry used Foulke, he brought in DeLo to pitch the tenth, and he, too, did his job.

Derek fit in perfectly with us idiots. He knew the job at hand, knew how important it was. He knew he was going to come in and use his talent and not think too much. That's why when he came into a tight game, he could relax out there on the mound.

In this situation Derek allowed runners to reach first and third, but with two outs got out of it. Then in our half of the inning Pokey Reese, a pinch runner for Mark Bellhorn, was on second with two outs and David Ortiz up. The Angels pitcher was star reliever Francisco Rodriguez, who was so good he was known as KRod. Mike Scioscia, the Angels' manager, was sure Rodriguez had nothing left after pitching 2⅔ innings, and he brought in Jarrod Washburn, a lefty, to pitch to the left-handed Ortiz.

Considering everything David Ortiz has done for us, I really can't believe that 2004 was David's first full season. The guy seems to be locked in all the time, because he goes out and works. He hits soft-toss before batting practice. He makes sure he gets in his tee drills. He works very hard for everything he gets. You have to respect that. He knows his body, what he needs to do. I still thank the Twins every day for letting us have our chance to get him.

In 2004 David hit .301, clubbed 41 home runs, and drove in 139 runs. And to think the only reason he got to play every day was because the year before Jeremy Giambi had gotten injured.

Ortiz stood in against Washburn, who threw him one pitch. David hit the ball the other way to left, over the Monster, winning the game and clinching the series.

The crowd went wild, and we celebrated again. Again because you don't know if this is going to be your last celebration, your last time in the playoffs.

We celebrated for some time, and after the game we went to a concert given by my friends the group Alterbridge. They actually waited for the ball game to end to start their show. When I arrived, I took the stage and sang four songs, even though I'm not very good. I can carry a tune, though I'm better with some tunes than with others. I like to think I did well. I sang the song "Open Your Eyes." If you go to the Alterbridge.com Web site, you can see a picture of me singing with the group after Game 3 of the Angels series.

We had to wait a day to find out whether we'd play Minnesota or the Yankees. I was actually rooting for the Twins, just because I hated all the hype that went with playing New York. We knew how tough the championship series was going to be. The thing about the Twins, though, is that we never play well in the Metrodome. That kind of scared me. A lot of guys didn't care who we played. We just didn't want the Yankees—we didn't think they were better than we were, we just wanted the series to be media free.

We were back in Boston hanging loose on my boat when the Yankees beat the Twins 6–5 in the final game. We didn't even have a workout that day. We took the day off to get ourselves together.

The next day we traveled to Yankee Stadium for media day. The reporters didn't bother us at home because they knew we'd be a captive audience when we got to the Stadium. When we arrived at the big ballpark in the Bronx, it was a zoo. Tons of people were there, far more than had been in Anaheim.

We worked out that day, and after I decided I'd done enough shagging during batting practice, for the first time in my 10 years in the big leagues, I walked out to Monument Park in center field in Yankee Stadium and chatted up the groundskeeper. We talked about how amazing the place was, how so many great players had walked through here.

"This rivalry is the best," he said. "I have to root for the Yankees, but I enjoy this series. It's what baseball is all about."

"Yes," I agreed. "You're absolutely right."

I decided to go out and get closer to the monuments and pay my respects to the legends of the past. That's something every ballplayer ought to do.

I found the Babe, and I went to visit with Mickey Mantle. I had always heard great things about the Mick, how he took care of his teammates, how he was all about heart. His teammates respected him so much. It was humbling to stand out there where he was being honored.

I stood beside the Babe.

This year, I thought, *you're going to be sorry the Red Sox traded you.*

Chapter 16

As Far Down as Possible

OCTOBER 2004

As a team, we were as prepared for Game 1 of the American League Championship Series as we were for any game during the 2004 season. The only question mark was the state of Curt Schilling's ankle. I knew that Curt had been in pain for most of the year. As the season continued, he started walking more with a noticeable limp. He wore an ankle brace, and when he was at home he used a crutch to help him move around. Some of the guys feared he might not even be able to pitch.

He did, but he wasn't sharp, and when Mike Mussina pitched a perfect game going into the seventh, the Yankees took an 8–0 lead.

After he departed, Curt was disgusted. He felt he'd let the Red Sox down. He knew he hadn't been sharp, didn't have anything, and he thought he'd set the tone for the whole series.

We didn't think twice about the hole we were in. We actually thought Curt's stuff had been okay. The Yankees had come out smoking the ball, but we had no intention of laying down.

"Okay, big deal," we said to each other. "Let's try to score some runs."

Our bats then got us right back into it as we scored four runs, courtesy of Bellhorn, Ortiz, Kevin, and Trot. The barrage combined to finish off Mussina.

The relief pitcher the Yankees brought in was Tanyon Sturtze. The scouting report on him said he threw a fastball between 88 and 91, and a sinker. But every time he faced us, he threw 94, 95, even 96, and he did it consistently. We thought, *Who's doing these scouting reports? What's going on? This guy is jacked up playing against us.*

Jason Varitek hit a long home run off Sturtze to make it 8–5. Tek hadn't hit much at Yankee Stadium all year, and of course, the reporters had been happy to let him know how horrible he hit there. When David Ortiz connected with a shot, it made the score 8–7. How things can change in a hurry with our team! Unfortunately, at this point in this game I'd struck out three times. I was shaking my head, thinking, *What's going on here?*

The Yankees scored two more runs off Mike Timlin to make it 10–7, and Mariano Rivera came in and finished us off. Once again, Mariano added to his saves record.

Despite the loss, we felt the momentum had shifted to our side, because after getting blown out, getting beat down, we'd come back strong.

"They got us," I said the next day, "but today we'll get them. They were lucky some of us didn't hit—mostly me." I'd struck out four times, and it's hard to win when your leadoff hitter goes 0 for 4.

Jon Lieber pitched against us in the second game. Lieber had been drafted by Kansas City the same year I had. That year the Royals had 5 of the first 42 picks. Michael Tucker was number 10, Jim Pittsley was number 17, Sherrard Clinkescale was number 31, I was number 35, and Jon Lieber was number 42. Kansas City could have kept us all, and they would have been pretty good, but the next year they traded Lieber away along with my high school buddy Danny

Miceli, for Stan Belinda. Hal McRae wanted Belinda, predicting he'd lead the Royals into the World Series. I can't tell you where Belinda took them but it certainly wasn't to the World Series.

Lieber is a sinkerball pitcher. He knows how to work. He hits the outside corner, and then he expands and expands the strike zone. Players love to see him pitch on getaway days because he works fast. When you're hitting against him, the biggest thing is to try and slow him down.

Pedro started for us. After the national anthem, Pedro walked in from the bullpen as the Yankee Stadium fans all shouted, "Who's your daddy?"

Pedro opened the game by walking Derek Jeter on four pitches, then hit ARod and allowed a single by Gary Sheffield to put the Yankees ahead 1–0. That Jeter is something. He always gets things going.

It was all Pedro allowed for the next five innings. He only allowed three hits, striking out six batters. He shut up the Yankee fans, but good. Unfortunately, we weren't able to do much with Lieber. In six innings he allowed one crummy single.

Our best offensive moment in Game 2 came in the sixth inning when I had a 16-pitch at-bat. I fouled off 10 pitches, but then I lined out. I was hoping I'd tired Lieber enough for Torre to take him out of the game.

Pedro made just one mistake, a pitch to John Olerud, who hit it into the right field stands for a two-run home run. Pedro didn't make a bad pitch. It was a fastball, middle and up, and Olerud turned on it. I was surprised when he hit it out. It got out in a hurry.

Pedro's nightmare became a reality, and once again he heard "Who's your daddy?" from the crazed Yankee fans.

Pedro kept his composure and took it all in stride. It wasn't his fault we'd lost. He'd allowed three hits. We didn't do anything against Lieber, who was pretty awesome pitching that night. But for Boston, Pedro was the center of the sports world, and if we lost when he was pitching, it had to be his fault.

After the game he put it all in perspective.

"Everybody's eyes were on me," he said. "Fifteen years ago I was standing under a mango tree. Today I'm the biggest thing on the planet."

We were down two games to none, and it was time to go back to Boston. Making it even more difficult emotionally was the thought that we'd have to go through the rest of the Yankee series without Curt Schilling. But then again, we hadn't even been sure he'd get to pitch in that first game. We held out hope that he could pitch in just one more game if we needed him.

What we really needed to do was hit as a team again. We needed to step up. We needed to turn the thing around. When you're down two games to none, it's pretty tough to come back, especially against the Yankees.

We went to Fenway Park on Saturday to play Game 3, but it started to pour just before game time, and the game was postponed until the next day.

During the 2004 season Michelle and I lived on the thirty-fourth floor of the Ritz-Carlton Hotel in a condo, and one of the crazy things we loved to do every so often was launch water balloons off our terrace. We never tried to hit people. We picked targets, like a big sign or a streetlight. No one ever got hurt. A couple times security came up to reprimand us, but Michelle, always witty and charming, would say, "How do you know it's *us* throwing the water balloons?"

"We saw you."

"It couldn't be me," she'd say. "I was too busy having sex with my fiancé for the last half hour."

Or if we had friends over, she'd turn around and start blaming them. She didn't fool anyone. Everyone knew it was her causing the trouble.

Anyway, after we lost these first two playoff games to the Yankees, we dropped a pumpkin off the balcony to see what would happen.

It started like this: after we got word of the rainout, we decided to go visit friends of ours who live a little north of us. We saw there was a pumpkin patch next door to their house. There were eight of us, and we decided to walk over and steal us each a pumpkin. Drinking might have been involved. Michelle grabbed the biggest pumpkin she could find and began running back to the house. I grabbed a flowerpot full of mums and started running. I blew right past her because her pumpkin weighed about 25 pounds. We were acting so silly, but it was a nice break from the pressure of the Yankee series.

I'd been the only one who didn't take a pumpkin, so the others made me go back and get one. I grabbed a very tiny one. When Michelle and I returned to our condo at the Ritz-Carlton, I decided to throw that pumpkin off the balcony to change our luck. I don't encourage people to steal pumpkins, or to throw them off tall buildings, but that's the kind of cra-zee thing that keeps you loose. We'd been under so much stress during the course of the season, and we were down two games to none. You have to be able to get your mind off the baseball field when you can.

I let that baby go, and I could see it drop all the way down to the ground, before it smashed into a million pieces. I was sure our luck had changed.

During the playoffs, I was suffering from migraine headaches the likes of which I hadn't experienced since my collision with Damian Jackson a year earlier. If it hadn't been for my chiropractor, Dr. Richard Green, I'm not sure I could have played. Not that it mattered. The next day we lost to the Yankees 19–8.

Bronson Arroyo started Game 3 for the Sox, and he gave up six runs in two-plus innings. We were tough. We came back. We tied it up. But then the Yankees scored seven, and we couldn't come back a second time. Then they exploded for five more, and the rout was on. There are only so many times you can come back. Those guys were hitting *everything*. Matsui had two home runs. ARod had a home run. Sheffield hit a home run. There I was standing in center field, watching the Yankees performing a Chinese fire drill as they continuously circled the bases and won in a rout. By the seventh inning, we were getting blown out so badly, I was hoping we could rest a couple guys and let Pokey Reese get his feet wet. Maybe get Dave Roberts an at-bat to keep him fresh.

By the eighth inning, the Fenway stands were half empty. The fans had booed so loudly they'd tired themselves out and left.

Now we were down three games to none against the Yankees. I knew we had to do something impossible. We talked it over.

"I don't know if the Yankees have lost four games in a row over the last ten years," someone said. "That just doesn't happen with the Yankees."

Curt Schilling walked around patting guys on the back.

"Hey, let's go," he said. "Tomorrow's a new day." So we walked around saying, "Tomorrow's a new day. There's not going to be any quit on this team. But just in case, let's start packing our bags."

We refused to admit defeat.

"Hey, the only way to do this is to rewrite history," someone said. "We're the team that can do it. We have nothing to lose now. We're supposed to lose now."

Remember the curse? It's all I'd heard about since the day I arrived in Boston three years earlier. We were *supposed* to lose. History said we couldn't come back from the depths.

I was sitting in the food room with Dave Roberts, who'd become one of my better friends on the team.

"We can do this," we said to each other.

We went back to our homes in a state of shock. I was feeling particularly stressed. In the three games, I was 1 for 13. Things weren't looking too good.

We began packing our bags, hoping to get some good mojo going, because when you don't pack, you get clobbered. So before Game 4, a bunch of us started packing to go home in the hopes we wouldn't.

Nobody wanted the season to end. I didn't want to start my wedding plans. I was scheduled to move homes when I got back to Orlando, and I didn't want to start doing that as yet. Guys didn't want to start hanging out with their wives quite yet. They didn't want to have to start the carpool or begin taking their kids to school. A bunch of us arrived for Game 4 saying, "Hey, come in, let's do this. Let's help each other." When we got to the ballpark, we were very, very relaxed.

Terry Francona wasn't quite so relaxed. We were down three to zip, and nothing he'd tried had worked. He was trying to figure out what to do, thinking he wouldn't have Schilling the rest of the way. Before Game 4, Terry said to the pitchers, "Everybody's in, so be ready." He knew he was going to have to use all the guys he had left.

One thing we all noticed before Game 4 was how angry and frustrated the media seemed to be. The reporters had been thinking, "This is the year," then all of a sudden we were disgracing the city by getting clobbered.

"How much longer can New Englanders take it?" Dan Shaughnessy asked. He added, "For the 86th consecutive autumn, the Red Sox are not going to win the World Series."

"Who among us needed this?" asked Bob Ryan.

The fans all have their dreams, and there wasn't one happy person in all of Boston. They wouldn't have been all that upset had we lost, but it was the way we were losing—the Yankees had scored 19 runs against us at home, for heaven sake.

Mark Bellhorn and I were taking a lot of the heat. Even though our pitchers had given up 19 runs, I stood before the reporters and took the blame.

"I'm the reason we're down three to nothing," I said. "Blame me. There's no one else to blame." I really felt that because I hadn't hit, it was my fault. But I also knew that by taking the blame, I'd take the pressure off the other guys.

Before Game 4 we also read the things the Yankees had said about us after the 19–8 loss. Gary Sheffield called us a "walking disaster." Mariano Rivera said we were done.

When I was asked about Sheffield's quote, I told them, "We're not walking disasters. We're *total* disasters."

But we were really pissed off by the Yankees' arrogance. Remember, you don't ever want to wake up a sleeping giant, and they'd crossed the line. On game day we discussed the Yankees' lack of class, saying, "They're not going to beat us. We're going to come back and rewrite history. We'll be the first team to come back from three and oh."

We wondered why the Yankees would make those comments. We had our backs against the wall. All they had to do was go out there and play. But they didn't. They lit a fire in us and under us. That fire was burning bright but we knew we needed to get our big bats going to start rewriting the history books.

Right before the start of Game 4 I called my teammates together in the clubhouse.

"Hey," I said, "this could be the last game a bunch of us play together. Let's not make it our last. Let's put it all together. We're not supposed to win. I haven't hit. I've let us down so far, but guess what, I'm going to keep going strong. We need everybody to pitch in. There's no pressure on us. All the pressure's on them. Let's not make this our last game together. Let's serve our Red Sox Nation proud. If we go out, we go out with a fight." I thought I'd end it on an up note.

"And just in case," I said, "start packing your bags."

Chapter 17

Miracle of the Century

OCTOBER 2004

Game 4 of the American League Championship Series began on October 17, 2004, and ended on October 18. The game started out as a pitcher's battle between Derek Lowe and Orlando Hernandez, who'd been reacquired from Montreal only to win eight games in a row and single-handedly save the Yankees' season. Hernandez—El Duque as he is called—pitched on the right days, because every time he pitched, the Yankees scored runs by the bucket-load. He also knew how to pitch. He's one of those 50-year-old Cuban pitchers with all the funky motions and all the funny pitches and different speeds, but he knows what to do. And he's got a lot of heart. If he doesn't have his good stuff, he starts innovating.

Our pitcher, Derek Lowe, began the game with the top five batters in the Yankee order having a .350 batting average against him. And in the third inning, Alex Rodriguez hit a long, two-run home run. At this point every sports fan in America figured we were done, and for good reason.

Then in the fifth inning we scored three runs. I scored one of those runs on a two-run double by David Ortiz. Of course, the next inning the Yankees came back against Mike Timlin and scored two runs to take back the lead. The fans who were booing him so loudly that night didn't know it, but Timlin had broken in as a rookie with the Blue Jays and won a World Series. The guy, who is getting up there in age, is a battler. He goes out there and gives his all every time. Mike never complains about how sore his arm is. He wants to pitch. He never knows when it's going to be his last time.

Down 4 to 3, Terry Francona made the wisest move he made in the whole series: he brought in Keith Foulke to pitch the seventh. Foulke was the reason *we* were in the championship series rather than the Oakland A's. We hadn't had a closer the year before, and Keith really liked it in Oakland and wanted to stay. But he went through the same thing I went through in Oakland. They couldn't afford to keep him, and they decided to go cheap. And when the A's blew a lot of games early, they fell too far behind to catch up. Of course, Oakland then went and traded for Octavio Dotel, but it was too late.

As I've said, to win it all, you need a closer who doesn't give a shit. If he blows a game, he's got to want the ball the next night. And he's got to be able to clear his mind, especially in the toughest situations. And in this game, Keith Foulke was stepping into a no-win situation. We were losing, but he still had to give us good innings for us to have a chance.

He shut them down, but we didn't score either, so when we batted in the bottom of the ninth, we were losing 4–3 with Mariano Rivera on the mound for the Yankees. A run down, we were three outs away from elimination.

Mariano then did a very un-Mariano thing when he walked Kevin Millar on four straight pitches that weren't even close.

Walks are what kills a team. It's a lot tougher for a team to get three singles in an inning. Three hits in one inning is *tough* to get. When the pitcher walks a batter, now you only need two hits, and that's so much easier. Look at us and the Yankees—we were the two teams that consistently drew the most walks, and we scored the most runs in the league. Our teams score a lot of runs each year by design. We were veteran teams, and veterans find a way. We take our walks. We extend the innings. That's what losing teams *don't* do.

It's a good thing Kevin Millar is slow, because it was a perfect opportunity for Terry to pinch run Dave Roberts for him. I might be faster from home to home or home to third, but Dave's a lot smaller than I am, a lot quicker. It takes a while for my big ass to get going nowadays. This was the perfect situation for Dave.

The Yankees knew he was going, but they just didn't know when. Billy Mueller was up. We remembered that Billy Mueller had hit a walk-off home run off Mariano earlier in the year, and we were hoping he could do it again. We also knew there was no one out and that we had three shots at a home run to tie it.

On the very first pitch, Roberts, who wasn't scared of anything and who knew he had to do something, took off and stole second. He made it look easy.

So now Roberts was on second with nobody out. All we wanted Billy to do was hit the ball to the right side and move Dave over to third to give us a better chance to score. Billy, as clutch as he is and as professional as he always is, did us one better. He singled to center, not only getting Roberts over, but getting himself on first, which was a huge relief to our fans, because we'd tied up the game and still hadn't made any outs.

Terry sent Doug Mientkiewicz to pinch hit for Mark Bellhorn, and he had Doug bunt Billy over to second. Doug had played for the Twins, where they play a lot of small ball. He did what he had to do. He got Billy over. We had two more tries to score the winning run— which we did not do.

I got up and hit a slow roller that Yankee first baseman Tony Clark couldn't handle. Mariano got a second out, and with runners on the corners, Orlando Cabrera came up. This time Rivera reverted to form. He struck Cabrera out. The game went into extra innings.

We brought in relievers Alan Embree and Curtis Leskanic, and the fans weren't happy about that. But nobody coming out of the pen was getting cheered because of what had happened the night before. I know the Boston fans were praying to God we could somehow hold them. On the bench we were saying the same prayer.

Embree and Leskanic were lights out. Those guys are the reason we ended up the way we did. For a pitching staff as beat up as they were to come in and shut them down like they did . . . They held the mighty Yankees through the twelfth inning.

We batted in the bottom of the twelfth. The Yankees were down to Paul Quantrill, who'd pitched about 100 innings. Every year Quantrill is up at the top in games pitched. He's a warrior who wants the ball. But when you pitch that much, by the end of the season your arm wears down. Joe Torre could have used someone else, but he wanted the rest of the staff rested if there were other games. He wasn't worried. He was thinking he was going to win, whether it was this night or the next. He already had used Mariano and Gordon in the game. Who else was he going to use? It was only Game 4, and he had a three games to nothing lead. He was not going to go to his starters, not yet.

Torre knew what he was doing. He had to be conservative. So Quantrill was his only choice.

The funny thing about this game: people kept saying, "Oh man, I stayed up so late. I'm worn out watching." Tell me about it. I was there.

As we went to bat in the twelfth, Mark Bellhorn and I were back in the clubhouse grabbing a banana. It was a quarter after one in the morning, and we needed some energy to keep going. We started to walk back down the corridor to the dugout, and I could see on the TV that Manny was on first. We stopped to watch Ortiz bat, and when he hit the ball out of the park, we sprinted down the concrete corridor and we ran out onto the field—about 10 seconds after everyone else, but in time to greet him at home plate.

As David crossed the plate, the joy in Boston was as incredible as anything I'd ever experienced. I felt so good for David. Here was a guy let go by his old team because they didn't want him at first base and didn't think he'd hit well enough to DH. We picked him up, and after we got him, no one worked harder. Every day he and Manny went down to the cages to hit with Ino Guerrero, a coach who is paid to throw batting practice for us whenever we want it. He's also from the Dominican, and he studied them and worked on their fundamentals. They had a routine that they began in spring training and maintained all year long. And boy, did it pay off!

We mobbed Ortiz, but we were still down three games to one. So we knew to go home and pack our bags for good luck. People now were beginning to think we had a chance, because Pedro was pitching the next game, and maybe Schilling would pitch Game 6.

Remember I said we were afraid if the Angels won one game, we'd be in trouble. Now we had won our first game, and we felt the Yankees were in trouble.

We were back at the ballpark before we knew it. Game 4 had ended at 1:30 in the morning, and after the game I did go home and pack, which took a good hour, and then I went to sleep. Game 5 was scheduled at 5 p.m. It was as though we'd never left.

Before the fifth game, every player had to pack, only we didn't know what we were packing for. If we won Game 5, we had to go to New York. If we lost Game 5, we had to go home. Our wives and fiancées were more distressed than we were because they had even less control than we did. All we could say was, "We don't know, either. If we win, we're going to New York. If we lose, we come back here, finish packing, and then we're rolling out in the morning."

We'd thought Game 4 was long and tiring, but we reached a new threshold of exhaustion in the next game, which went 14 innings.

Pedro wasn't as sharp as usual, and in the sixth with the bases loaded he gave up a double to Derek Jeter to give the Yankees a 4–2 lead. The hit was a little flare, but it really didn't matter how he'd done it. Jeter doesn't have the most hits in playoff history for nothing. He's Mr. October. He comes up big. Maybe you take ARod over a 162-game schedule, but in one game I'd go with Jeter any time.

Tom Gordon pitched for the Yankees in the eighth, and that man Ortiz got up and hit another home run. David was on fire. He was a driven man, picking up a lot of guys. He was the guy who kept us going.

On the bench he was a cheerleader, coming up to guys and saying, "Hey, let's go. Let's go." He was anxious and couldn't wait to get up to bat. He wanted the spotlight on him. He knew this was a big series, knew what we'd gone through the year before. He knew he could carry us through, though. He swung a powerful stick, but he also had hard work and heart behind him.

He's a big guy, all right. But when you meet him, he's lovable, joyful, cheery, a great guy to have around. The Twins missed that. A.J. Pierzynski, a good friend of mine who caught for them, told me, "When Ortiz left, a lot of heart left the Twins." It was his everyday shouting and horseplay in the clubhouse that was missed after he wasn't around.

After Ortiz's homer closed the gap to 4–3, Gordon walked Kevin Millar, just one more time when Millar got on base in a crucial situation. Kevin took a lot of abuse during the season when he wasn't producing, but he kept swinging the bat, kept taking his walks, and he ended up with a decent on-base percentage. As I've said, the problem Kevin faced was that he was losing playing time to Doug, and Kevin wanted to be a big part of what we were doing. I thought Kevin did a great job for us.

And once again, Terry sent Dave Roberts in to run for him. Trot Nixon was the next batter. Gordon knew Dave was going to steal. He kept throwing over to first to hold him on, but we all knew that Gordon would have to throw home eventually, and when he did, Trot singled to center, sending Roberts around to third. Not a lot of runners are as good at going from first to third as Roberts. I don't know if Millar could have made it.

At this point Joe Torre took Gordon out and brought in Mariano Rivera. With Roberts on third, and Jason Varitek up, Torre was looking for a strikeout. But Tek hit a long fly ball to center, and Roberts scored, tying the game.

Like Game 4, this game also went into extra innings. I should have won it for us in the eleventh. We had runners on first and second with no one out. Paul Quantrill was in again, a sinkerball pitcher. I was up with orders to bunt the runners over, setting things up for Cabrera, Manny, and Ortiz, and I was confident and relaxed with what I had to do.

I offered at the first pitch and popped out to the catcher.

I just shook my head, because nothing had gone right for me in this series. I once was a guy who put down 30 bunts in a season. In 2004, I attempted to bunt exactly 3 times, and I popped out three times, the last in this crucial situation.

I started hearing the boos, and rightly so. I felt as small as dirt. I really thought I'd batted myself off the team.

If we lose this game, I thought to myself, *I'm not going to be back in a Red Sox uniform. No way.*

You can do so much during the season, but the post-season is what matters. We still had runners on first and second with one out, and I was praying that Orlando Cabrera would do something to pick me up.

He grounded into a double play. Now I felt even worse.

I went out into the field, expecting to really hear it from the Fenway fans. But we have some really great fans out there in center field.

"Johnny, we're all right," they said. "Just get the job done the next time."

"Come on, let's go, John. The game's not over. Make something happen."

They were very supportive. I was shocked. I didn't hear one nasty comment, which is the way it used to be in Boston. I was pumped. They were rooting us on.

We almost lost it in the thirteenth. Ordinarily Doug Mirabelli catches Tim Wakefield, because Jason Varitek has such a tough time with Wake's knuckler, but Terry wanted Tek's bat in the lineup and left him in there. Tek gave us a few scary moments. He allowed three passed balls. He let Hideki Matsui go to second and then to third from first, and he let Gary Sheffield get on after missing strike three.

As I stood in center field, I was feeling bad enough about not getting that bunt down, and I didn't want to lose the game on all those passed balls. I was trying to think like Terry. "Do you pull your catcher out of the game because he can't catch the knuckleball?" We were very scared for Tek—and for us.

One more passed ball, and we would have lost, but Wakefield struck out Ruben Sierra and Tek somehow held onto it, and the threat passed. When Varitek came in, he looked like a deer in the headlights.

"I can't believe how much those balls are moving," he said to me. "They're doing the loop de loop."

Wakefield's knuckler was working so good that night, Tek said he was surprised he caught that last strike to Sierra.

In the fourteenth inning the Yankees brought in Esteban Loaiza. He's another guy who throws a lot of innings and seems to run out of steam late in the season. A couple years ago he was the best pitcher in the league pitching for the White Sox, and then the Yankees traded Jose Contreras for him. Contreras throws a 94-mile-an-hour splitter and we were happy the Yankees traded Contreras away, because we thought he had the best stuff on the Yankee staff.

That was another reason we thought we had a chance. Over the years, whenever the Red Sox made a personnel decision, it would turn out to be the wrong one. It would come back and haunt us–the curse. We'd pick up a talented player, and he'd have the worst month of his career, and then it would be too late for him to turn it around.

Now it was happening to the Yankees, and I felt something good was going to happen for us. I led off the inning. I didn't want to make another out and get booed again. At this point I was 2 for 24 with seven strikeouts in the ALCS.

I remained positive. I wasn't looking to walk. My goal was to hit a home run and send the Fenway crowd home happy. But Loaiza didn't throw me many close pitches, and I walked. Loaiza got the next batter, and then he walked Manny. You have to be very careful pitching to Manny. Loaiza was making tough pitches, but Manny had a great at-bat. He battled pitches. Loaiza was throwing the ball outside the strike zone, and the ball would drift back over the out-side part of the plate, but Manny kept spoiling them, fouling them off. On one pitch he was spoiling, Manny almost won the game with a hit down the right field line. And then he walked, and the guy who'd been carrying our team so far, David Ortiz, came up.

I was standing by second base, waiting. Meanwhile, Loaiza's ball was really moving. He'd throw the ball right over the middle of the plate, and then it would move, and Ortiz kept fouling them off. I knew what Ortiz was trying to do, to hit a home run and end the game. And with all that pressure, he kept fouling and battling.

Loaiza threw another pitch, and Ortiz hit it softly into center field. As soon as I saw the ball hit, I raced toward third, intending to score. In the back of my mind, I was thinking, *Please don't let me make another Derek Jeter highlight.* I wasn't sure how deep the ball was, but I knew if it was anywhere near Jeter, he was going to catch it.

Bernie Williams was playing center field, and I wasn't sure whether he was going to catch it, either. But I knew Bernie couldn't play shallow because of Ortiz's power. As I rounded third, my prayer was aimed at Jeter. *Please don't let Jeter pull off another miracle play!*

I put my head down and hauled ass home. I didn't even have to slide. But before I scored, I made sure I took my batting helmet off, because if you leave it on and score, the guys slap you hard on the head.

Earlier in the season I scored a game-winning run and left my helmet on, and Gabe Kapler came over and head-slapped me hard. I'd had that concussion the year before, and it really hurt.

"Kapler, no more," I said. "I can't take it."

I decided the next time I scored a game-winning run, I'd make sure to take my helmet off to keep from getting smoked.

Now we were only down three games to two. We were in a posi-tion where we could joke with each other again.

"Guys, what are we doing?" I asked. "We could be driving home right now, but now we've got to go to New York."

In the clubhouse we were absolutely ecstatic, though our plans for Game 6 were up in the air because we didn't expect Curt

Schilling to pitch. And from what we heard, when he woke up the morning of the game, he was in such pain he wasn't expecting to pitch, either.

Before we arrived, Curt went to see Bill Morgan, who by now has become the most famous and most popular doctor in the country. I doubt Dr. Morgan will have to buy a meal in Boston ever again. Bill Morgan diagnosed what was causing Curt's pain, and he designed an operation that would allow him to pitch a couple more times. No one had ever tried the operation before, so Dr. Morgan first practiced on a couple of cadavers.

Curt wanted to pitch. He just didn't want to permanently damage his ankle and put his career on the line for a bunch of idiots. When Dr. Morgan assured him that the operation would give his ankle enough support that he'd be able to pitch without hurting himself worse, Curt decided to give it a shot. Not too many people would have done that. But Curt had come to Boston to be a part of history, to go down in folklore, to ride off in the sunset. Fans remembered Carlton Fisk's home run, the Dwight Evans catch in right field. Curt didn't know it, but he was about to add a treasured image to Red Sox Nation's scrapbook. Millions would remember him and his bloodied ankle for the rest of their lives.

Game 6 was played in Yankee Stadium, where the Yankee fans were still expecting to win, even though we'd just made a series of it again. In our clubhouse, we were elated that Curt Schilling would be taking the mound, and we knew without a doubt that we were going to win.

Jon Lieber, who was pitching against us, had been pretty darn good the last couple times he'd faced us. Lieber hadn't lost a game since August. But he was going on short rest, and most important, he was going while we had the momentum.

As Curt was retiring the Yankees in the first inning, I was standing out in center field saying to myself, *Let's try and score some runs early. Let's take the pressure off Curt.* We were tired of stressing. All the games had been pressure cookers, and it was great to watch as Curt retired the first eight batters he faced. He was mowing them down.

In the fourth inning we had two outs when Kevin Millar doubled to left, took third on a wild pitch, and scored on a single by Tek, who'd fouled off several pitches before connecting. Cabrera singled, and Mark Bellhorn, who'd been vilified all series long, hit a ball over the fence in left center field.

I was in the on deck circle. I could see clearly that the ball had gone over the fence, hit a fan in the gut, and dropped back onto the field. When the umpires made Mark stop at second, I threw my hands up in the air. I couldn't believe it. I went to Terry Francona and told him, "Hey, that ball was a home run." Before Terry went out and argued, Derek Lowe ran upstairs to watch the replay on television. He came back and told Terry, "You've got to argue it."

Terry went out and reported what Derek had seen. The umpires got together in a group, and they ruled it a home run. Normally, things like that don't get changed. Normally, the curse being the curse, those calls always go in the Yankees' favor. It was pretty amazing for us to watch the umpires reverse the call in our favor and get it right.

Bellhorn's three-run homer gave us a 4–0 lead.

Schilling pitched a four-hitter during the seven innings he pitched. One of those hits was a home run by Bernie Williams in the seventh. Curt then retired the next two batters and walked off the field. We were just ecstatic because of what he'd done for the team, but Schilling being Schilling, he started to fight with Francona even though his sock was covered in blood.

"Yeah, I'm good to go," he said. "Let me go back out there."

"No, I can't let you go back out there," Terry said. "What you did for us was amazing, and I'll always be grateful. Let the bullpen come in and get the job done."

Terry chose Bronson Arroyo to pitch the eighth. He'd gotten beat up the night before, but he was fresh. With his sharp slider going, he seemed to be the best choice.

Miguel Cairo led off the inning and doubled to start another Yankee rally. Then Derek Jeter singled him in to make the score 4–2. I was standing in the outfield thinking, *Son of a bitch, the curse is coming back to haunt us. The curse is about to bite us in the ass.* Keith Foulke got up and started to heat up, but he was going to need time.

Alex Rodriguez, the next batter, then made a play that will always make him a disgrace to Red Sox fans and other ballplayers. People couldn't believe he did what he did. He hit a slow roller to Bronson, who ran down the first base line to tag him. I was out in center field, and all of a sudden I saw the ball roll all the way down the right field line. I couldn't see what Alex had done. I had no clue, so I was wondering, *What's going on here? The ball shouldn't have done that. Did Babe Ruth grab the ball and throw it down the right field line?*

Jeter scored on the play, and Rodriguez was standing on second base. We were now up by only 4–3, with a runner on second and nobody out. And guess who was coming up? Gary Sheffield, Matsui, and Bernie Williams.

This is unimaginable, was what I was thinking. *We just might have lost our season right here.*

In all my years of playing the game, I'd never seen anything like that. *How did the ball get from Bronson's glove all the way to right field? Did I miss something?* Then I saw first baseman Doug Mientkiewicz going nuts. Jumping up and down, he went straight for the first base umpire.

While we watched the commotion, all three Red Sox outfielders—Manny, Gabe, and myself—gathered around second base. We were trying to figure out what had just happened. Orlando Cabrera came out and talked to us.

"That son of a bitch just slapped the ball out of Bronson's hand," he said. "You can't do that. What is he doing slapping at the ball like that? What was he thinking?"

Manny and I were both incredulous.

"What?" we said. "He slapped at the ball?" I couldn't believe it. I hadn't seen the play with my own eyes, but based on what I'd just been told, there was no way the umpires would let this pass, was there?

And what was great, the umpires—Randy Marsh and his crew—again got it right. They ruled that Rodriguez was out, and they made Jeter go back to first. At least we can look back and say,

"That didn't cost us the game." No player wants an asterisk next to a win, and I'm sure in hindsight A-Rod, having been informed of the rule, wouldn't have wanted a play like that to tip the balance. I know I wouldn't, if I were in his place.

You have to give a lot of credit to Randy Marsh and the other umpires. Randy Marsh is one of the best in the game. His crew got it right, which was great, and somehow we got out of the inning still leading 4–2. Sheffield and Matsui, who'd been so hot all season long, suddenly stopped hitting after Game 3. Who'd ever have thunk it?

Keith Foulke came in and pitched the ninth, and it would have been too easy for him to just come in and finish them off. Instead he walked Matsui and Ruben Sierra. With two outs, Tony Clark came to bat for the Yankees. I was scared, because of Tony Clark's home run potential. One swing, and we would have lost. He had the muscle to knock the Red Sox out of the season and send us home.

But Foulke threw him a tremendous change up, and he swung for strike three. The game was over, and the series was tied.

And again, an excitement washed over us that is hard to describe. We had that feeling that we were going to rewrite the history books. We also went back to the hotel and packed before the game to give us luck, continuing what we'd done since we were down three games to none.

After the game Kevin Millar, Jack Daniels, and I got together in the clubhouse with about a dozen of the other Red Sox players. We passed out paper cups and poured each guy a shot of Jack.

"Here's to changing history," Kevin said. "Let's not do what we did last year. Let's finish this thing off and go on to the World Series."

We were never so together as we were that night. We just knew that this year we weren't going to be denied. We also knew the Yankees were feeling the pressure. They went from talking smack about the Red Sox—"They're a walking disaster"—to meeting us in Game 7, where it was anybody's ball game.

We had Derek Lowe going for us, and I was confident he was

the perfect pitcher for the job, because he was an idiot like me, just going out there, a guy who played for the love of playing, who didn't worry about anything but sticking to his game plan, throwing that sinker and getting guys out. I knew he'd be tired, and I knew he'd be sharp, because when he's tired, his sinker sinks even better.

When I stood in center field and watched his pitches, I could see he was on. That night he also threw a change up, which nobody could hit.

The Yankees started Kevin Brown, the hired gun who'd come to New York and worn out his welcome when he punched a wall, broke his hand, and had to miss several weeks late in the season. Kevin had had 20-game winning seasons. He starred for Texas, Florida, San Diego, and Los Angeles. The Yankees signed him to a shockingly huge contract so he could take them to another World Series win. Before the 2004 season he'd always gotten the job done. He goes about his business. He's a warrior who thinks he should win every game, who never gives up.

Unfortunately for Brownie, this wasn't his day. It was mine. And I couldn't have picked a better game for it. When I went to bat in the first inning, I knew he was a sinkerball pitcher, and I knew if I got behind in the count, I'd be in trouble, because after throwing first-pitch strikes, the Yankee pitchers throw tough pitches that are hard to hit. They put them in perfect spots, and then I have to chase bad pitches. I chased *a lot* of bad pitches in the first six games. When you're behind in the count a lot, you have to. You have to defend the plate, you have to battle a little more.

Prior to Game 6, Ron Jackson, our hitting coach, came up to me and said, "Hey, John, let's get you in the cages." I'd always been a "see the ball, hit the ball" sort of guy, but I was struggling, and Ron, whom we call Papa Jack, wanted me to go back and work on my fundamentals. Papa Jack wanted to make sure I had my best game going. If I still didn't succeed, at least I could say, *I did the work. I did all I could.*

Ellis Burks, who was on the DL at the time, also encouraged me to do that.

"Let's get in there," he said. "Let's work hard, because you're going to be the difference-maker. You're going to be the man." Everyone knew I was hitting poorly in the series, and they were very supportive.

So before Games 6 and 7, I hit off the tee, and I took soft-toss, where a coach lobs the ball up in the strike zone, and you hit it, all the while working on your mechanics.

After the 19–8 debacle, we'd decided not to take batting practice anymore, because it was making us feel tired. Nothing was working. We felt we had nothing to lose.

We didn't take BP before Games 4 and 5, and it had rained in New York before Game 6, so we couldn't take it, and though we had a beautiful night before Game 7, again we decided to skip batting practice. We didn't want to change things. We didn't want our pitchers to go out and shag flies or even the position players to shag flies and get tired.

"Let's just show up and kick some butt," we said.

Before the game Adam Hyzdu, a young outfielder who'd just come up from Pawtucket, said to me, "You're made for this. You're made for Game 7—for reversing the curse."

Kevin Youkilis set up a dozen chairs for me to run over and knock down.

"Relax," Terry Francona told me, "have fun. This is your game."

"This is your game," our bench coach, Brad Mills, said. "Right now is your time," said pitching coach Dave Wallace. I was pretty amazed how all these guys still had faith in me. Two games before, I'd as much as traded myself off the team. The team pats you on the back and keeps you going.

I led off the game. Kevin Brown was throwing his sinker, and I was feeling good at the plate. I could tell that my work in the cages had helped. Brown threw me a sinker, and then he threw me another sinker, which I hit on a line past Jeter at short for a single.

As I stood on first base, I knew I needed to make something happen. I have the green light so whenever I want to steal, it's okay with Terry. I didn't think we'd score too many runs off Kevin Brown, so I figured we should play a little small ball. He doesn't have a particularly good move to first. He's herky jerky, and sometimes he can be slow to the plate. And sometimes he throws his splitter in the dirt.

I was able to steal second, and then Brown struck out Mark Bellhorn. Manny was up next, and he lined a ball that I thought Derek Jeter was going to catch. I had to freeze momentarily to make sure it got through, and when I rounded third Dale Sveum, our third base coach, waved me home. Yankee left fielder Hideki Matsui hustled for the ball, threw it to Jeter, and Jeter threw a pea home to beat me by a hair. In fact, I was sure I was safe. I thought I got my foot in, but you can't argue close calls.

I'd barely put my helmet down when the next batter, David Ortiz, shocked the world by hitting Brown's first pitch into the right field stands in Yankee Stadium for a 2–0 lead.

Derek Lowe, who pitched like an idiot—lights out great—had some breathing room. That home run was so huge. So was a fantastic inning by Derek.

We batted in the second inning against Brown. Kevin Millar singled, and then Brown, who didn't have it, walked Bill Mueller and Orlando Cabrera to load the bases. I was up next, and I guess Joe Torre didn't want Brown pitching against me. He yanked Brown out of the game and brought in Javier Vazquez, who was supposed to be the Yankees' savior but who'd stopped winning after the All Star game. I had a feeling Vazquez would try to get ahead of me, because then he could go to work on me, throwing his change up and changing speeds. I knew he was going to throw me a fastball, and I guessed that he figured I'd be leaning over the plate, looking for a fastball away. I was actually looking for a fastball in, and I was thinking if he threw it there, I'd hit it out of the park. *Come on, big fellow, pitch it in. Let me see it.*

Vazquez's first pitch was a fastball in. He didn't throw me a bad pitch. He actually jammed me. But from the hard work I had been doing in the cages, I was able to adjust, get my balance back, and when I swung, I was hoping I'd gotten enough of it for it to go out.

Thank goodness right field in Yankee Stadium is short! With one swing of the bat, I'd drive in four runs. The crowd fell silent. It was a different story in Boston, where the entire city and all of northern New England erupted into a joyful celebration that probably never will be duplicated. I was told that when I hit that ball out, it was as though an earthquake had struck the Boston area. And as the Red Sox fans went nuts, there were aftershocks for hours.

On the bench the team was going crazy. I remember as I ran around the bases deciding it wouldn't be right for me to smile, that I wasn't going to be happy until the game was over and this series was over.

I also knew that a six to nothing lead over the Yankees wasn't enough.

Those guys can score six runs with their eyes closed, I told myself. So the team was joyous, but I wasn't smiling. The players were so pumped up and happy for me. All of Boston was happy for me. It was just such a great, great feeling.

That home run is always going to be part of the history of Boston, the history of baseball. I started the season with long hair and a beard, and then after I hit that home run, for some fans I became God—or maybe I should say Jesus. It's hyperbole, obviously, but I'm telling you the feeling. It was just incredible. Thousands of Red Sox fans had been led to believe the Sox would never win the big game during their lifetimes. Well, here was proof that their lives were about to change.

While I was in the moment, even with the goose bumps I had, and as much as I wanted to shout out, I knew I couldn't be totally happy because the game wasn't over. It was only the second inning, and there was a long way to go.

In the bottom of the second, Derek hit Miguel Cairo with a pitch. That guy was a royal pain in our butt. We kept putting him on base all year. He was supposed to be a utility infielder, but for some reason, when he played against the Red Sox, he was a star. And after Cairo came up, we knew what was coming up after him: a very potent All Star lineup.

Derek Jeter singled, and drove him home to make it 6–1. Terry got Mike Myers and Curtis Leskanic up in the pen, but Lowe finished the inning just fine.

What was so huge for us was that the bats of Rodriguez and Sheffield remained silent. All year long Sheffield had been the guy who hit the ball often and hit it hard. But after the third Yankee game, he stopped hitting, thank goodness.

In the fourth Orlando Cabrera came up with Vazquez still on the mound. He had an eight-pitch at-bat, and again he walked. I was the next batter. After hitting a grand slam the at-bat before, I was feeling totally relaxed and comfortable. I figured he'd start me out with a fastball on the other side of the plate—outside—and that's what he did, and I drilled it into the upper deck in right field. And this time the Red Sox fans sitting in Yankee Stadium, quiet before for fear of arousing the anger of the Yankee fans, were feeling less timid, and as I rounded the bases I could hear the cheers. Before I touched home plate, I again took off my batting helmet to keep Gabe and the other guys from bashing me on the head. Also, it was a chance to show off my great hair.

"You are the man," the guys kept saying, "the best leadoff hitter we've ever seen." Dave Roberts, a leadoff hitter himself, couldn't stop singing my praises.

"You're not only the best leadoff hitter I've ever seen," he said, "you're the best player I ever saw. I can't believe the rest of the league doesn't realize how important you are or how huge you are." He was embarrassing me.

"All right," I said. "The game's not over yet." We were up 8 to 1, but I still refused to smile. We were playing the Yankees, and we had not—yet—overcome the curse.

But Derek Lowe that night was unhittable. He was throwing an absolutely incredible change up that looked like a slider. Whatever it was, the Yankees couldn't hit it.

Terry took Derek out after six, and in the seventh he brought in Pedro. I don't know why he did that. When Pedro came in, I felt the Yankee players were salivating. Pedro was a starter, and he hadn't had great success against the Yankees, and in the inning he pitched, the Yankees scored two runs and made the Red Sox fans very nervous. The Yankees were hitting cannon shots, but they were right at people. We felt lucky that they'd only climbed back to 8–3.

In the top of the eighth Mark Bellhorn hit a two-run home run off Tom Gordon, bringing the score to 10–3, and we were able to breathe a little bit more.

We weren't sure whether Terry was going to bring Pedro back to pitch the eighth. We were kinda hoping he wouldn't. The Yankees had perked up when he came in, because they'd wanted to shove it in Pedro's face so badly. Pedro versus the Yankees always added something extra to the atmosphere. The Yankee fans, having something to cheer about, got back into the game.

Terry decided to go back to his usual relievers, and he used Mike Timlin in the eighth and Alan Embree in the ninth. We had a big lead, they got them out no sweat, and we didn't need Keith Foulke.

To me, Mike Timlin could well have been our team's MVP. That's how we felt about him when he took the mound. We knew he'd throw strikes and was going to keep us in the game. We just thought the world of him.

Alan Embree got the final out, a ground out by Ruben Sierra. I was so happy for Alan. Some pitchers only get to be on SportsCenter when they give up home runs. Embree will always remember the feeling of being the pitcher who got the final out in our incredible four-in-a-row comeback win against the Yankees in the 2004 American League Championship Series.

We ended up in a pile on the mound at Yankee Stadium hearing a lot of cheers from our no-longer-intimidated fans. I like to think that even Yankee fans felt happy for us. Of course, they wanted to win, but they'd witnessed the biggest, most spectacular comeback in the history of the game. If there was a team to do it, it was us idiots. People liked us, even Yankee fans. They liked the energy, the free-spirited way we went about playing the game.

What I remember most after the final out was that Orlando

Cabrera bent down to pray, and when he came up he was wearing a pair of swimming goggles. You see, he knew he was about to get sprayed with champagne, and he didn't want any to get in his eyes. *Man, that is so dang creative,* I said to myself. *This is one of the best moves I have* ever *seen.*

After the final out, I allowed myself to smile. As I sat in front of my locker, answering questions from the media, I felt one overriding emotion: relief. Our team had played 162 regular season games, and every single one had been played as though it were the last game that was ever going to be played. And after we played the Angels in the three most important playoff games in Red Sox history, we then got down to the Yankees three games to none and faced being labeled the goats of Boston for all time. And as far as I was concerned, it was all my fault. I hadn't done squat, and I'd let my team and Red Sox Nation down.

But the fact was, we stuck together. I didn't quit, and we didn't quit. We stayed together as a team. All season long we had never relied on one guy. Every night it was somebody different, whether it was the big guns, Manny and David Ortiz, or Pokey Reese, Curtis Leskanic, or me. It was a total team effort. It even trickled down to the guys who were sitting on the bench rooting—guys like Kevin Youkilis and Adam Hyzdu.

We knew we'd just done something very special, and to hear the people in Yankee Stadium applauding us—well, the emotion was overwhelming. Of course, we were now going on to the World Series—the curse wasn't quite broken yet. We didn't know whether we were going home to face the Cardinals or the Astros, but the important thing was that we were going home to get ready to play in the World Series.

The celebration was memorable. The wives got to come into the clubhouse and celebrate with us. Meanwhile, we were being pulled every which way—the media just wanted us and wanted us, for good reason. You couldn't talk enough.

For most Red Sox fans, it really didn't matter whether we won the World Series. They'd rather we beat the Yankees than anyone in the National League anyway. Beating the Yankees was better than erasing any old curse, though we'd have the opportunity to do that as well. Red Sox Nation was euphoric. They'd just witnessed what felt to them like the greatest event in the history of the world. I thank my lucky stars I had the chance to be there and be part of it.

Chapter 18

The Curse Is Broken

I didn't watch much of the Cardinals-Astros game that decided the National League pennant, because Michelle and I, Kevin Millar, Mark Bellhorn, Dave Roberts, Kevin Youkilis, and a couple of the other Sox were at the Lucky Strike, a bowling alley right next to Fenway Park, for a Godsmack charity concert. The group performed in front of maybe 300 fans, and when it was time for them to play the song "I Stand Alone," Sully, Godsmack's lead singer, called Kevin Millar up on the stage to sing it, because whenever he came up to bat at Fenway, the PA announcer would play the song over the loudspeaker. For a white guy Kevin has pretty good rhythm and a pretty good beat, but Kevin being Kevin, he never took the time to listen to the words. So when they began to play, Kevin went, "Time out. Hold it. Can you get Johnny Damon to come up here and sing it with me?"

I knew a lot of the words, so I jumped up there, and we had a ball.

There was no mosh pit. It was an acoustic show that was aired on the radio. I've been in mosh pits, but I'm a little wary after what happened to Drew Bledsoe a couple years ago. He was on stage, and he jumped into a mosh pit, and I was told he landed on someone and hurt the guy something serious, so I kinda stopped doing that.

Periodically, we'd peek at the ball game on the TV in the bowling alley. Two former Red Sox started, Roger Clemens for the Astros and Jeff Suppan for the Cards. The game was pretty close early on, but then the Cardinals pulled away.

We knew how great a lineup the Cardinals had. We'd faced them in the spring and we'd played them in interleague play the year before. Their lineup had included Edgar Renteria, Albert Pujols, Reggie Sanders, and Scott Rolen. Then they'd traded for Larry Walker to go with them, and they got *a lot* better. The Cards were knocking the cover off the ball. They were a force.

Since the American League had won the All Star game, we had the advantage of playing the first two games at Fenway Park. We had a day off before we had to play them, so I went out on my boat. I relaxed and had fun and stayed loose, just as had been my pattern all year long.

I arrived at the ballpark at 3:00 in the afternoon. Coming any sooner just meant more chaos. Once I arrived, I grabbed a sandwich like I normally do and then walked into the clubhouse where everything was crazy. I had press, radio, and TV interview requests, but I was also bombarded by representatives of sporting goods companies, who wanted to give me their best stuff. All kinds of reps—shoe reps, glove reps, batting glove reps. Each had lines of goods labeled "2004 World Series."

Puma, my shoe company, always came up with the wildest designs. Earlier in the year Puma had made a black shoe with white flames on it hand-painted by an artist. When I wore the shoes, they really stood out.

Before the game we had a meeting with Papa Jack, our hitting coach, to go over the pitchers. The coaches have to study them so they can tell us how these pitchers are going to approach the game.

But as I've told you, a lot of guys, including me, don't want to hear what a pitcher is going to do, because if I'm looking for a certain pitch, and then he doesn't throw it—which happens most of the time—then I'm pissed off at the scouting report. Pitchers change, and as hitters you have to change when they change.

So to me, these meetings are worthless. I don't want to know. Again, it's why I called our team idiots. To us, it's better not to know. Ignorance becomes an advantage. See the ball, hit the ball.

What I prefer to do is talk to the hitting coach right before going up to the plate.

"This is what he threw me the last at-bat," I'd say.

"Just look for a curveball the first pitch."

To me, that's a lot more helpful than listening to what the pitcher's tendencies were during the last series. If the guy's throwing well, he's going to be tough. Then you have to scratch and find some way to beat him.

I'd say this applies to most of the team. We're just not very bright or intuitive about the way pitchers are going to pitch us. We know if they make a mistake and throw a pitch across the heart of the plate, we'll drive the ball out of the ballpark. No one on our team tries to slap it. Our hips rotate, and we let her rip. We're an extra base hitting team—doubles and home runs. We love the fact that John Henry and Theo put together this kind of team. And our fans love it, too.

In 2003, the Boston Red Sox had a better slugging percentage than the 1927 New York Yankees with Babe Ruth and Lou Gehrig. That number is pretty amazing. It says that we're the masters. And I still think that in 2003 we had the best ballclub around. Now in 2004 we were going to prove it.

In my career I've had some thrilling moments—I had 15 hits in a four-game series to tie the American League record. I had 3 hits in one inning. Getting to go to the All Star game in 2002 was also thrilling. But going to the World Series, that was something I'd dreamt about ever since I was a kid.

When you're a Little Leaguer, you don't dream about hitting a grand slam in the seventh game of the American League Championship Series. No, the dream is about hitting a home run in the World Series. You play to be a champion. You live to be a champion. When you make it to the World Series, you're one step closer to that dream.

When you go into the World Series, you know this is the big dance. You know that not only all of America, but the whole world, will be watching.

You also know that after it's over one team will go home victorious and will ride in a parade with millions of fans cheering. The other team will just go home.

We went into the series with the intention of sweeping in four games. We didn't want to go to Game 7, like we had against the Yankees the last two years. We wanted to save the Red Sox fans from having to suffer and pray as much as they'd been doing over the last 86 years. We weren't going to mess around. Going in, we decided that *every* game would be played like it was our last. *Every* game was a must win.

The way the rotation worked out, Tim Wakefield started Game 1 of the World Series for the Sox. Terry had been using him as the long man, the guy who came out of the pen to keep the game close and shut the door. The problem was at the end of the season Wake really didn't have good stuff. He was getting hit pretty badly. That's why he was the odd man out.

Pedro and Schilling weren't ready to pitch, and Derek Lowe had pitched Game 7 against the Yankees. Bronson Arroyo had been hit hard his last time out, so he got shifted over to the long man role, and that put Wake in center stage for Game 1.

We felt confident he could get the job done. We also felt that no matter what happened, if the Cards had to face a knuckleballer, it would screw them up, get them off balance for the next two nights against Pedro and Schilling. Wake was the first knuckeball pitcher to start a World Series game since 1948.

After Wake retired the Cards in the top of the first, I led off against Woody Williams and immediately established a pattern for the entire series by wearing out the opposing pitcher early. The Cards saw how focused our team was every at bat.

We were especially focused for a bunch of crazed lunatic idiots, who actually become very smart when we prepare for a game. We put our minds on the line. We put our hearts on the line.

I ran the count to three and two and then fouled off four straight pitches before doubling into the left field corner the opposite way. When David Ortiz homered, we led.

Jumping out to the lead allowed everyone to relax. We were ahead 7 to 2, but then we made a series of errors that hurt us. Kevin Millar threw a ball away, Bronson made a bad throw, and Manny, trying to be aggressive on the play, overran a routine fly ball, catching his spikes and falling down as the ball fell behind him. The fans were pretty upset because in an important game like that, any error can be devastating. In the dugout we took it all in stride. We told Manny, "Hey, no big deal. We're gonna score, and we're gonna win, so don't worry about it." This is our team. Everybody picks everyone else up.

When Millar came in, Francona had a smile on his face.

"Next time," he said, "don't throw it. Just hold onto it. You'll help us out a lot more." Millar had to smile. Stuff happens.

We could have sulked and said, "We're making errors because the curse is working its voodoo on us," like the media wanted us to do. But when we told Manny, "We'll pick you up," we meant it.

The Cardinals threatened in the eighth against Keith Foulke. With the score still 9–9, he had runners on the bases with two outs and Jim Edmunds up. Jim Edmunds is a clutch hitter who doesn't look lost too often, but against Foulke, he was completely lost. Foulke struck him out three times in the series. In this case, Foulke threw a change up in the strike zone that Edmunds took looking, ending the threat.

We were so locked in. It was just a matter of time before one of us did something to win it for us. Varitek led off the ninth and hit a ball to Edgar Renteria that should have been a single, but the Boston scorekeeper, who cost me at least four hits during the season, ruled that Renteria, who went a long way and tried to backhand it, had made an error. What happens is that when you watch the TV re-play it in slow motion, you say to yourself, "He could have made that play," but I can tell you, it's a lot harder doing it in real time. Either way, Tek was safe on first. Mark Bellhorn batted against reliever Julian Tavares, a hard thrower who didn't allow many home runs. He got two strikes on Mark, but then threw him a pitch that Mark crushed high and deep off the Pesky foul pole in right field for two runs and a 9–7 victory.

Standing in the on deck circle, I had the best view in the house. I was so happy for Bellhorn. He won the game and set the tone for the rest of the series. And by hitting that home run, he picked Manny up and let him relax and prosper during the rest of the series.

After the game we were very excited, happy that we'd won, that we were one up on the Cards. We weren't overconfident at all. We had one goal: to win Game 2.

The guys in the media kept asking, "Do you guys think you can continue to win with the [horrible] way your defense played tonight?" Negative, negative, as always, wanting to concentrate on the errors.

My answer, and everyone else's was, "We just won a ball game. What difference does it make how we did it? We just won, so what's the big deal?"

Unfortunately, when some reporters don't like your answer, they come back and try to ask the question again, and a third time if they feel they have to.

Finally, I just say, "I'm done," and I walk away. You go to take a shower, where they can't follow you, and you get ready to go home.

The big story of Game 2 was the appearance of Curt Schilling. He'd spent the whole day in the trainer's room. He was suffering from a dislocated ankle tendon, and he was in such pain, none of us wanted to be in the trainer's room when he was being treated. We left it to Dr. Morgan, who before the game had cut on him and then stitched him back up to ease his pain and allow him enough relief to pitch. The other reason we left him alone was that on the day he pitches, he wants his privacy, doesn't want anyone talking to him so he can study his charts.

At game time, it was 48 degrees in Boston. We play in perhaps the coldest weather of any ballpark in America, which we look at as an advantage. We don't mind the cold as much as the other guys.

Curt pitched six innings on his bum ankle, allowing four hits and not one single run in six innings. He became a legend that day. In the World Series there have been moments that people who love baseball talk about all their lives. They talk about Grover Cleveland Alexander and how he came into the World Series drunk and struck out Tony Lazzeri to win the World Series for the Cardinals in 1926. They talk about Enos Slaughter scoring from first base on a single for the Cards in 1946. They talk about Carlton Fisk's home run in 1975 against the Reds. And now baseball fans will talk about Curt Schilling having his ankle operated on before a game against the Cardinals and going out and beating them. What an amazing performance! Curt had signed with the Red Sox for the express purpose of bringing a world championship to Boston. And on this night he did more than his share to make that a possibility.

We had three two-out, two-run hits in the game. In the first inning Jason Varitek drove in two with a triple, the second game in a row we scored in the first inning. Mark Bellhorn, whose hitting was so important in the post-season, later had a two-run double, and Orlando Cabrera hit a two-run single off the Monster.

Billy Mueller made three errors at third base, for a total of eight Sox errors in two games, but the errors only cost us a run, and we beat the Cards easily 6–2. Billy was in the dumps after he made those plays, but he shook them off like a champ. Our whole team did. Keith Foulke had another situation in the eighth where he needed to strike out Jim Edmonds to prevent runs from scoring, and once again he struck him out looking.

When the game was over, the fans were happy, and they were also anxious about what would happen next. We needed to win two more games to remake New England into nirvana, but those fans also knew what had happened in the past, and they were afraid to hope for what they thought had once been impossible—a world championship.

Like the opening playoff Angels series, we went into Game 3 saying it was a "must" win. We didn't want the Cardinals to gain any momentum and take the series back to Boston. We wanted this series over as quickly as possible, because of what was on the line: the end of human existence as Red Sox Nation knew it.

The matchup was between Pedro and Jeff Suppan, and of course, we gave the edge to Pedro. Suppan had pitched for us the year before, and we knew what he could do. He didn't throw hard, but he was a veteran who knew how to mix up his pitches. We also knew that the Cardinal hitters had been quiet and that there was always the possibility they would break out.

Pedro knew this would be the defining moment in his career. The year before, the Yankees had beaten him in Game 7. So far he'd pitched well for us in the playoffs, but he wanted—needed—to win in the World Series to define himself as perhaps the greatest pitcher in Red Sox history.

Pedro retired 14 batters in a row. He allowed two infield singles and a double by Edgar Renteria, allowing not a single run in the seven innings he worked. He finished his evening by striking out 3 of the last 4 batters he faced, including Albert Pujols, the Most Incredible Player in the National League; Jim Edmonds; and Reggie Sanders. Pedro was simply magnificent, as he'd been almost all year long.

I don't know why Pedro often doesn't get the respect he deserves. Part of it is that everyone expects him to be awesome every time he goes out there. You always expect him to shut out the other team or give up one run. But he kept us in there almost every game. It seemed this year that every time he pitched, we failed to score much.

Whenever Pedro does badly, it's magnified in the press. Against the Yankees, Pedro struggled, but so did a lot of pitchers. When he said "The Yankees are my daddy," he gave people a chance to criticize him.

Against the Cardinals in the World Series, he shut up all his critics. He struggled in the first inning when he allowed the Cards to load the bases with two outs, but he got Jim Edmonds to fly out to Manny.

When Manny hit a long home run in the first inning, we didn't look back. Manny hit in his thirteenth post-season game in a row. Only Hank Bauer and Derek Jeter with 17 have longer streaks.

The play everyone will remember came in the third inning. The Cards had runners on second and third with nobody out. Terry had our infield play back, conceding a run on a ground out. Suppan was the runner on third. But when Larry Walker hit a hard ground ball to second, I thought for a second that Mark Bellhorn might throw Suppan out at home. When Bellhorn threw to first for the out, I thought, *That's okay. Even though we're giving them a run, we got a big out.* But Suppan didn't run home to score the run. He took a few steps and stopped.

I think what happened is that when Bellhorn throws, his sidearm motion is such that you can't be sure where he's throwing it. I'm sure Suppan thought he was going home, so he stopped. Then there was chaos. Without hesitating, David Ortiz, who was playing first, whipped the ball over to third, and even though Suppan was pretty close to the bag, Bill Mueller made the tag. Wow, what a shift in momentum for us!

Since we were playing in St. Louis, we weren't using the DH, and before the game reporters were questioning why Terry was playing David Ortiz at first base instead of Doug Mientkiewicz. We'd made a lot of errors in the first two games, and the reporters wanted to know if putting Ortiz at first would make things worse defensively.

Terry made exactly the right move. Our strength is our offense, and David had powered our offense all year long. He needed to be in the lineup, and he showed everyone on that play that he isn't bad on defense, either.

After the double play, Pedro cruised the rest of the way.

After the game, which we won 4 to 1, everyone surrounded Pedro and gave him a hug. I stood there feeling proud for him, happy he'd won arguably the most important game of the year.

Taking a three games–to-nothing lead after coming into Busch Stadium, we felt like we were in control. Of course, what we heard from the
press and the fans was, "You guys were down three to zero to the Yankees and the Yankees ended up losing it. Are you thinking about that?"

"We expect to win tomorrow night," was our answer. We were so
locked in. We didn't want to give the Cardinals a chance.

Before Game 4 most of the players were passing around their extra
uniform tops, getting the rest of their teammates to sign them as
World Series champs. I couldn't believe they were doing that. We
hadn't won it yet, and I was the only player on the team who refused
to pass his jersey around.

In Game 4 we faced a pitcher by the name of Jason Marquis. I
remembered facing him in spring training when I was with Kansas
City, and he was with the Braves. He was throwing hard, about 95
miles an hour, with a sharp slider. After he struck me out, I went
back to the bench and said, "This guy is incredible. He's got the best
stuff I've seen in a long time."

In 2004 he put it all together. He still has great stuff, and he's
aggressive, and he has a great demeanor on the mound. But I was so
dialed in, it really didn't matter who was pitching on this day. It
could have been Babe Ruth himself. I'd done my extra work in the
batting cages, and I was determined. My balance was perfect, my bat
speed was there, I never felt more comfortable at the plate, and I
knew before I led off that something good was going to happen.

I went up there looking for a fastball across the middle of the
plate. I figured Marquis was going to start me off with a strike and
then start throwing that curveball. The Cardinal crowd was ener-
gized, and I decided to go up there hacking. His first pitch was a
ball. I was looking for something to drive, and when he threw me a
strike where I was looking, I got my bat on it with a perfect swing. I
knew I'd crushed it, but I hit it so low, I didn't know whether it
would hit before the wall or go over.

The ball flew out of the ballpark, and the fans were stunned. In-
stantly, the wind went out of the Cardinals' sails.

Trot Nixon drove in the other two runs with a bases-loaded double. He hit it on a 3–0 count. Terry let him hit. Terry has faith in us. He even let me, the leadoff hitter, swing at 3–0 sometimes. You play better when you have the faith of your manager, when you know everyone is backing you, everyone has confidence in you.

Terry believed in having his hitters hit, and Trot hit it solid. He's so strong, and I thought it was going to be a grand slam home run, but it came up short.

The three runs were all that Derek Lowe needed. He made them look sick. What a fun game to watch! I thought Derek was making them miss on sliders, and later I came to learn he was throwing change ups. Derek was tired, as I've said, that's a plus for a sinkerball pitcher. They were swinging, but they weren't hitting anything.

Derek had everything working in the final game. That was one of the finest games I ever saw pitched. The Cardinals had *no* chance.

The irony was, we actually kept them in the ball game. We had chance after chance to score again, but didn't. We couldn't capitalize, and we were worried the Cards would come back on us, but Derek took care of that.

He pitched seven shutout innings, and then Terry used Bronson, Alan Embree, and the consistent Keith Foulke, who easily could have been voted the Series MVP, to close it out.

While we were batting in the eighth, my stomach was starting to turn, so I went up into the clubhouse to grab a banana. I saw the clubhouse guys getting out the champagne, and I told them, "Don't put up the plastic yet."

Curt Schilling, who was sitting there, understood what I was saying. Whenever a team has a celebration, the clubhouse guys put up plastic to protect everything inside the players' lockers.

"Don't worry," Schilling said, "the plastic's not going up until it's time."

In the Cardinals' ninth Albert Pujols singled off Keith Foulke, and from my outfield vantage point I knew which fans were Red Sox fans, because I could hear the murmurings, the dread that the curse would come back and hit us. You could hear their, "Uh oh." But

Keith got Scott Rolen to hit a long fly ball to right. It looked scary coming off the bat, but it didn't have legs, and Trot caught it. Then for a third time Keith struck out Jim Edmonds looking for out two.

Edgar Renteria was the game's final batter. Edgar is one of the most feared hitters in the game, but he swung and hit a slow, easy roller back to the mound. Keith gloved it, and then he started jumping up and down, even though he hadn't yet thrown the ball to first base.

It's funny, I don't remember Keith fielding a single ball during the regular season. During spring training he took hundreds of balls during pitchers' fielding practice, and a couple of times he'd had balls hit off his legs, injuring him. How ironic that he didn't get to field a ground ball until the very last ball hit in the World Series! After he began celebrating, he realized that he'd better throw the ball over to first. It was the perfect ending to the perfect year.

We went on the field after the game, jumping up and down and congratulating each other, celebrating the winning of a world championship—something that hadn't occurred since 1918.

"We're going to be out here for a little while," Curt Schilling said. "The clubhouse guys have to get the clubhouse ready for us."

I remember looking around and being happy for guys such as Alan Embree, Ellis Burks, Tim Wakefield, Johnny Pesky.

After the game we went back to the clubhouse and celebrated all night long with John Henry, Larry Lucchino, and Theo Epstein and their families. They'd bought and run the Red Sox, and they'd done all the right things to make us a better team. They went out and got Curt and Keith. They changed the clubhouse, bent over backwards to give us everything we needed to feel comfortable. We owe them so much.

Players were dancing, the champagne was washing over our heads; our eyes burned.

It's funny: you work so hard for so long to accomplish something, and when you finally achieve it, the immediate celebration lasts such a short period of time. After all the congratulations and the champagne shower and interviews, we threw on our clothes, got in our cars, and went home. First comes all the noise and commotion, and then silence, which gives you a chance to sit back and reflect on what you've done. Gradually, it began to sink in that we'd shocked the world—or at least the world that follows baseball. We'd made history. We'd done something that will be remembered lovingly until the death of the last Red Sox fan who watched that last World Series game. Fifty years from now, people will talk about where they were that day and what they were doing. And they'll mention all their dead loved ones who never got to celebrate the way they did.

Yankee fans can throw away their "1918" hats. And they can retire their catcalls of "Bucky Dent" and "Bill Buckner." And Red Sox fans can stop talking—at least for a little while—about Carlton Fisk's home run against Cincinnati. From now on, they'll have even more magical moments to cherish.

We got an idea of what our triumph over the Yankees and the Cardinals really meant when Boston held a parade for us that Saturday morning. I woke up very early that day. My brother, James, and my friend Roger Hernandez were in town, and they wanted to go out to Fenway Park, where the parade was to begin. Because all the streets were closed, the police had to escort us from my apartment in the Ritz-Carlton to the ballpark.

When we arrived in the hotel lobby, the place was mobbed. When the fans saw me, they began to close in to get autographs, but I have a policy not to sign when I'm home—whether it's in Orlando or Boston. I'll sign at the ballpark before the game, and I'll sign in a restaurant if you come up to me before they put the food on the table, but never at home. I feel bad about it, but if you sign one, you have to sign them all, and there's just not enough time.

"Never at home," I say.

If the fans ask why, I say, "If you knocked on the door of my house in the country, you'd be on my property, and I might mistake you for a thief—might take out my shotgun. I wouldn't know why you were coming onto my property, so I might be reaching for my gun."

"You have a point," they say. You have to be tough about it.

After I apologized to the fans we made a mad dash to the police car. During the drive to Fenway, people were lined up 10 deep along the streets. You couldn't move. And when we got to the clubhouse to link up with my teammates, it was so crowded there we couldn't breathe. Family members were there, and there were a ton of people I'd never seen before, asking for autographs.

"Man," I marveled, "this is absolutely crazy."

We rode the parade route in amphibious ducks, and there were a couple extra seats on our duck so James and Roger got to ride with Michelle and me, Dave Roberts, Pokey Reese and his brother, Dave McCarty and his wife and two kids, and a few media types. It was tough for the kids because the parade lasted four hours, and there was no place on the duck to go to the bathroom and no time to stop. We had to find the kids bottles in which to pee. Roger filled up four water bottles.

We drove around the city of Boston, waving to millions of fans. Since the duck could ride in the water, we rode some of the route on the Charles River. The World Series trophy accompanied us part of the way. I can't wait to get my personal World Series trophy. I hear it's pretty cool.

The parade never stopped, except when the traffic wouldn't let us continue. The crowd was going nuts. We were only able to travel at 5 to 10 miles an hour. Cops walked with us the whole way, a long walk on a chilly, rainy day. But Boston had planned it with precision. We couldn't have asked for anything better.

The town had waited for this for so long. I'd expected things to get a little crazy, but the fans were gracious and well behaved. They'd been preparing for this for years.

For me, the parade's highlight was a sign that Manny held up, "Jeter is playing golf. I like this better." Somebody threw a baseball up for Pedro to sign and hit him in the head. I got hit by a girl's panties. That was much better. One girl held up a sign, "Johnny, marry me. I'm easy." There were a lot of signs that said, "Mrs. Johnny

Damon." Another read, "Johnny, take me to the prom." I thought, *Oh man, sixteen will get you twenty.*

The way it is now for high-profile athletes, when you meet a girl, you have to ask for her birth certificate, and you also have to ask her about her desires and how much money she makes—to make sure she's not after your money. You have to ask her if she's psycho, or if her ex-boyfriends are psycho. Nowadays, you have to be really careful.

As a kid growing up in Orlando, Florida, I never dreamed any of this hoopla might happen. One event I did fantasize about, though, was getting to be the star athlete who appears in the commercial and says, "I'm going to Disneyland."

I know people who worked at Disney, and they told me that after my two home runs against the Yankees and our World Series win, I was being considered for the company's commercial. But they also told me that because of my long hair Disney chose not to pursue it, which just goes to show that no matter how famous you might become, it's still possible to become a victim of intolerance, stupidity, and discrimination.

I couldn't believe it. Every night when I'm home, I get to watch the fireworks that end the evening at Disney World. I was disappointed and very hurt.

Universal Studios, Disney's competitor, decided to honor me, until they found out I'd already agreed to appear there at Jimmy Buffett's charity event for Hurricane Relief. I was advised to skip the Hurricane Relief event so I could have my own celebration, but I'd promised Jimmy I'd be there, and I wouldn't go back on my word. Not only that, but my home had sustained $25,000 in damage from the hurricane, and I knew it could have been a lot worse.

The city of Orlando stepped in and on November 11, 2004, gave me my day. Mayor Buddy Dyer proclaimed the day mine. Some critics tried to ruin the honor by saying the ceremony shouldn't be held on Veterans Day. They didn't know my dad was a veteran who'd served for 20 years. They wanted to be negative, but I was determined to stay positive, and it worked out great because during the ceremony I honored all those men who'd fought for America in past wars, including my father and those who were fighting in Iraq at the time.

We had a great turnout for my day. There were tons of Red Sox fans and dozens of friends. All I'd wanted from the city of Orlando was to be recognized, and I was very grateful for that. The Disney decision, so be it.

The night after the parade in Boston I appeared on *Saturday Night Live* as part of a whirlwind tour. Seth Meyers, who's a huge Red Sox fan, arranged it with Lorne Michaels, the producer. Kate Winslet, who's one of the most beautiful women I've ever seen, and very polite, was the host. Eminem sang. Lorne Michaels and the whole cast were incredibly nice.

They do two shows, a rehearsal show in front of a live audience, and then the show you see on TV live at 11:30. The first time I went out there, I was supernervous. In our skit, Seth Myers says, "Everyone's been ragging me here, so forget you all, I'm going to hang out with my friend Johnny Damon."

At that point I walked out to tons of cheers. I had one line, "Let's get out of here, Seth." Except, not having any acting experience, I didn't know when to start talking. I was supposed to wait for the applause to die down before I said my line, but the first time I didn't wait long enough, and I was drowned out. The second time I did it just right.

Doing the show made me realize how nice those people are, how down to earth. And I was surprised by how many had rooted for the Red Sox. One girl, Amy Poehler, a huge Red Sox fan, was so beside herself she wouldn't let go of me.

After the show, I went out and had a few drinks with the cast. It was the day before Halloween, and a lot of people were in costume, and sure enough, I ran into a girl dressed up as Johnny Damon. She was as much in shock at seeing me as I was at seeing her. The paparazzi were snapping pictures, and I was loving it.

A bunch of us from the team spent the next day in a hotel

room in Boston signing memorabilia items to be sold on Home Shopping Network. Then on Monday I flew back to New York to appear on the David Letterman show. That was a treat. The Donnas sang, and Anne Heche, who's beautiful and very sexy, was also a guest. I didn't get to talk to her, but just being in the same room as all these stars is *very* cool.

I also appeared in a movie directed by the Farrelly Brothers called *Fever Pitch* with Jimmy Fallon, who used to be on *Saturday Night Live.* They shot me in a couple of scenes at Fenway in a game we won, and then after a game we lost, they asked me to do another scene, but I refused, because we'd lost and it didn't seem right. They eventually rewrote the script to change the ending because we'd beaten the Yankees and won it all, so in November I flew up to Toronto with Jason Varitek and Trot Nixon and finished filming.

I'd love to do some acting, and there's been talk of my being involved in a one-shot reality show, but I know what my purpose is right now: to play baseball.

Winning the World Series as part of the Red Sox has certainly changed my life. Mostly, of course, for the better, but some aspects have been awful. One day I went to my son's T-ball game. Before I even arrived, the parents had told all their kids to run up to me to get my autograph. I hadn't even parked my car when the mob surrounded me.

I wanted to spend the time with my son, Jackson, but so many people descended on me that I had to jump over two fences and run away. One kid even jumped over the fences to follow me. I was so impressed, I signed for him.

It's gotten better because I've learned how to say "no." I went three times to watch Jackson play, and by the third time, I'd trained the crowd to stay away. I turned away everyone, didn't sign even one. That stopped folks from bothering me and allowed me to enjoy the game.

I enjoyed visiting my kids' school. Before we won the World Series, the other kids knew my kids pretty well. After we won, my son and daughter became the most popular kids in school, and now my kids have big grins on their faces, because when I walk in the other kids chant their name. My son and daughter now know they have the coolest last name—Damon.

I know it won't last forever, so I've tried to accommodate media requests, especially in the Orlando area. At the same time, I've been trying to enjoy my friends, and I've moved into two new homes, one in Boston and one in Orlando. Best of all, on December 30, 2004, Michelle and I got married. It was five days of fun, merriment, and rock and roll.

Michelle and I are looking forward to returning to Fort Myers, as the 2005 Boston Red Sox try to accomplish something special for only the second time in their history: win two straight American League championships. It won't be easy, because this year George Steinbrenner and his Evil Empire will probably spend $300 million in salary trying to beat us. He's already signed Randy Johnson and Carl Pavano to his all-star lineup, but I'm confident that John Henry, Larry Lucchino, and Theo Epstein will work their magic again and give Red Sox Nation another exciting team of champion idiots. To date we've lost Pedro, Derek Lowe, and Orlando Cabrera to other teams, but Theo has signed three excellent starters: David Wells from the Padres, Matt Clement from the Cubs, and Wade Miller from the Astros. And Theo replaced Orlando with Edgar Renteria, who may have been the best shortstop in the National League last year. We may not win every game, but I promise you, we will *try* to win every game. And if we should lose one, it won't be because of the Curse of the Bambino. It'll be because in this great game of baseball, you win some, you lose some, and every once in a while, you get rained out.

I'll always cherish being a part of the 2004 World Championship Boston Red Sox. No one will ever be able to take that away from me—nor, I'm proud to say, from you.

JOHNNY DAMON
CAREER STATISTICS

YR	TM	G	AB	R	H	2B	3B	HR	RBI	BB	SO	SB	CS	SBP	AVG	OBP	SLG
1995	KCA	47	188	32	53	11	5	3	23	12	22	7	0	1.000	.282	.324	.441
1996	KCA	145	517	61	140	22	5	6	50	31	64	25	5	.833	.271	.313	.368
1997	KCA	146	472	70	130	12	8	8	48	42	70	16	10	.615	.275	.338	.386
1998	KCA	161	642	104	178	30	10	18	66	58	84	26	12	.684	.277	.339	.439
1999	KCA	145	583	101	179	39	9	14	77	67	50	36	6	.857	.307	.379	.477
2000	KCA	159	655	136	214	42	10	16	88	65	60	46	9	.836	.327	.382	.495
2001	OAK	155	644	108	165	34	4	9	49	61	70	27	12	.692	.256	.324	.363
2002	BOS	154	623	118	178	34	11	14	63	65	70	31	6	.838	.286	.356	.443
2003	BOS	145	608	103	166	32	6	12	67	68	74	30	6	.833	.273	.345	.405
2004	BOS	150	621	123	189	35	6	20	94	76	71	19	8	.704	.304	.380	.477
		1407	5553	956	1592	291	74	120	625	545	635	263	74	.780	.287	.351	.431

■ In Boston's 10–3 win in Game 7 over the Yankees, Damon belted two home runs, including a memorable grand slam against Javier Vazquez, and finished with six RBIs to tie an American League Championship Series record.

■ Damon hit a leadoff homer against St. Louis in Boston's 3–0 victory in Game 4 of the World Series as Boston ended its 86-year championship drought.

■ Damon had his best all-around season in 2004 by batting .304 with a career-high of 20 home runs, 94 RBIs, and 123 runs scored.

- One of the game's premier leadoff hitters, Damon has scored 100-or-more runs for seven consecutive seasons.
- Damon was chosen for the 2002 American League All Star team.
- On June 27, 2003, Damon became the second player in Major League history to collect three hits in one inning with a single, a double, and a triple against the Florida Marlins. Boston's Gene Stephens was the first player with three hits in an inning in 1953.

THE 2004 WORLD CHAMPIONSHIP RED SOX TEAM

POSITION PLAYERS

Mark Bellhorn
Ellis Burks
Orlando Cabrera
Cesar Crespo
Johnny Damon
Brian Daubach
Andy Dominique
Nomar Garciaparra
Ricky Gutierrez
Adam Hyzdu
Gabe Kapler
Sandy Martinez
Dave McCarty
Doug Mientkiewicz
Kevin Millar
Doug Mirabelli
Bill Mueller

PITCHERS

Terry Adams
Abe Alvarez
Jimmy Anderson
Bronson Arroyo
Pedro Astacio
Jamie Brown
Frank Castillo
Lenny DiNardo
Alan Embree
Keith Foulke
Bobby Jones
Byung-Hyun Kim
Curtis Leskanic
Derek Lowe
Mark Malaska
Anastacio Martinez
Pedro Martinez

Trot Nixon

David Ortiz

Manny Ramirez

Pokey Reese

Dave Roberts

Earl Snyder

Jason Varitek

Kevin Youkilis

Ramiro Mendoza

Mike Myers

Joe Nelson

Curt Schilling

Phil Seibel

Mike Timlin

Tim Wakefield

Scott Williamson

Principal Owner .... John W. Henry
Chairman .... Thomas C. Werner
Vice Chairmen ... David Ginsberg, Phillip H. Morse, Leslie B. Otten
President/Chief Executive Officer .... Larry Lucchino
Director .... George J. Mitchell
Chief Legal Officer, New England Sports
       Ventures .... Lucinda K. Treat

PARTNERS

Theodore Alfond	Michael Egan	Arthur E. Nicholas
William Alfond	Ed Eskandarian	Frank Resnek
Ben Cammarata	Michael Gordon	Samuel A. Tamposi, Jr.
David D'Alessandro	John A. Kaneb	Martin Trust
Thomas R. DiBenedetto	New York Times Co.	Jeffrey Vinik
	(Russ Lewis, Jim Lessersohn)	

FRONT OFFICE

Chief Operating Officer .... Mike Dee
Executive Vice President/Public Affairs .... Dr. Charles Steinberg
Senior Vice President/Fenway Affairs .... Larry Cancro
Senior Vice President/Corporate Relations .... Meg Vaillancourt
Special Assistant to the Principal Owner .... Sylvia Moon
Executive Assistant to the President/CEO .... Fay Scheer
Special Assistant to the President/CEO .... Jonathan Gilula
Senior Advisor/Baseball Projects .... Jeremy Kapstein
Senior Director of Broadcast Services .... Chuck Steedman

Assistant to the Executive Vice President/
    Public Affairs .... Kerri Moore
Assistant to the Senior Vice President/
    Fenway Affairs .... Beth Krudys
Executive Assistants .... Barbara Bianucci, Jeanne Bill,
                                    Kathleen Fleming
Executive Assistant/Corporate Relations .... Laurie Smith
Special Projects Coordinator .... Adam Grossman
Financial and Business Analysis .... Tim Zue

BASEBALL OPERATIONS

Senior Vice President/General Manager .... Theo Epstein
Vice President/Baseball Operations .... Mike Port
Assistant General Manager .... Josh Byrnes
Special Assistant to the General Manager/Scouting .... Bill Lajoie
Special Assistant to the General Manager/
       Player Development and International
       Scouting .... Craig Shipley
Senior Baseball Operations Advisor .... Bill James
Director of Baseball Operations/
       Assistant Director of Player Development .... Peter Woodfork
Assistant to the General Manager .... Jed Hoyer
Coordinator of Major League Administration ...... Brian O'Halloran
Traveling Secretary .... Jack McCormick
Instructors .... Jim Rice, Luis Tiant, Carl Yastrzemski
Administrative Assistant .... Jean MacDougall
Medical Director .... William J. Morgan, M.D.
Head Trainer .... Jim Rowe
Assistant Trainer/Rehabilitation Coordinator .... Chris Correnti
Assistant Trainer .... Chang-Ho Lee
Equipment Manager and Clubhouse Operations .... Joe Cochran
Assistant Equipment Manager .... Edward "Pookie" Jackson
Visiting Clubhouse Manager .... Tom McLaughlin
Video/Advance Scouting Coordinator .... Billy Broadbent

MINOR LEAGUE OPERATIONS

Director of Player Development .... Ben Cherington
Director of Minor League Administration .... Raquel Ferreira
Special Assignment Instructors .... Dwight Evans, Tommy Harper,
                    Frank Malzone, Johnny Pesky, Charlie Wagner
Coordinator of Florida Operations .... Todd Stephenson
Minor League Equipment Manager .... Mike Stelmach

SCOUTING

Director of Amateur Scouting .... David Chadd
Director of Scouting Administration .... Jason McLeod
Assistant Director of Professional and
      International Scouting .... Tom Moore
Advance Scouting Coordinator .... Galen Carr
Scouting Assistant .... Amiel Sawdaye
Administrative Assistant/
      Scouting and Player Development .... Victor Cruz

ACCOUNTING AND FINANCE

Vice President and Chief Financial Officer .... Bob Furbush
Vice President and Controller .... Steve Fitch
Director of Finance .... Ryan Oremus
Central Purchasing Administrator .... Eileen Murphy-Tagrin
Payroll Administrator .... Diane Sutty
Assistant Controller .... Robin Willis
Staff Accountant .... Cathy Fahy
Accounting Staff .... Kim Birn, Lou Stathis, Tina Yong

ADVERTISING, PRODUCTION, AND ENTERTAINMENT

Director of Advertising, Television,
      and Video Production .... Tom Catlin
Manager of Scoreboard and Video Production .... Danny Kischel
Advertising Production Coordinator ....Megan Kaiser
Advertising and Production Assistants ...... Jon Mancini, John Carter

BALLPARK PLANNING AND DEVELOPMENT

Vice President/Planning and Development .... Janet Marie Smith
Planning and Development Coordinator .... Paul Hanlon

COMMUNITY RELATIONS

Manager of Community Relations .... Vanessa Leyvas
Manager of Community Athletic Programs .... Ron Burton, Jr.
Community Relations Coordinator .... Sarah Stevenson
Community Relations Assistants ..... Colleen Reilly, Sheri Rosenberg

FAN AND NEIGHBORHOOD SERVICES

Director of Fan and Neighborhood Services .... Sarah McKenna

FENWAY PARK OPERATIONS

Vice President .... Joe McDermott
Director of Security and Emergency Services .... Charles Cellucci
Director of Facilities Management .... Tom Queenan
Director of Event Operations .... Jeff Goldenberg
Director of Grounds .... Dave Mellor
Assistant Director of Grounds .... Charles Brunetti
Manager of Event Operations .... Dan Lyons
Manager of Fenway Park Enterprises .... Marcita Thompson
Director of Grounds, Emeritus .... Joe Mooney
Facilities Maintenance .... Donnie Gardiner,
Glen McGlinchey, Tom Barnard
Stadium Operations Staff .... Al Forester, Bob Levin

HUMAN RESOURCES AND OFFICE ADMINISTRATION

Director of Human Resources
and Office Administration .... Michele Julian
Human Resources Administrator .... Adis Benitez
Administrative Assistant .... Christine Collins
Receptionist .... Molly Walsh

Switchboard Operator/Receptionist .... Christina Robinson
Office Administration Assistant .... Jared Pinkos

INFORMATION TECHNOLOGY
AND TELECOMMUNICATIONS
Director of Information Technology .... Steve Conley
Senior Systems Analyst .... Randy George

LEGAL DEPARTMENT
Vice President and Club Counsel .... Elaine Steward
Staff Counsel .... Jennifer Flynn
Law Clerk .... Laura O'Neill

PUBLIC RELATIONS
Director of Public Relations .... Glenn Geffner
Media Relations Coordinator .... Peter Chase
Media Relations Assistant/Credentials .... Meghan McClure
Media Relations Assistants .... Mark Rogoff, Drew Merle

PUBLICATIONS AND ARCHIVES
Vice President/Publications and Archives .... Dick Bresciani
Executive Consultant .... Lou Gorman
Director of Publications .... Debbie Matson
Manager of Publications and Archives .... Rod Oreste
Coordinator of Alumni and Archives .... Pam Ganley
Staff Photographer .... Julie Cordeiro

SALES AND CORPORATE PARTNERSHIPS
Vice President/Sales and Corporate Partnerships ...... Sam Kennedy
Director of Corporate Partnerships .... Joe Januszewski
Director of Client Services .... Troup Parkinson
Senior Manager of Season and Group Sales .... Corey Bowdre
Senior Manager of Premium Seating Sales .... Sean Curtin
Manager of .406 Club and VIP Services .... Carole Alkins
Premium Seating Services Coordinator .... Stephanie Nelson

Sponsor Services Coordinator .... Laura Reff
Account Executives .... Kim Cameron, Tyler Fairchild,
Jordan Kogler
Red Sox Kids Club Coordinator .... Gillian Lewis
Sales Assistant .... Peter Pachios

TICKET SERVICES AND OPERATIONS

Director of Ticket Operations .... Richie Beaton
Director of Ticket Services and Information .... Michael Schetzel
Senior Manager of Season Ticket Services .... Joe Matthews
Manager of Ticket Services ....Marcell Saporita
Manager of Ticket Accounting Administration ....Sean Carragher
Senior Advisor/Ticket Operations .... Ron Bumgarner
Ticket Services .... Naomi Calder, Sandi Quinn, Frank Marion
Ticket Operations .... Barbara Cuddy, Peter Fahey,
Gary Goldberg, Lisa Lindsay

About the Authors

Johnny Damon has spent more than a decade playing Major League baseball. A feared contact hitter and base stealer, Damon is only one of four players in baseball history to drive in more than 90 runs from the leadoff position. He lives with his wife, Michelle, in Central Florida and has a twin boy and girl.

Peter Golenbock has written numerous *New York Times* bestsellers, among them *The Bronx Zoo* with Sparky Lyle, *#1* with Billy Martin, and *Balls* with Graig Nettles.